Winning the
Cash Flow War

Winning the Cash Flow War

Your Ultimate Survival Guide to Making Money and Keeping It

Fred Rewey

Special Foreword by
best-selling author
Robert G. Allen

WILEY

John Wiley & Sons, Inc.

Published by John Wiley & Sons, Inc., Hoboken, New Jersey.
Published simultaneously in Canada.

For general information about our other products and services, please contact our Customer Care Department within the United States at 800-762-2974, outside the United States at 317-572-3993 or fax 317-572-4002.

Wiley also publishes its books in a variety of electronic formats. Some content that appears in print may not be available in electronic books. For more information about Wiley products, visit our web site at www.wiley.com.

Library of Congress Cataloging-in-Publication Data:

Rewey, Fred.
  Winning the cash flow war: your ultimate survival guide to making money and keeping it / by Fred Rewey; special foreword by best-selling author Robert G. Allen
     p.   cm.
   ISBN 0-471-71153-5 (cloth)
   1. Finance, Personal.   2. Investments.   3. Retirement income—Planning.   I. Title.
   HG179.R3946 2005
   332.024—dc22

                                                                    2004024104

Printed in the United States of America

10 9 8 7 6 5 4 3 2 1

Dedication

Special thanks . . .

To those of you that are defending our country, and way of life, in real battles
around the world. No disrespect is intended by the theme of this book and
I know that without your efforts and sacrifices none of us would be able to enjoy
the freedoms we possess. My thoughts, and thanks, are always with you.

To Jon Richards for introducing me to the idea of educating others and also what
eventually became the Cash Flow industry—it forever changed my life.
Not a month goes by that I do not miss his mentoring and guidance.

To the team of Brian W. Kelly, Benny Powell, Rommel Manabat, Mike Judy,
and Chi Wang: Thanks for helping me make this book a reality and
putting up with my numerous changes and additions.

To Pamela van Giessen: Thank you for your belief in the book and your support.
I am sure this is just the beginning of many projects we will do together.

To my daughter, Mikayla. I look forward to watching you grow and
I hope you accomplish everything in your dreams.

Lastly, and most importantly, I want to thank Tracy, my wife. A vastly
accomplished person in her own right, her unwavering support
and belief in me has made this possible to share with others. Any success
I have is a tribute to her. I only hope that I can return a fraction
of the love and support she has given me.

Contents

Foreword

Robert G. Allen

"Nothing I do will change my finances."

"In this world, the rich get richer, and the poor get poorer."

"It's not what you know, but who you know that really matters."

"The only way I can ever make it is if I win the lottery..."

"I should just give up!"

Those are some pretty depressing sayings...and ones I've encountered far too often by far too many people. The only thing sadder is when I think of how many people would be better off if they simply realized one thing: It's *all* a load of hogwash.

You can change your finances for the better. You're the only one who can...and the only one who will. The rich aren't the only ones who get richer. And there are quite a few rich who get poorer as well.

It *is* about what you know. I have met a lot of influential people over the years, and not one of them *made* me a success. I did. Gaining connections is just a piece of the puzzle—it's not the key. Knowledge is.

And if you think the lottery is even a viable salvation, then have I got news for you. *Getting* money is the easy part. So many lottery winners go broke fast because they don't know how to *keep* their new-found wealth.

As for giving up, you wouldn't be holding this book if that was even an option for you.

But I'm getting ahead of myself. Perhaps I should introduce myself first. My name is Robert G. Allen, and over the past three decades I've written *several* best-selling books. My first book, *Nothing Down* has been updated *three times* and has sold more copies than any other real estate book in history. I've also written books on how to make multiple streams of income and even a book on utilizing the Internet for profit. Recently I co-wrote a book along with my good friend Mark Victor Hansen (a.k.a. the *Chicken Soup for the Soul* guy) titled *The One Minute Millionaire*. I've also taught numerous seminars throughout the country over the years and helped create thousands of prosperous students who are out there making money in the trenches each and every day.

Fred gave me a copy of his book and asked if I would be willing to write a foreword. After reading it, I jumped at the chance. You see, while I've spent years teaching people how to make money, I never fully covered the topic that Fred handles so well with this book: How to *win* the cash flow war, how to *keep* the money you make, and how to *make* the most out of it.

As it says in his analogy, cash flow *is* war. Many of the lessons contained in this book are ones I wish I had known 30 years ago when I was starting out. I would have saved myself a world of pain. But instead, I went through the school of hard knocks . . . the kind of learning you only get being in the trenches, the way Fred has. It wasn't easy, and I wouldn't wish anyone to go through it. So please save yourself the heartache and use this tool. In fact, I encourage you to think of it as your manual for the greatest *tool* of all—money.

That's right—money is a tool. Not a goal. You use money to do what you love to do. Best of all, when you're doing what you love to do, the money comes naturally. Maybe not at first—but eventually it comes—if you stick with it. Do you think great comedians like Eddie Murphy, Bob Hope, or Steve Martin started out with this goal: "I want to become a millionaire by making people laugh, then I'll retire to do what I really want"?

I doubt it. They just did what they did best. And the money came. Slowly at first, but then in truckloads. Comedian Jim Carrey has often told his story of being down and out and writing himself a million-dollar check. But even he sought his goal by doing what he loved doing—and he's still doing it. When you're living your dream—no matter how financially successful you are—why would you want to retire?

What about the presidents of the Fortune 500? They make several million dollars a year. Why do they do so well financially? It's because they love the game of business, and they have polished the skills necessary for success in the corporate world. The financial results are just how they keep score.

I read a study in which the employees and executives of a major company were asked what they would do if they won $10 million in a lottery. Eighty percent of the rank-and-file employees said they would immediately quit their jobs. Asked the same question, only 20 percent of the executives said they would quit. Why would 80 percent stay even though they were now financially independent? Because they find a lot of happiness and fulfillment in their day-to-day activities. They love what they're doing. They're not leaders because they make so much money. They make so much money because they love to lead.

Imagine what you would do if you won $10 million in your state lottery. Would this make you happy? Sure. (Whoever said money doesn't bring happiness doesn't know where to shop!) What would you spend it on? A larger house in a better neighborhood? How about a nicer car? Pay off those debts? Buy some new clothes? Give a little away to your favorite charitable cause? Blow a few thousand for the heck of it? Sock some away for a rainy day? And, of course, you'd quit your job and do what you love to do, right?

Seriously, how would you spend your time if you didn't have to worry about money? Want to know a secret? Most people never bother to ask themselves that question. They just assume that if they win that $10 million jackpot, they'll be happy forever. But money isn't the goal, and far too often people who fall into money are left with an empty, directionless feeling. Achieving money was their goal; it should only have been a means for achieving their goal.

At the Robert Allen Institute, one of the most important lessons I teach is that money doesn't come first. What most people are really seeking is the ability to spend each day doing something that they love to do. Rather than looking for happiness in some future goal of financial freedom (like almost all Americans), you want to find something that fulfills you every step of the way.

And we all know that money is the *tool* for achieving that kind of freedom, not the goal itself. Just like a hammer, in the right hands it can build a house, while in the wrong ones it can give you sore thumbs. It's all in how you use it.

This book shows you step by step the process to win your battles and wage your war for financial freedom. Fred shows you an arsenal of tools you never knew existed—the very secrets that the wealthy use in their everyday lives.

I applaud Fred for delving into this tricky subject as successfully as he has. This field guide through the Cash Flow War will not only make you into a Cash Flow Warrior, but a Cash Flow Winner! But you have to do your part. And now that you know what is at stake—the freedom to achieve your goals—I'm sure you will. You may have lost some battles . . . now you're prepared to win the war.

God bless,

Robert G. Allen

Preface

This Means War!

We're in trouble financially! Every day, thousands of Americans file for bankruptcy. In 2002, over 1.5 million noncommercial bankruptcies were filed—nearly double the number of filings only 10 years prior. And today, consumer bankruptcies account for over 97 percent of all filings. Overall consumer debt broke over one trillion dollars in 1999, and has continued to rise. Nearly half of all consumer debt was credit card–related.

Simultaneous to these startling statistics is the fact that banks and credit card companies continue to become more profitable. It is indeed startling to realize that the old axiom is actually is true: "While the rich get richer, the poor get poorer."

If these facts don't scare you, they should! Every indicator points to things getting worse, not better. The conclusion is simple: Americans need to learn how to survive financially. Even more alarming is the realization that these are just the symptoms of a problem afflicting millions of Americans. The problem? Each of us, every day, is fighting a battle. Not only are we unprepared and unarmed—many are unaware a battle is even taking place!

You Can Win This War

My name is Fred Rewey and I wrote this book to help you win your own personal Cash Flow War. You may not even realize that you're involved in a war for financial survival, but I can assure you that you are. Take a look around you. Every single day your credit cards, mortgages, tuition bills, medical bills, and car payments (and on and on) are laying in wait to ambush you and your dreams of a better life and a comfortable retirement. If you are like most Americans, you're virtually *drowning* in debt.

There's nothing easy about easy credit—the credit card companies aren't your friends, and the only reason they're so willing to lend you money is that they stand to make large profits as you struggle to pay off your balances. The same goes for your mortgage company, and for any other institution that is just begging for the opportunity to advance you some cash, or to loan you money for a major purchase. They're only doing so because they can make tons of money from your interest payments.

In fact, just about every company you deal with every day is only in it for the money. And there's nothing wrong with that! The people that run those companies know how to make money, and they're making a nice life for themselves. But here are some of the questions you need to ask yourself: Why should I be the one paying everybody? Isn't it time for me to get paid?

I can tell you this: If you read my book and apply the lessons you'll learn in each chapter, you'll be able to answer those questions in a positive fashion. You'll be equipped with the proper weapons to stave off all those ambushes, all those hidden expenses and land mines—and you'll learn how to use the weapons I'll provide you to start winning some financial battles of your own. By applying the lessons I show you, someday in the not-too-distant future you'll be able to look yourself in the mirror and say, "I did it. I won the Cash Flow War."

I can help you. Just like all successful generals and leaders need to learn battle tactics and military strategy before they ever assume command, I can supply you with all the knowledge, weapons, and ammunition you need how to win the

Cash Flow War. Think of this book as your personal Boot Camp, and think of me as the lead instructor of your War College. And remember that I do this daily: I speak on cash flow matters before thousands of people each year, and tens of thousands have seen me deliver this message on television. Each year I personally induct people into the prestigious Million Dollar Club and I host the largest Cash Flow convention in the nation.

I began helping others when I started my Cash Flow career in 1992, and not long after that I was offered an executive position with one of the country's largest institutional investors. As assistant vice president, I helped identify and implement ways to increase their production as well as create new programs for others. And all the time I was learning more about money, finance, and its effect on people and their financial lives.

I became a guest speaker for the numerous trade organizations and assumed the presidency of the American Cash Flow Association in January 2000. In the years since I first started my business on my kitchen table, I have founded or played a part in many other enterprises in more professional surroundings. These diverse companies include Diversified Investment Services (a cash flow purchasing company), Exposure One (a marketing firm), and Web-based businesses Man Inc., Cigar Secrets, and NoteInvestor.com.

I'm ready to help you take command of your situation, and to show you how to gather your forces and deploy your troops for maximum success in the Cash Flow War. Are you ready to gear up, enter into combat, and experience the thrill of running a successful offensive? Are you ready to experience the thrill of victory and to enjoy your new financial future? I thought you were!

Get-Rich-Quick Schemes Don't Work

Let me be clear about one thing right up front: This is not a get-rich-quick program or book. Let me repeat that: This is not a get-rich-quick opportunity. I firmly believe that as far as get-rich-quick things are concerned, there are really only two ways in our world to do it. One is to buy the winning lottery ticket and the other is to go to the casino and pull the *right* one-armed bandit. And statistically speaking, if you're pinning your financial hopes on that happening, you're more likely to be struck by lightning . . . five times!

What I'm going to tell you about in this book requires actual work. It requires that you actually read this book and think about the things you learn in it. At the same time, I want to assure you that the things you will learn are all well within the grasp of the average person, and you won't need a doctorate in economics to win your personal Cash Flow War. Just take a look at me—I succeeded when the odds were stacked against me. Believe me, if I can do it, you can do it!

Now that we're crystal clear that I'm not offering you a secret get-rich-quick plan, and that you've actually got to do some work, we can get started. And if you're still reading, then you're in this for the long haul and want to get the upper hand in your personal finances. I can guarantee you there will be many things in this book that you will be able to apply successfully to your own life—some immediately. In the chapters ahead, I'll outline just what actions you need to take to enable you to win your own personal Cash Flow War.

With all that said, the question *you* should be asking now is *Just who is Fred Rewey and why is he telling me these things?*

I'd like to take the opportunity to tell you a little bit about myself, just so you'll see that I understand what it is to owe money, to feel like there is no way out, and to feel so defeated that you think there is no way you'll ever achieve your dream lifestyle. And then, I'd like to tell you that no matter how bad you think things are financially, you should take heart and *then take action*. I went from bankruptcy to living comfortably—without any money worries—and I can show and tell you how to do just the same. Hopefully, you won't be starting this process from as deep in the hole as I was, but whatever your financial position is at the start of this book, if you apply the lessons you learn along the way, your situation will improve by the end of the book!

How I Found Myself at the Bottom and Ended Up Declaring Bankruptcy

I was born in Milwaukee, Wisconsin, and my family, like many others, moved around the country a little bit. So I've lived all over the place, although I spent most of my school years in San Francisco and around the Bay area. After I graduated high school in 1984, I realized that I really had no clear career path, and that I just didn't know what I wanted to do with my life. I had friends who knew what they wanted to do, and I was a little bit jealous of them—they were in college, and working towards a four-year degree, while I was just kind of knocking around and taking some junior college courses, working different jobs.

In fact, I worked a lot of different jobs: I guess I had a short attention span. I did a little bit of everything. I studied acting at the American Conservatory Theatre and in Oxford, England. I did stand-up comedy, and was a DJ on the radio. I worked as a graphic artist, a computer operator, sold Christmas trees, and ran a forklift. I have been a cook, waited tables, bartended, and managed restaurants. I tried numerous other jobs and none of them ever really felt right to me, and certainly none of those jobs earned me the kind of money that I really wanted.

As I was trying to figure out what I wanted to do with my life and working all those various jobs, I was also spending money freely. I was young, and people kept offering me credit, so I kept on taking it! Before long, I found myself getting into some deep water with my credit card debt, and eventually I was having a hard time making the payments on all those high-interest cards, paying my car loan, and affording basic living expenses. I was in over my head, and I didn't know what to do about it.

I ended up declaring bankruptcy in 1988, and my first marriage failed not long after that. I have to say it was a pretty low point in my life. No money, no significant other, and I still didn't know what the heck I wanted to do with my life. And to make matters seem even worse at the time, I couldn't even turn to credit cards for entertainment or to bail me out any longer! Obviously something needed to change for me.

Looking back on it all now, I realize that I didn't owe all that much, but at that point in my life it seemed like an awful lot of money to me. I realize now I could have found a better path than bankruptcy: I could have managed my money better, but I didn't really have the knowledge or tools to know what to do. And why was that? I know now that I was simply uneducated in the area of personal finance. There are two things they don't teach you in school, two pretty important things. And they are how to handle your money and how to handle relationships.

Well, after failing miserably at both money management *and* personal relationships, I decided that it would never happen to me again. So I started out on a several-years-long investigation to find out everything I could that would help me succeed where I had previously failed.

What I Decided to Do About It

So there I was, back in 1988, bankrupt and alone. I was pretty ticked off at the whole bankruptcy issue. Although I don't blame the credit card companies, because I believe in taking personal responsibility, I felt a victim of the system. Nobody had ever taught me how to deal with finances. So there was really only one thing I could do. I started to read everything I could. I read any book I could find that dealt with finance or credit cards, I picked successful people's brains, and I started asking questions wherever and whenever I could. I spent a lot of time in the library—remember, this was in the dark ages, back before there was all this information floating around on the Internet!

To make a long story short, I set out to learn how banks and credit card companies made money. I figured since they had taken all my money, they must be pretty good at it. I found myself back in school again. I took night courses, and I learned about buying foreclosures, VA loans, and HUD houses. I took these courses because I was trying to figure out how I could ever afford to buy my own home! I took continuing education courses, anything I could find to better myself, to learn how to work within the system—and, more importantly, how to *beat* the system.

I learned everything I could in a classroom environment. And I learned everything I could outside of the classroom. I worked with a professor, and he showed me the note business (I'll explain the note business fully in Chapter 22). I moved things around in my 600-square-foot apartment and I set up a home office. The professor helped me in my first business. I gained a lot of practical experience there, and I even grew to eventually teach courses with him on personal finance.

And I did all of this while I was still working in the restaurant business. I still had to pay my bills while I was learning all this! I'm not going to kid you, while I was learning a new business, I was making a lot of mistakes; I had to learn entrepreneurial skills and I had to learn how to manage my time.

Here's What Surprised Me the Most

What really amazed me away about all these new things I was learning was the fact that I, for the most part, wasn't really learning anything "new" at all. Everything you need to know about personal finance, and how to make some real money for yourself, has already been figured out. Wealthy people already knew these things, and it wasn't like you had to be born into their circle. You didn't have to go to an Ivy League school, and you didn't have to know a secret handshake; the knowledge was right there for the taking. It only required a little diligence and some hard work to learn how to become wealthy.

I began to realize that wealthy people knew things that most of us don't. I started to believe that schools had failed me. They should have taught me some of the easy-to-apply realities of finance, because when it comes right down to it, most of what you really need to know is simple. It's not that hard to use a financial calculator (you'll learn how in Chapter 12) to figure out a car loan or a mortgage; these should be basic survival skills that could be taught in one semester in college or as a course in your senior year in high school.

We should have been taught how credit cards operate, and what to look for in a loan. Some of this information is not new, but it certainly is hard to find in this world. Despite the need for this information, we still aren't taught any of this growing up, which is why young people just starting out are still making the same mistakes I did, and why we have more and more bankruptcies occurring every day.

Some of it is learning restraint, some of it is accepting personal responsibility, but a lot of it is that people just don't have the information they need to make informed decisions. Until now! Once people read this book, they'll be armed with all the knowledge I, and others, learned while out there in the financial wars. Now, people will have the opportunity to learn the very things they should have learned in school and be prepared to control their financial destiny.

Barring catastrophic illness or some other terrible event beyond their control, when most people go into debt it's a conscious decision. They decide they need this house, or that car, or they need to take such and such vacation. So they take out a loan, or they take out their MasterCard. And the debt grows and grows, and the interest mounts up. It's not hard to let that sort of thing get out of control—believe me, I've been there!

I am not saying credit cards and other such tools are evil or should be destroyed; actually, what I believe is quite the opposite. I believe credit can be a powerful tool to help you achieve financial independence and win the Cash Flow War—if it is used properly, and if you know the rules of the game. I use credit all the time—but *how* I use it is important. Too many people make critical mistakes unknowingly.

This book could stop that from happening to a lot of people. Someday I'd like to get this book into the hands of every high school senior in America. It would save a lot of people an immense amount of grief!

Our schools do a pretty good job of teaching kids how to read and write and do math, but they don't teach anyone the basics of what they need to know to run their life; or to put it another way, I've never applied for a bank loan where they asked me how to find the radius of a circle. I'm sure it's important to know how to calculate the radius of a circle, but I'm a lot more certain that knowing that won't help me to wisely use a credit card, how to pay off my mortgage sooner, or how to get a better deal on a car loan!

Where I Am Now

So here we are, 17 years after I first declared bankruptcy, and 16 years after I got mad at the system and decided to do something about it. And where did I end up? Well, I'm typing these words from a nice house in Orlando, Florida, and my wife just went to pick up my teenage daughter from her horseback riding lessons. Let me tell you, keeping a horse is not cheap. (Did you know that in addition to boarding a horse you have to feed it as well? Now I know where the phrase "Eats like a horse came from!") All joking aside, I feel very good about the fact that when my daughter expressed an interest in horses, my wife and I were in a financial position to allow her to pursue her dreams. In my spare time I golf, scuba dive, play volleyball, race cars, ride motorcycles, and fly stunt kites. And we vacation when and where we want.

I'll give you some concrete examples of the way I can now live my life, now that I've learned and applied all the winning battle tactics. My wife and I have no outstanding bills and we can pay cash for just about everything. We had paid off all four years of our daughter's college education by the time she was 10, we recently remodeled our house and paid cash, and we invest heavily in notes, real estate, and various other items. And last but certainly not least, our retirement accounts are fully funded. Everything I own is paid off (except leveraged investments) and I don't have to think about my retirement ever again. And I have a long way to go to before I want to retire anyway, because I'm still having a good time working!

I know we are well off financially and we are certainly thankful for it. If we want to buy a new car, we buy one. If we want to take a vacation, we take one. It is that simple. I don't believe that money should ever be the deciding factor in what you want to do. But we all live in the real world and unfortunately it takes money to do many of the things we want to do. But, I also know it is not that hard for many other people to be in the same situation I am—with the proper tools, training, and information.

My wife and I started out by opening up our own company, Diversified Investment Services. I became president of the American Cash Flow Association several years ago, and I fly all over the country speaking to thousands of people each year. I speak about personal finances, the cash flow industry, entrepreneurship, and self-employment. I keep in touch with my clients and students through my own weekly e-letters and weekly conference calls. To top it all off, I serve as publisher of the *American Cash Flow Journal* and I am a member of the National Speakers Association.

Please understand that I'm not telling you these things to show off. In fact, I wanted to dial this section back a little bit, but my friends and colleagues insisted that I put all this stuff in here. I just want to make sure that you understand that it is possible for an average person to rise up from bankruptcy and failure and achieve the American Dream, however you may personally define that dream. You already know where I came from, and now you have seen what I've accomplished. And there's nothing I have accomplished that you can't do just as well, or better! Once you're armed with the weapons you need to win the Cash Flow War, the sky is the limit.

Last I'd like to thank you for buying this book. I sincerely believe that if you read the whole book, and follow the hard-fought advice I've learned over the years, then you can follow thousands of others I have trained and accomplish your own personal goals. So, here's wishing you congratulations in advance on your upcoming victory in the Cash Flow War. Now let's get started!

Frederic M. Rewey

How to Use This Book

> *Friends come and go, but enemies accumulate.*
> —Thomas Jones, author

This book is divided into four parts. I call them the "phases of financial independence." Your road to winning the Cash Flow War will go through these four different phases. I suspect you may already have some knowledge of them now—or perhaps not. Although I would prefer it if you read this book from cover to cover, I understand that not everyone will need advice on every subject—although I would bet that you'll find at least a few new weapons for your Cash Flow War arsenal in each chapter.

So, feel free to skip around this book, concentrating on areas where you need the most help. In any case, this book is going to help you put it all together. Rest assured, those that have already won the war know this stuff! Let's just follow in their footsteps.

In the first part of this book, **Evaluating Your Troops**, we'll take a look at the basics of cash flow. This is where we get to know our surroundings, and find out what works for us and what works against us. We'll look at everyday things that you can do to change your prospects of victory in the Cash Flow War—we'll also look at basic areas like setting a budget, and how to figure out your net worth. This part will give you a real good idea of where you stand and where you need to be.

In Part Two, **Understanding The Battlefield**, we'll take an in-depth look at the sort of things that I believe we should have all learned. Unfortunately, this sort of everyday financial awareness is not taught in our schools, although I believe a lot of disappointment and heartbreak could be warded off if it were. Here's where we'll learn the ins and outs of credit cards, basic banking, loans of all sorts, and insurance issues. This is the stuff that they don't want you to know.

In Part Three, **Mastering the Rules of War**, we'll move forward. After Parts One and Two, you will now have a better understanding of the players in the cash flow war. In Part Three, we'll start using advance techniques with our newfound skills. It's time to take the next steps—it's time to get proactive. We all know there's more to life than living from paycheck to paycheck, so this part of the book will deal with how you can start making your money *work for you—and keep your money from others.*

In Part Four, **Building on Your Victory**, we'll take a more in-depth look at building your own business, and your investment vehicles, as well as how to take your financial success to the next level. It is this area of the book that will help ensure your financial success for generations to come.

Allies and Enemies

What I wouldn't give to have known who my friends and enemies were when I started out. In the beginning everyone seems to want to help you out. It is only later that I learned they were all so friendly because I was the one on the wrong side of the cash register. I want to make it easier for you. Look at the little icons off to the sides. You'll find these sprinkled throughout the book, and you should pay special attention to them.

Allies

Your **Allies** are special tips and techniques that will help you turn the tide of the battle just when you need them most. Think of these guys as the cavalry that comes roaring in over the hill just at the right moment in old westerns. Get to know your Allies, and when you see them pop up in the text in the upcoming chapters, make sure you pay special attention to them. These are your tried-and-true foxhole buddies, and they'll never steer you wrong.

Your **Enemies** are to be avoided at all costs. When you see these pop up in the text, make sure you pay special attention to them as well. If you ignore your enemies, you run the risk of setting yourself back in winning the Cash Flow War. I've clearly marked the enemies throughout this book. Remember, knowing who your true allies and true enemies are is half the battle, so when you see these icons pop up in the book, listen up.

Mail Call: This will reveal quotes or thoughts from the field that will help to shine the spotlight on a particular point we are discussing.

By the Numbers: Helpful statistics or quick facts that will help to easily explain a particular point.

Action Items: What to do and how to do it! This is your opportunity to put a technique or strategy to immediate use.

Land Mines: Step carefully, you're in a mine field! Call them what you want: snakes, scorpions, people that sell Tupperware, land mines, whatever scares you. Watch out for these. I'll be using this icon to clearly point out situations that may look okay to the untrained eye, but are guaranteed to blow up if you step into them unawares. These are the opportunities that are too good to be true, the schemes that seem foolproof on the surface, and the hidden dangers that await the unwary investor.

Marching Orders: These are friendly tips on how to use what you've learned in each chapter.

Ready? Let's get started!

Part One

Evaluating Your Troops

What would you attempt to do
if you knew you could not fail?

Robert H. Schuller, author, *Possibility Thinking*

Evaluating Your Troops

> *Living at risk is jumping off the cliff and building your wings on the way down.*
> —Ray Bradbury, author, *Bradbury Stories*

Now that you know my story as well as how to identify the *Allies* and *Enemies* in this book, it is time to get started.

The first section of this book is going to help you understand where you are financially and where you want to be. I suspect that you are saying, "Fred, I just want more money." I understand that. Wanting more money may be your goal, but we have to figure out *how* you are going to do that. The good news is there are numerous ways to get there and all we have to do is start at the beginning and follow in the footsteps of the successful people ahead of us.

I'll be the first to admit, in the beginning, some of this is the "boring stuff" that people may have already heard: "I need a budget." "I know I should have goals." "I should figure out my net worth, even though I know it is not where I want to be." Take a few extra minutes on the first section of this book and you will already have done what most people will not. The wealthy know this. Financially independent people know this. And now you know it.

The next few chapters are all about getting started. Here is what you can expect in the first part of this book.

Chapter 1: What Does Victory Mean to You?

It is human nature to question just about everything. It is also human nature to need to know where we are going and when we are going to get there. But more importantly, you need to know *why* you are going there. I don't believe you can fail in your mission to win the Cash Flow War as long as you follow this book and always remember for what, and whom, you are doing this. Let's get started on the right foot and make sure you are motivated to *finally* make a real positive change in your life.

Chapter 2: Planning Your Defense: Basic Training

Here you are going to learn the importance of a record-keeping system. I know— it sounds boring and you have no doubt heard it before. So if that is the case, is it a coincidence that the rich have a record-keeping system and the less fortunate do not? I don't think so. Let's learn the reasons why a simple record keeping system can help you win the war—once and for all.

Chapter 3: Financial Assessment Test

If we are going to win the war, we need to know where we are starting from. You certainly don't set out on a drive across the country without a map and, hopefully, you know your starting point. The same is true here. Let's find out where you are (financially) starting from. You can only move up from here and you may find some "hidden money" that you didn't know you had.

Chapter 4: Understanding the Importance of Budgeting

Maybe "budgeting" is not everyone's favorite word. It is a word that makes some people think they have to give up everything they enjoy. Well, rest assured that is not my thought at all. We are all adults here. I believe you can make the right decisions as long as you have all the information you need—and that does not mean you have to give up all your favorite things. Even millionaires have a budget. Budgeting is more about knowing where your money is going, and it is an important part of a cash flow winner's strategy.

Ready? Let's get started...

1

Welcome to the Cash Flow Academy

What Does Victory Mean to You?

> *I learned that the only way you are going to get anywhere in life is to work hard at it. Whether you're a musician, a writer, an athlete or a businessman, there is no getting around it. If you do, you'll win—if you don't, you won't.*
> —Bruce Jenner, Olympic gold medalist

Some people seem like they're just lucky. There are always some young kids that seem wise above their years and you know they will not have a thing (financially) to worry about. I was not one of those people; but now I help educate and create them. One of my biggest reasons to write this book was to help people avoid the mistakes I made. I'm going to help you be one of the lucky ones.

I used to think that wealthy people had secrets I would never learn. I almost always accepted what life sometimes offered as opposed to running out and getting what I wanted. I am glad I didn't and I am glad that you, too, have decided to make a positive change. The fact is that the wealthy do have secrets, but anyone can learn them, and that's what I intend to show here. The winners of the Cash Flow War are not born, they are created.

We already know what can happen to the losers in the Cash Flow War. In the worst-case scenarios, the losers face bankruptcy, increased chances of ill health, social and marital problems, and even stress-related death. But what do the winners get? What can the winners of the Cash Flow War expect?

Relief from financial stress is just the tip of the iceberg! This is a war for financial freedom that we're talking about!

Simply put, by winning the Cash Flow War, money will never be a determining factor in your day-to-day decision making again. Think about that for a minute. Imagine deciding your next vacation or gift not based on budget, but on what you really want to do or get. Obviously, if you're looking to buy a Rolls Royce or a Leer jet, money will play a role. They are attainable, but let's walk before we run.

Initially, if you apply the strategies learned in this book you'll never have to worry about finding the money to live a comfortable lifestyle again. In the end, I believe that is where most people want to be—simply not worrying about money.

When I was young I wanted items like a trip to Europe, a Harley-Davidson Motorcycle, a Porsche, lots of vacations, and even an air hockey table (don't ask). What do you want? Would a comfortable lifestyle, for you, be to own a nice house and provide for your family? Or do you want to own a home and a vacation home? How many cars do you want? How much money in the bank is "enough" money? Try and be honest with yourself when you answer these questions.

What you need to decide is what a "pleasant lifestyle" means to you. You need to figure out just what it would take, realistically, to achieve the feeling that you are financially secure. This level of security is different for everyone, and you need to figure out what it would take for you personally to be able to declare yourself a winner. After you have that set in your mind, you need to sit down and develop some clear goals and objectives.

Developing Goals and Objectives: Writing Your Battle Plan

I remember very clearly years ago, when well-meaning people would tell me "Fred, you need to visualize your goals if you're ever going to get ahead." One mentor of mine suggested that I write down what I wanted on a post-it note and put it on the mirror. Heck, I had so many dreams and goals I could have stuck them on my body and ran around the house looking like Big Bird! I used to think that setting goals was a waste of time. I was wrong. Goal setting and "To Do" lists are some of the biggest secrets to success.

There are two types of people that go to the store: those that have a list and know what they are going to get, and those that wander up and down the isles thinking "Do I need this?" and "Do I need that?" The aisle-wanderers end up taking five times as long, spend a lot more money, and still miss items they should have bought.

The best part about a list is that you know if you are on track. When you cross out items on your grocery list when you get to the end, you know you get to leave. And you can't tell me that when you cross out that last item there is not a brief moment of satisfaction. I know there is for me.

Here's your first lesson in the *Winning the Cash Flow War* boot camp: choosing and following a course toward short- and long-term financial goals. Without clear-cut financial goals and specific plans for meeting them, some people can just drift along, plugging away at their jobs, and more or less leaving the future to chance. Imagine trying to drive from San Francisco to New York *without* directions or a map—good luck! If you have a clear idea of where you want to go, it follows that you will be better able to gauge whether or not you're getting there, doesn't it? If you have a battle plan written out, then you'll be able to stay on track and win the Cash Flow War. Obviously, since you are not there now, something in your current battle plan (or lack thereof) has to change.

> **Unless you do something in your life to make change, nothing in your life will change.**

Mail Call

Five Stage Program for Setting Financial Goals

Stage 1: Get out a piece of paper and write down your financial goals. This was fun for me; it is like a "wish list." Don't leave anything out! Think about whether you're saving to send your kids to college, buy a new car, saving for a down payment on a house or a vacation home, paying off credit card debt, mortgages or loans, planning for retirement, buying new furniture, putting in a pool—you get the picture. List everything you can think of!

Stage 2: Now take those goals and break them down into four categories: short-term (less than one year), medium-term (one to three years), long-term (five years or more), and lifetime goals.

Stage 3: Educate yourself! This was one of the most important things I did to turn my life around; I wanted to learn everything I could to improve my financial outlook. You're well on your way with this book. You can also use this book as an introduction to everything. If you find a particular subject in here that intrigues you, continue to pursue it. But remember, in the Information Age the sources are vast. That is why you should first narrow the scope of what exactly you want to learn. Once you have successfully done that, you will be more easily prepared to take the steps necessary to learn what you need. Please be aware you don't want to get stuck in a cycle of continually searching for knowledge. There is an old saying that goes, "The more you know, the more you find you don't know." It would be impossible to know everything there is to know on any subject. It goes without saying, however, that the more you know, the better off you will be. But it is far better to know a lot about a specific subject than it is to know a little bit about a lot of subjects. Later, you will want to sign up for my e-letter at *www.winningthecashwar.com*. With this book and a little effort, you can learn enough to make educated decisions that will increase your net worth many times over. Then identify small, measurable steps you can take to achieve these goals, and put this action plan to work.

Stage 4: Make sure you can evaluate your progress by achieving little goals along the way towards your final objectives. Review your progress monthly, quarterly, or at any other interval you feel comfortable with. But make sure you check yourself against your goals at least semi-annually to determine if what you're doing is actually working.

Stage 5: Re-write your goals and objectives. The bottom line is, things change. You may find yourself ahead or behind on your goals—you may want or need to change them after you complete this book. If you're not making satisfactory progress on a particular goal, reevaluate your approach and make changes as necessary. If you've overshot a goal, maybe you had set your sites too low to begin with. If you took a realistic approach to Step 1, you might find that you are well ahead of where you wanted to be and you need to set the bar a little higher. If you were unrealistic, you might need to reset the bar a little lower. Be flexible.

Staying Motivated

Motivation: Sometimes I think that is what it all comes down to. I don't know how many times I heard the same message about finance until I finally took action and decided to change my life. I ordered countless programs and books (some good, some not), and still did nothing. Then, one day, I decided that I had had enough and that it was time to get moving—the idea of never trying to better my life was more annoying than the fear of actually doing it.

Once you've set your goals and objectives, one of the most difficult things to do is stay motivated. I can't emphasize this enough. We usually have no trouble getting excited about things initially, but once it actually begins becoming work—we find ourselves easily distracted. I am going to try and help you stay focused throughout this book. Although you may not see the changes right away, rest assured they are happening.

> **Make your first goal to read every page in this book—whether you think you know the information or not.**

Action Items

I have seen some of the most unlikely success stories come out of extraordinary circumstances. People that were battling education issues, geographical issues, and even physical or emotional issues have become formidable professionals in their chosen industry. Conversely, I have seen some of the most talented and educated people do nothing. If I were forced to pick what separates these people and I had to reduce it to one element, I would have to say it is motivation and commitment.

With proper motivation (commitment, drive, and a take-no-prisoners mentality), almost anything can be accomplished. I have seen it time and time again. It is interesting that most people really don't know what motivates them. What motivates you? You should be able to answer that question right away without significant thought. But realistically, lots of us really don't know what motivates us, or we think in terms of goals that are too extensive.

Mail Call

> **Find out what motivates you. If you read books and journals on psychology (not something I would recommend without purpose), you will note that some experts believe that we are always motivated by one of two circumstances: the *pursuit of happiness* and the *avoidance of pain*.**

The first big motivator for people is the *pursuit of happiness.* Perhaps you want to buy a new car, take a vacation with the family (or without the family), pay off some credit cards, or simply save money for a future goal. The pursuit of the "reward" can be very motivating. The reward does not need to be big, just something you would enjoy as a symbol of your achievement.

The second is the *avoidance of pain.* It is the opposite of the pursuit of happiness. Perhaps you are motivated by your inability to get a new car or pay off that bill or go on vacation. It doesn't matter how you are motivated. Either method can be very effective. Matter of fact, people can choose opposite motivators for the same thing. You will often go back and forth depending on the issue at hand.

The best example is a trip to the gym. People do not go to a gym at 5:30 AM because the idea of lifting a bar with metal discs on the end is fun. They don't get to take it with them. When they finish, it just goes back on the rack where they started. People do not go during their lunch hour to walk up mock steps that go nowhere for entertainment. It's not sport and for the most part, it is not a game.

So why do people do it? It boils down to one of two reasons. The pursuit of pleasure: They like how they look, they like how they feel, they want to lose weight, they want to do better in some physical activity, etc. These elements can be strong motivating factors.

The people on the other side of the gym are working just as hard, but are motivated by other factors: the *avoidance of pain*. They are concerned how they would look if they didn't work out or if they gained weight or if they aren't in shape to play with their family. Either motivational factor works, but the people are there for entirely different reasons and accomplish the same outcome.

So look closely at what motivates you. Study yourself and move forward. Are you nervous about introducing yourself to a new business contact that you keep hearing about? What if he or she can help you close more deals than you ever have before? What if it is the best call you ever could make? How can you afford *not* to follow through on something that could lead to great potential?

In the end, if you're doing things right, you will lead a life free of financial stress. Because you will have the motivation to accomplish everything you set out to do—or at the very least make an attempt.

Find out what motivates you and move forward. I can guarantee that if you discover what motivates you, and you let that motivation drive you, nothing will stop you from accomplishing your goals.

Never Forget That You're Fighting for Financial Freedom!

According to the Administrative Office of the U.S. Courts, for the fiscal year ended June 30, 2003, the number of bankruptcy filings was 1,650,279—the largest number of cases ever filed in any 12-month period. And according to some industry analysts, over the next 30 years 38 percent of all American households will be administered through the U.S. Court system. Now, I think that projection may be a little high, but it does underscore my point. We're in a war here—and far too many of us aren't winning!

Although we'll be discussing bankruptcy (and more importantly how to avoid it) in Chapter 19, I'd like to show you some statistics here to illustrate just how close a lot of us may be to losing the Cash Flow War. Although there are numerous ways to measure our failing battle, bankruptcy can clearly be seen as a concrete example of a major defeat, so I'll use it to hammer home the seriousness of the situation. Here are some not-so-cheerful facts from our friends at the Administrative Office of the U.S. Courts:

The 2003 national rate for filing personal bankruptcy is one in 78.8 households, or about 1.27% of all households.

Personal Bankruptcy Filings increased 9.6 percent in the 12-month period ending June 30, 2002.

Non-business filings totaled 1,613,097 for the 12-month period ending June 30, 2003, up 10 percent from the 1,466,105 cases filed in the 12-month period ending June 30, 2002.

It's No Longer a Private Affair

And if you do happen to lose your personal battle and fall into the bankruptcy trap, everyone will know it. As late as November 2003 all consumer bankruptcy information—including name, address, social security number, assets, liabilities and account numbers—continue to be available online for Chapter 13 Plans. In addition, court records also report the names and ages of children. This data is available to everyone as a public record. There is legislation currently pending to restrict access to some of your data, but as of 2004 this is the way it is.

Clearly, something is wrong with the battle plan these people falling into bankruptcy are following. And I think the first thing wrong is that these people don't realize they are in a war! In the end, all the government statistics and public embarrassment were not a concern of mine. Providing for my financial future and the financial future of my family was. I suspect it is the same for you. By virtue of you buying this book (and actually reading it), you're doing something about it. That is the first big step to take on the way to your eventual financial freedom.

Marching Orders for Chapter 1

✔ Write down your Battle Plan (goals and objectives).

✔ Sort your Battle Plan into a timeline.

✔ Determine what motivates you.

Planning Your Defense: Basic Training

> To be prepared for war is one of the most effectual means of preserving peace.
>
> —George Washington, United States president

Planning Your Defense: Basic Training

The good news about winning the Cash Flow War is that all we really need to do is follow the lead of other people who are already successful. And this is the sort of good news that you should be seeing on TV, but nobody ever shows it. Seems like all we ever hear about is crime, violence, and death—you almost never hear a success story. Think about it: Other than announcing this week's lottery winner, what do you ever hear on the local news that helps people better themselves? Not much. But there really is no shortage of positive stories out there; you just need to look a little harder. There is also no shortage of successful people out there. I personally know a lot of them and I've learned from them, and in this book I'm going to tell you what I learned and what you need to know to be successful.

We've already established that you and I are indeed in a Cash Flow War—and that the stakes are incredibly high—but what can we do about it? The answer is actually quite simple. I learned years ago that there are only three things you must do to succeed: *acknowledge, learn, and apply.*

I'm excited you've made the first positive step towards being an effective winner in the Cash Flow War. This shows you realize there are things you could be doing more efficiently to maximize your chances for personal victory. In order to begin correcting anything, *acknowledging* there is a problem is critical. Most people are able to do this. Most people know that there is something in their lives they would like to fix.

Guess what? You're already doing the second step! Reading this book and learning the information it contains is one method of gaining the knowledge you need. It is certainly not the *only* way to gain knowledge. In fact, I encourage you to continually seek out *learning* in all aspects of your life. But for now, this book is where we start. I know a lot of people who have stopped at the first step. They think that's all life has to offer and they just have to deal with whatever cards are dealt them. Not true! I suspect if you didn't think you could do better, you wouldn't be reading this book. You're looking for ways to do better.

The third step and final step is to begin *applying* what you learn—to arm yourself, and to familiarize yourself with the weapons that you'll be using in the Cash Flow War. This may sound simple—but this is where most people stumble. We all know someone in this category. As a matter of fact, for several years even I was in this category. I have a good friend named David who always has great ideas and has learned a lot about several things. But in the end, he just can't apply what he has learned. It's the only thing keeping him from being a success. People like David unfortunately don't apply what they've learned. For some it is fear of change, for others, they just don't ever think they have all their ducks in a row— they never feel the time is right to take a chance. Well, this won't be a problem for you. I'm going to show you how to successfully apply what you've learned.

The first weapon you'll learn how to wield in your basic training for the Cash Flow War is a record-keeping system. Pretty boring, right? But keeping good records may be among the most important tasks you will learn. So let's take a look at how you can implement a proper record-keeping system that will enable you to maximize your resources and deploy your assets in the most favorable manner—in other words, let's start kicking some financial butt!

Record-Keeping Systems

The biggest advantage in a record-keeping system is that you *know* where your money is going. You may be saying "Fred, I know where my money goes. It goes to groceries, bills, gas, etc." Well, my answer to that is simple: You're probably right, for the most part, but you don't have a complete picture yet—and that is dangerous.

One of the worst things you can do is make a decision (or, in our case, create a budget) with only part of the information. Or, as a wise man once said, "A *little* knowledge is a dangerous thing." What he meant was that if you only know half of what you need to know, you're making decisions based on only a fraction of information. We're here to find out all that we need to know. Having just a *little* knowledge is not good. It's like trying to bake a cake when you have only half of the proper ingredients, and so you decide to just make up the other half of the ingredients—have fun eating that cake, but please don't send me any.

Record keeping will give you a full, accurate view of your finances. I couldn't believe the results the first time I did this. I had no idea how much money I spent on little things like lunch or a few sodas. My friend Robert calls this sort of spending "leakage"—money that seems to disappear without any trace. If that is the case, when I first took a serious run at record keeping, the Hoover Dam must have broken! I found literally *hundreds* of dollars a month that were just falling through the cracks.

Now the light pops on—suddenly record keeping is not so boring after all. Especially if you're going to get "paid" for it. The most important part of an effective, efficient record-keeping system is to build the proper foundation and get it set up right. Later in the book we will talk about making it "scalable"— especially if you plan to include a small business or if your saving and investment activity grows. "Scalable" simply means we'll adopt a system that will be able to grow with you. Believe it or not, in a little while you will need a system that can handle *positive* cash flows such as savings, stocks, rental homes, and other investments. Keep in mind you don't need some wild elaborate system for most of the purposes we'll discuss in this book, but you must have *some* system.

> **An accurate record of your spending will be one of the most important things you can do in the beginning. We need to know the battlefield and what we are fighting!**

Allies

The simplest system is to just use your checkbook and pad of paper. Record every single check and deposit slip, along with the details of that transaction. If the item is not in the checkbook (as most of your cash items will not be), write it down on the pad of paper. Make sure that *all* transactions are recorded in the checkbook and on the pad of paper. Leave nothing out. Even the smallest fifty-cent purchase should be written down.

You are going to do this for your first two weeks, and then for a total of 30 days. The reason we'll start with two weeks is to get a quick picture of your situation as you progress through the book. However, you will not have a complete picture until you get at least 30 days. Remember, a *little* knowledge is a dangerous thing; you've got to do this for at least 30 days!

You can also use journals that record cash receipts and cash disbursements. Journals or ledger paper that fit into a notebook are available at office supply stores like OfficeMax or Office Depot. Again, make sure you record all transactions in the appropriate journals. I know there are many software products available today that have these journals included in them (for home PCs as well as for popular handhelds like Palm Pilots). They'll do the math for you, but the basic principles of an old pen-and-paper system are the same that are followed in the software products. So if you plan to use software, remember that you'll just be typing in the entries we talk about rather than writing them down. It's the same principle though—just like Ray Davies says in that old Kinks tune "Low Budget," you need to "count every penny and watch where it goes."

Allies

There are great software programs out there like Quicken® and Microsoft Money® that will enable you to keep all your records on your home PC. Many of these products also have the ability to do some basic reporting and create some nice-looking graphs and charts.

Land Mines

Always remember, with a software record-keeping application, to back up your information often to a removable storage device like a CD or a diskette. If you don't, when your computer inevitably crashes (and they all do, sooner or later) you could be left up the creek without a paddle!

Don't forget (and here's something that you can't do with software): You need to keep the originals of all receipts, invoices and order forms. You can put all of them for one specific month in one envelope. Or, you can keep all the receipts in one file folder and all the invoices in another. The important thing is to decide what you're going to do it and then make sure that you do it consistently.

Try and keep your filing system simple—decide what you need to file and set up a system that makes sense to you. Don't forget the little things, like making sure you label your folders so they can be easily read. If you're making this effort in tandem with your spouse or partner, it usually works best if one person is in charge of the records. The other partner, however, must be familiar enough with the system to be able to take over if necessary, or to file items when it is necessary.

> Keep all financial records for at least six years after tax returns are filed. You never know when Uncle Sam will come knocking, and the best defense against any tax problems is to have all your ducks (or receipts, in this case) in a row.

Action Items

Checklist for Good Records

✔ **Open a business checking account (if needed).** If you are running a home business, don't use your personal checking account for your business. The cost of another account is minimal compared to the confusion of business matters in your personal account. You will also find you may not be able to deduct certain items if you mix business with pleasure.

✔ **Pay all bills by check or debit card.** On each check, note what was purchased with that check. This is your record of having paid bills and enables analysis of expenditures.

✔ **Get receipts for cash.** Make sure when spending cash that you have a receipt including the purpose of each expense.

✔ **Endorse all checks immediately.** Endorse checks "for deposit only" to your account in your bank.

✔ **Deposit receipts often.** Don't keep cash or checks around your home or place of business. They invite theft, they can get lost and the money should be put to work for you immediately. Also, take copies of all checks you deposit!

✔ **Label bank deposit slips completely.** They provide a good record for sources of income and back up sales records.

✔ **Balance bank account monthly.** Do it when the statements come from the bank.

✔ **Practice good record hygiene.** Keep clean, neat, and consistent records.

Don't get discouraged if you can't immediately find a record-keeping system that works correctly for you. This whole process will probably involve a little time and error. Remember to be diligent—count *every penny* and watch where it goes.

What Sort of Records Can I Toss Out?

After you're doing this for a while, you'll probably need a nice file cabinet to keep your stuff in—but you really don't need to keep *all* of your records around forever.

For instance, my friend Bill has his tax returns for the last fifteen years. That's overkill! How long should you keep tax records? The Internal Revenue Service has three years in which to audit federal income tax returns—except, of course, when Uncle Sam decides to bend his own rules. In unusual cases, if you failed to report more than 25 percent of your gross income, the government has six years to collect the tax or to start legal proceedings. Also, there are no time limitations if you filed a fraudulent return or if you failed to file a return. But if you pay all the taxes on what you make, you don't need to hold onto the stuff for more than three years. Personally, I like to keep seven years' worth to help measure my progress.

But you don't have to keep everything. You can lighten your record load by discarding certain checks and bills once they have served their purpose. For example, you can throw away weekly or monthly salary statements after you check them against your annual W-2 Form. But save canceled checks that relate directly to any entries on your tax returns, and keep all medical bills for three years to back up your canceled checks.

If You Really Want to Keep Some Detailed Records

You should keep two home files in addition to your safe deposit box at the bank. In the safe deposit box you should keep important papers like your mortgage, insurance information, and wedding and birth certificates—things that would be difficult to replace if you lost them.

The two home files are your *active file* and your *dead storage file*. Your *active file* will hold:

- Unpaid bills until paid

- Bill receipts

- Current bank statements

- Current cancelled checks

- Income tax working papers

After three years, move these items to your *dead storage file*.

There are other items which should always be kept in your *active file*. These include:

- Employment records, such as résumés, recommendation letters, and health benefit information

- Credit card information, including the number of each card, by company name

- Insurance policies

- Copies of wills

- Family health records

- Appliance manuals and warranties

- Education information, such as transcripts, diplomas, etc.

- Social Security information on benefits and regulations

- An inventory of what's in your safe deposit box (you might store a key in the inventory folder)

Finally, keep a record book of the whereabouts of your important papers. If you use a loose-leaf binder, you will be able to change papers easily or copy a page or two.

The book should contain a list of all your savings and checking accounts. This way you won't become one of the missing depositors who have forgotten their accounts or who have died without telling relatives about them. Also, include the name and branch of the bank where you keep your safe deposit box.

The book also should have all of the family members' social security numbers, and all of the insurance policy information. Finally, if you're a family guy or girl, make sure someone else knows and understands the family record-keeping system—and keep the book in a safe place.

What You Need in Your Home Cash Flow Command Center

Okay, it's time for you to take the controls, Captain. Don't worry, there are plenty of resources at your disposal (and I'll show you how to find them in later chapters), but let's make sure you have everything you need to run your own Cash Flow Command Center.

At the most basic level, all you need is a chair, a lamp, this book, a financial calculator, a pen and some paper, and a place to keep your files. That's all you need to get started. I'll explain financial calculators more fully in Chapter 14, but for now you should just know that your regular garden variety calculator is *not* a financial calculator. Don't get all flustered about the financial calculator. They're not that hard to operate and they're one of those things that I was talking about in the Introduction that rich people know about and the rest of the world doesn't.

However, if you can afford to add some things...a good computer with a high-speed internet connection, an inkjet printer, some of the software I mentioned previously, a separate business phone (if you have a home business), and a comfy work station would really do the trick. You can get all of these things with one phone call to a company like Dell or OfficeMax. None of these items are strictly necessary, but you may find they will make things easier.

Marching Orders for Planning Your Defense: Basic Training

✔ **Develop a Record Keeping System.**

✔ **Set up a Home Office.**

✔ **Work on developing the right attitude.**

✔ **Track all spending for two weeks.**

✔ **Track all spending for 30 days.**

Financial Assessment Test

> *A billion here, a billion there and pretty soon it adds up to real money.*
>
> —Senator Everett Dirksen

Checking Up on Your Financial Well-Being

If you and I were on a journey across the country we would need a map. And we would certainly need to know where our starting point is. This chapter is all about how to find out where the starting point is for you, the Cash Flow Warrior.

In the last chapter we learned that we need to track our spending. If we don't know where the money is going (and often we don't), it makes it almost impossible to make sure it is in the right place. If you are like I was, you no doubt found a few surprises along the way.

This is a good place for us to examine just how well you're doing in the Cash Flow War so far. Remember, we're still in boot camp—don't get frustrated or upset if the results you achieve in this chapter are a little disappointing. The whole reason you're reading this book is that you want to improve on these results the next time you objectively look at your finances. In this chapter we'll fill in a questionnaire about your financial situation, and then take a look at how to figure out your personal net worth. By the end of the chapter you should be able to gauge pretty well just how far you have to go to meet your goals.

Net Worth Test

Here's a little test I put together to give you a quick snapshot look at your financial health. It's not scientific, but between this test and the personal net worth section in this chapter, you will have a pretty good feel for where you are. You can then gauge yourself against where you eventually want to be financially. Answer each question with *yes* or *no*. If the question doesn't really apply to you (like if you're single and the question refers to a spouse or partner) then give yourself a break and answer *yes*:

1. Do you know your net worth?

2. Are you making what you feel you are worth?

3. Do you live in the neighborhood that you desire to live in?

4. Have you paid off your mortgage?

5. Do you own a rental or income-producing property?

6. Do you own a vacation home or a timeshare?

7. Have you avoided having to pay mortgage insurance?

8. Do you pay your credit cards off every month?

9. Do you pay your other monthly bills in full each month?

10. Do you pay cash (or use a debit/check card) for everyday expenses (groceries, lunches, gasoline, etc.)?

11. Do you have at least three months' worth living expenses, or $6,000, put aside in case of emergency?

12. Do you have a 401(k), IRA, Keogh, or a defined benefits pension program?

13. Do you have more than one retirement account?

14. Besides your emergency money and your retirement plan, do you save or invest regularly?

15. Do you have any idea how much you need to save every month to retire at your targeted age?

16. Do you even have a targeted retirement age?

17. Do you have adequate life insurance?

18. Does your spouse/partner have adequate life insurance?

19. Do you have car insurance?

20. Do you have health insurance?

21. Does your insurance cover long-term disability?

22. Do you agree that Social Security will not cover your retirement expense?

23. Do you (and your spouse/partner) have a will?

24. Do you spend less than 25 percent of your gross income on rent or mortgage payments?

25. Are you investing or saving money every pay period?

26. Do you save 10 percent of your gross income each month?

27. Do you know the interest rates on your checking, savings, and credit card accounts?

28. Do you know the interest rate on your mortgage or car loans?

29. Have you looked at your credit report lately?

30. Do you balance your checkbook monthly?

31. Do you keep track of your monthly expenses?

32. Do you read about improving your personal finances? (Hey, look, a freebie question: You're doing it right now!)

33. Do you have a long-term financial plan?

34. Do you have short-term financial goals?

35. When you contemplate a purchase, is the cost your first concern?

36. In the last year, did you purchase anything that your parents would never have been able to afford?

37. Were you able to take a nice vacation in the last year?

38. Can you not worry about how much you spend (within reason)?

39. Are you completely satisfied with your financial status?

40. Do you see yourself winning the Cash Flow War?

Summarizing the Results

Okay, now let's add up your results. Award yourself one point for every *yes* answer. Forty questions answered *yes* would give you a perfect score of 40. Don't worry, if you didn't get all 40 correct: That just gives you something to build on. Check your score against these generalized grades:

0 to 15 points: You're currently in dire need of a variety of financial self-help remedies. First off, get yourself on a budget immediately! We'll look closely at budgeting in Chapter Four. But be aware that you are currently at risk of suffering a few big defeats in the Cash Flow War. One financial setback, such as a job loss or accident, can really hurt your chances of immediate economic recovery. But take heart—by using just some of the strategies in this book, you will see a phenomenal improvement in your situation!

16 to 30 points: You're doing well enough for yourself and your family, but you could do a lot better. Let's just say that you're definitely on the right track to meeting your goals and objectives. However, now is definitely not the time to declare victory. As a matter of fact you are at a crossroads—let's make sure we take the right path! You need to keep working out the details of your personal financial plan and keep on learning more about the Cash Flow War. You've got a good jump on the enemy and all you need to do is to refine your tactics.

31 to 39 points: Life is good. Your hard work has paid off, and your personal financial plan has all the potential to keep you in great economic shape. But it's *still* not time to declare victory: You need to continually update your goals and objectives and make sure that they still fit the changing needs of your life's circumstances. Be sure to update your plan frequently, the real world changes around you every minute. You've come this far, and after all such hard work, you don't want to lose a few battles because you fell asleep on guard duty.

40 points: What's the title of *your* book? Time for you to help others!

Calculating Your Net Worth

Now that you may have an idea of where you are (or at least how you feel), let's move on to a more in-depth way of gauging your financial health. The last test was a little bit of fun, but calculating your net worth will really give you a good idea of where you are in your personal Cash Flow War. When I first calculated my net worth, it was pretty depressing. I certainly had a long way to go to win the Cash Flow War but then it dawned on me that that I could only move up from where I was!

Interestingly enough, your income has *nothing* to do with your net worth. This was illustrated most clearly when I reviewed the documents produced by some students of mine. Bill and Donna had a combined income of $128,000 while Chris and Mary had a combined income of $43,000. When they both did their net worth statements, Chris and Mary had a positive net worth of $112,000 where Bill and Donna had a *negative* net worth of $23,000. This is actually not uncommon. In most cases, it is not the money you make, but what you do with the money available to you.

If you just take a look at your cash-flow analysis over a single year, it really doesn't give you a good picture of the cumulative impact of those habits on your financial worth. You really need to sit down and do a net-worth statement. This may sound like we're straying into an area where we'll need a certified public accountant to help us out, but all you're really doing is adding up what you own and subtracting what you owe. At the end of it all, you'll know exactly what you're worth financially. Let's hope you're pleasantly surprised. If not, that's okay too; we are going to change that. Remember, achieving awareness of your current financial state is one of the most important things we can do at this point.

Determining your net worth is a three-stage process. First you need to figure out the value of everything you own, and then you need to figure out exactly how much money you owe. In the third stage, when you total up the figures, you'll find your net worth.

First Stage: Add Up All Your Assets

Grab a pen and paper (you can also use the worksheet in this chapter) and a calculator.

First, start with cash: whatever you have on you, what's in your checking account, and whatever you may have stashed away somewhere. Then add in the balance of your savings accounts, CDs (certificates of deposit), and money market accounts. If you have U.S. savings bonds, check their current values with a bank or go to the Bureau of the Public Debt Web site (*http://www.publicdebt.treas.gov*) to find out what they are worth.

Take a look at any life insurance policies you may have. Do you have a cash value policy? Only policies that have been paid for and have cash value have these; most policies out there are "term" and do not have a cash value related to the amount of premiums you have paid on them. However, some policies actually have a cash value if you needed to cash it in. Call and check with your insurance agent or see if there is a table in the policy that tells you what the policy is currently worth. If you have any annuities, they also have a cash value, known as the surrender value. Call your agent to find out what they're worth presently.

If you have a traditional defined-benefit pension plan, or have profit sharing at work, you can add in values for these as well. It's kind of tough to figure out what these are worth, so the best way is to call the human resources department at work and ask them to tell you the amount you could hypothetically withdraw if you quit your job today. Let them know why you're asking; you don't want to start anybody thinking about having to replace you! Even though these values will increase as time goes on, you can only add in the dollar figure they are currently valued at when you're figuring out net worth.

If you have an IRA, 401(k) plan, or Keogh, or a similar plan, list its current balance. You should be getting regular statements on these, so this shouldn't be hard to determine.

A lot of company-provided 401(k) plans have account access online. You can look at your balances at any time.

Remember, if you are looking at a pre-tax account like a 401(k) or an IRA, you would have to pay tax (and penalties) if you took that money out prior to retirement age (currently 55 or 59½ depending on the plan type). For the purpose of this exercise, use the full amount because that is what it will be worth (aside from increases) when you finally withdraw it at retirement.

Enemies

If you own a home, this is probably your biggest asset. You need to be careful you assign it an accurate value. Don't just list what you paid for it; or worse yet, don't take a wild guess. You can go to *www.realtor.com* to find out what similar homes are selling for; just enter your zip code and then fill in the form that asks what type of home you're looking for with information that describes *your* home. This is a neat site; currently you don't have to register or provide any information, so whatever you do is private. Do the same thing with any other real estate or business interests you own as well.

If you own any financial assets such as stocks, bonds, and mutual funds, the value should be clearly stated on the most recent statements from your funds or broker. Again, you can get an up-to-the-minute picture if they have online Web access.

You can get a pretty good idea of what your car or other vehicle is worth by consulting a car price guide, such as the Kelley Blue Book or the NADA Official Used Car Guide, published by the National Automobile Dealers Association. Kelley is online at *www.kbb.com* and you can find the NADA listings at *www.nadaguides.com*. NADA will give you prices on anything from a snowmobile to a car to a boat. Banks that make auto loans usually have hard copies of those guides, as do many public libraries. But if you end up in a library, you might as well go online for the pricing—the information will be more up to date.

Don't expect a dealer to ever give you the prices you find in one of these guides. If you're going to sell vehicles and you want top dollar, you need to do it privately. Check the paper for similar items and see how much they are selling for.

Land Mines

You'll have to make ballpark figures for the value of household furnishings, appliances, and other personal belongings. Try and be conservative in your estimates. One way to come up with a quick figure is to say that whatever is inside your home is worth 25 percent of the value of the home itself. So if you have a $100,000 home, then the items in it are worth about $25,000. You'll probably get closer to the real value if you do a piece-by-piece estimate, and then cut that total by 50 percent. If you have antiques, furs, jewelry, or collections of stamps, coins, comics, baseball cards, and so on, try to figure out the current market value of them. Don't use the price you paid, as they have probably shifted in value since purchase. If you're a collector of any kind, then you already know that people publish price guides on everything! Check those guides out for estimated market value.

> **Remember: The value of a collectible is really what you can actually *sell* it for, not necessarily the appraised or book value. Want to be safe? Deduct 35–50 percent off those book values or check on some recent sales at places like eBay.**

Total up all those items listed in the preceding paragraphs, and you'll have the current value of your total assets.

Second Big Stage: Total Up Your Liabilities

This is the part that isn't so much fun, but it also shouldn't be too difficult. Liabilities are obvious, and whoever you owe money to probably sends you a reminder of the debt on a regular basis.

Start by adding the total of all your current bills. Next, list the total balance due on every credit card and home equity or similar loan you have taken. Don't forget your car loan. Your home mortgage is probably your biggest single liability, and the year-end or monthly statement from the lender should show exactly how much you still owe on it, and what your real estate taxes are—or you can call them for the balance. Go through all your mail and checkbook and make sure you list every single debt you owe. Don't leave anything out! Everything you owe is a liability that cuts into your net worth.

Third Stage: What's the Bottom Line?

Just subtract your total liabilities from your total assets and the number you end up with is your net worth. I can almost guarantee that the number is not what you'd like it to be. It's very possible that it's a negative number, especially if you have credit card debt and a car loan. Don't get too upset by this number; it's not uncommon to have a negative net worth. Most people are in the same boat. What separates you from others is that you're actually taking the first steps in your march towards winning the Cash Flow War.

I can guarantee that you're one of the only people in your neighborhood who actually knows what his or her current net worth is. You need this information so you can use the weapons you will discover in this book to start to figure out where to beef up your assets and trim your liabilities.

And if you ended up with a net worth in the millions, check your math! If it still shows you that you're worth a few million, put down this book and go play golf or something, because you've obviously already won your Cash Flow War. But, if you're like most people who go through this exercise, you now have a firm foundation to start planning on.

Use This!

You can use this worksheet to figure out your net worth; obviously, you'll need to do some serious calculations to fill in some of the blanks. To use this worksheet, fill out the appropriate fields under assets and liabilities, and then perform the addition and subtraction.

Cash War New Worth Worksheet

Assets

Cash in savings accounts _____

Cash in checking accounts _____

Cash on hand _____

Certificates of deposits   _____

Money market funds   _____

U.S. savings bonds   _____

Market value of home   _____

Market value of other real estate   _____

Cash value of life insurance   _____

Surrender value of annuities   _____

Vested equity in pension plans   _____

Vested equity in profit sharing   _____

401(k) or 403(b) plans   _____

Individual retirement accounts   _____

Keogh plans   _____

Stocks (individually owned)   _____

Bonds (individually owned)   _____

Stock mutual funds   _____

Bond mutual funds   _____

Real estate investment funds   _____

Other investments   _____

Collectibles   _____

Precious metals   _____

   Total of assets   _____

Estimated Market Value

Household furnishings   _____

Automobiles   _____

Boats, other recreational vehicles _____

Furs and jewelry   _____

Loans owed to you   _____

   Total of other assets   _____

Liabilities

Balance owed on mortgages   _____

Auto loans   _____

Student loans   _____

Home equity credit line   _____

Other credit lines   _____

Credit card bills   _____

Other bills   _____

Total liabilities   _____

Total assets   _____

    minus

Total liabilities   _____

Net worth   _____

Are You "Okay" or Do You Want to Do Better?

Now that you've taken an objective look at your finances, tell the truth: Are you "okay" or do you want to do better? I already know that you want to do better, and by going through this process you already have a better grasp of your financial status than you've probably ever had before. You know the areas where you are doing well, and you know the areas in which you have room for improvement.

> **Sometimes you hear someone sum up your thoughts perfectly. Every time I try and describe how people get "comfortable" with their financial situation (even if it isn't good). I am reminded of what one of my Cash Flow graduates, Kristi, always said. "I was beginning to feel that living an adequate life was going to have to be good enough, that it was all I could have . . . I now know that there is so much more out there."**

Mail Call

Don't get down on yourself because you're not a millionaire yet—if you were, you would have already won the cash war. Many people believe that millionaires have some secret that "normal folks" don't have access to—a secret that allows them to accumulate immense fortunes. Others think millionaires are just naturally smarter than most people. Then there's the belief that there is an "inside" group of well-connected people who somehow pick and choose who will become the newest millionaire. And of course, there are those who feel millionaires were just plain lucky.

Obviously, most of these theories are silly. Millionaires are ordinary people no smarter than you are. Very few got where they are by being lucky—and fewer still had enough "luck" to maintain their wealth. There isn't a secret "insiders" group somewhere—at least none that I've ever been invited to. But the truth is that most people who have won the Cash Flow War do have a universal secret. They all share a mindset that helped them succeed. They all know most of the items in this book. They all know the rules of engagement in the Cash Flow War. They have all taken *control* of their financial future.

We know now where we stand or, more importantly, what our starting point is. In the coming chapters I will share with you my personal strategies, philosophies, and mindset on building the kind of financial freedom most people only dream about. These are the techniques I continue to use every day to build as well as retain my own wealth. More importantly, these simple-to-use strategies can be applied to your life to achieve the same results I have seen. I firmly believe that you can easily put these strategies to work for you. I know that if you do, then you will more easily find the success you've been working toward. And the next time you sit down to figure out your net worth, you may just get up from the table feeling like a million bucks.

Marching Orders for Financial Assessment Test

✔ **Take the Financial Assessment Test.**

✔ **Figure out your net worth.**

✔ **Don't get downhearted: Keep your eye on your final goals and objectives.**

4

Understanding the Importance of Budgeting

> *I'm living so far beyond my income that we may almost be said to be living apart.*
>
> —E. E. Cummings, poet

Budget—The very mention of the word used to make me cringe. I used to think that it meant nothing other than "learn to do without." Let me tell you, nothing could be further from the truth! Adhering to a good and comfortable budget helps to assure that you are staying on track in your Cash Flow War campaign. The big trick for me was learning how to create a "livable" budget. You need to create a budget that works for you—not against you!

I knew a waitress named Ann; she was a single mom with three kids. Ann asked me to help her out with a basic budget, so I sat down with her one night and went over all of her bills with her. It turns out that she was doing pretty well; she was actually living within her means and making all the payments that she needed to. Now, Ann didn't have a lot of wiggle room in her budget, but we still found a way for her to put away five percent of what she makes every month. It's not a lot, but it's a start—and if Ann can find a way to do it, I'm pretty confident that you can, too.

Mail Call

> **Budgeting is one of the most underestimated tools in winning the Cash Flow War. I often hear people say, "I don't have enough money to make a difference." Well, by the end of this book you'll see how just a little money, put in the right place, can go a long way.**

Now that you know your net worth and have an idea of where your money is going, it's time to figure out what you should be doing with your money. You need to sit down and sharpen your pencil and create a livable budget. And somewhere in that budget 10 percent of your net income that you can invest and start supplying the forces that will be out in the trenches winning the Cash Flow War for you!

I can't emphasize enough the importance of budgeting—you simply must know how much money you have to spend and where you are spending it. It amazes me that the vast majority of people do not track their monthly spending. Budgeting is one of the most powerful weapons in your Cash Flow War arsenal and it does not deserve the "restrictive" reputation that it has. When people think of budgets they think they have to "go without." But as I mentioned before, that is simply not the case. As a matter of fact, you may find *more* money for the things you like to do.

Thankfully, budgeting it is one of the easiest weapons to learn how to use and master. The bottom line is that creating a budget means tracking your *personal* cash flow—knowing just how much money comes into and goes out of your pocket every month.

Mail Call

> **Record keeping only shows you where your money goes. Budgeting will help you make sure it goes to the right place.**

Whatever you may have found out about your current status when you figured out your net worth in Chapter 3, the simple act of developing a workable budget is the first step in gaining complete control over your financial future. Just look at what a budget will help you to achieve:

- The ability to track your personal cash flow.

- Complete control of your finances.

- A roadmap for saving and investing money on a regular basis.

- An easy way to identify and eliminate unnecessary expenses.

- A sensible planning process for upcoming events and major purchases.

- And—perhaps most importantly—if you have a family or a partner, a concrete base upon which to build discussions about the priorities for where your money should be spent.

Budgeting Basics

I'll take you through the basics of budgeting with the assumption that you'll be doing it the time-honored way—with a sharp pencil and a piece of paper. But if you can use a financial management program like Quicken® or Microsoft Money®, your budgeting job could be a lot easier. Today's software choices can help you categorize where every cent goes each month, and can print out graphs and reports from your computer. They're definitely worth the investment for the budgeting process, and they'll also help you with the record keeping we discussed in Chapter 2. But don't get discouraged if you cannot access one of these programs; you can do just as good a job of creating a budget without them—they just make it a little easier.

My buddy Steve has a very elaborate budgeting system in a computer worksheet. He must have spent hours evaluating and adjusting it. His sister Maryanne uses a legal pad of paper and a pen. So who has the better system? They both have a good system—use whatever method works best for you!

Using software or not, the basic principles of budgeting are the same. Just like the record keeping we talked about in Chapter 2, it's not the tools you use to do the job at hand; it's the amount of time and thought you put into it that will yield the greatest rewards. I'll discuss budgeting in such a way that it won't matter whether you're using a software program or a pencil and a piece of paper.

There are five basic steps to creating a workable budget:

1. **Determining your total monthly income.**

2. **Determining your total monthly expense.**

3. **Analyzing your expenses.**

4. **Evaluating spending habits to look for areas to cut expenses.**

5. **Tracking your spending to make sure it stays within pre-set limits.**

Sounds pretty simple, doesn't it? Well, in reality, it is pretty simple. The hardest part is to maintain self-discipline once you determine your budget. Since you've already expressed an interest in doing a little work to make a better life for yourself and your significant others, I'm sure you're ready, willing, and able to apply a little self-discipline to make your budget work. So, let's begin!

Step One: What's Your Monthly Income?

This one is the simplest step. How much money do you make on a monthly basis? You should have this information from Chapter 3. If your income fluctuates wildly due to factors like commissions or overtime pay, figure out what your average monthly income is or use a figure slightly lower—that way your budget is not thrown off on a "lower month." Make sure you include all sources of income. When you're figuring out what your salary or wage is, make sure you use the take-home figure. Exclude any money you make that goes directly to Uncle Sam—however painful that may be.

Here's what to include in your monthly income:

- Take home salary and/or wages

- Any income from self-employment. Do you moonlight or freelance on the side?

- Retirement pay, pension payments, annuities and any money from the government such as Social Security, disability, or unemployment

- All interest and dividends

- Alimony and/or child support

- Rent—paid *to* you!

- Income from trusts

- Any other source of consistent income you may have.

Total up all these fiugres; this is your total monthly income.

Allies

> When computing an average income for budgeting purposes, always stay on the low side. After all, if you create a budget based on less than you actually make, then you'll be that much further ahead of the game!

Step Two: What Are Your Total Monthly Expenses?

This could be the most painful part of this process—you need to be completely honest with yourself when you sit down to figure this out. Again, you should have this figure from our exercise in Chapter 3. You need to include everything here, ranging from your mortgage payment down to the pack of gum you pick up when you put gas in your car. As we mentioned in Chapter 2, the easiest way to go about this is to pick a thirty-day period and keep a record of everything. Collect all your bills, your credit card statements, your checkbook register, and get receipts for your groceries, gas, or anything else you buy with cash. It's very important that you don't leave anything out, even little items like lottery tickets and sodas. Get a receipt for absolutely anything you buy, and anything you can't get a receipt for, write down what it cost and add it to the pile.

Here's a partial list of what you may have to include in your monthly expenses:

Household

- Groceries

- Cleaning supplies

- Maid service

- Laundry

- Dry cleaning

- Home improvement projects

- Tools

- Towels, linens

- Furniture (indoor and outdoor)

- Clothing

Transportation

- Car payments

- Car insurance

- Gas

- Maintenance—oil, windshield wiper fluid, etc.

- Car repairs (take an annual figure and average it out monthly)

- Airfare

- Commuting costs (train fare, tolls, parking, etc.)

- Rental cars

- Any public transportation costs

Basic Shelter

- Mortgage or rent

- Home insurance

- Taxes

- Electricity, gas, or oil

- Water

- Garbage pick-up

Personal Care

- Hair cuts, perms, manicures

- Make-up

- Medical, dental, vision (premiums prescription costs, co-pays, over-the-counter remedies)

- Weight loss, diet products

- Vitamins and nutritional supplements

Entertainment

- Cable TV or satellite service
- Eating out
- Bars, clubs, etc.
- Beer, wine, liquor
- Gambling (football pools, lottery tickets, etc.)
- Movies
- Sporting events
- Sports expenses (greens fees, bowling, gym costs, etc.)
- Lessons
- Club fees or dues
- CDs, DVDs, VCR tape rentals and purchases
- Books, magazines

Other

- Credit card payments
- Other loan payments
- Child care
- Tuition
- School supplies
- Special items for baby/elderly
- Kids' allowances
- Vacation
- Donations to church or charity
- Gifts (holidays, birthdays, wedding, baby shower, graduation, anniversary, etc.)
- Emergency fund
- Coffee, soda, cigarettes, etc.

Communication

- Telephone
- Cell phone and/or pager
- Internet access
- Voice mail
- Postage

Savings

- Pay yourself first—10% of your total monthly income should go to savings and investments. More on this later!

Obviously, you'll need to figure out a monthly average for some of these items such as car repair. When you are done, add it up. This is your total monthly expense.

Step Three: Analyzing Your Expenses

Here's where we can start to make some positive improvements to your situation. You need to look at your expenses and figure out what are fixed expenses, what are variable expenses, and what are discretionary expenses. The second and third categories are where we'll be able to find you some wiggle room!

Here's a partial list of what to include in each category of your monthly expenses:

Fixed Expenses

- Mortgage or rent
- All loans
- Insurance premiums
- 10% of your total monthly income for savings and investments
- Commuting costs: What does it cost to get to work?
- Tuition

Variable Expenses

- Utilities
- Water and garbage
- Some communication costs
- Gasoline
- Groceries

Discretionary Expenses

- Health and beauty costs
- Entertainment costs
- Some communication costs

- Donations
- Gifts
- Maid service
- Dry cleaning
- Lawn service
- Pool service

This is really only a partial breakdown, because you'll have to figure out into which of the three groups many of your personal expenses fit. For example, even though I have all entertainment costs listed under Discretionary Expenses, you may feel that going to the gym is absolutely essential to your health so much so that you consider it a fixed cost. Others may feel that gym fees are discretionary. Only you can decide which group each of your expense fall into—you're the one who's going to have to live with this budget!

Step Four: Evaluating Your Spending

Action Items

Start evaluating your spending by determining how much you need to trim. To do this, simply subtract your monthly expenses from your monthly income. If your take-home pay is $4000 per month and your list of expenses came to $4600 per month, you obviously need to trim $600 or more per month.

Positive cash flow: Do you have money left over? Then you're spending less than you make and are in good shape. You may still be living paycheck to paycheck, but at least you are a little ahead of the game. Apply the extra money to one of your credit cards or other debts, and if you still have money left over, you should consider bumping the 10 percent savings and investment figure up! I'll show you just how you can apply this money most effectively to your credit cards in Chapter 6, and we'll begin discussing investment vehicles in Chapter 15.

Negative cash flow: If your expenses are more than your income, remember that the simple key is to always spend less than you earn (later we'll talk about *earning more* instead—which is my personal preference). If you can't find ways to cut expenses, then you'll need to step back and really evaluate what you currently view as necessities.

Here's a quick list of eight easy budget cuts:

1. Forget about going to first-run movies. Movies can be ridiculously expensive. Rent a video or DVD and stay at home (or at least try and hit the cheaper "matinée" prices).

2. Buy groceries and necessities like toilet paper in bulk. I know it will seem like an enormous expense the first time you do, but your weekly bills will be reduced dramatically. Don't get locked into brand-name food items—buy whatever is on sale.

3. Don't forget to check your local superstores for food items that are on your grocery list. Things such as snacks, chips, and even cold cereal are much cheaper at my local warehouse store then they are at the grocery store. Add that to your basic list of needs, and try to hit the big store only once a month. This will also reduce adding impulse items to your grocery cart.

4. Pack a brown bag lunch to work.

5. Use an energy-saving water faucet in the shower. You could cut your bill by 30 to 50 percent. Set your air conditioning system two degrees warmer, and your heating system two degrees cooler.

6. Stop smoking. If you can't do that just yet, buy generic, or buy online from one of those sites that can sell them tax-free.

7. Keep a snack drawer at work of homemade goodies or things you bought on sale. Keep snacks and a little cooler full of soda or water in your car to avoid stopping at stores and drive-throughs.

8. If you have a home phone and a cell phone, consider dropping the home line or converting to minimal service.

These are simple, easy-to-do items that won't really affect your quality of life and can be implemented immediately. Some expenses, like insurance or a house payment, are harder to reduce than others. Look at the expenses that are more flexible, like entertainment or food, and find ways to cut back. Try to reduce expenditures in every expense group. Many expenses will probably have to be cut back until your spending is brought under control and bills are paid. Don't let this get you down! The figure you need to cut out may seem a little tough at first, but if you look hard enough at your expenses list, you can usually find a few items that are easy to cut.

> Some people find it hard to give up too many things. By all means, you need to live a little along the way, but some small sacrifices today will add up to big dividends later! Think about that hot sports car you wanted 10 years ago. You can probably buy that same car now (in mint condition) for 40 percent of what it originally sold for. The person who bought the car in the beginning is most likely in financial trouble! Patience is definitely your friend.

Mail Call

Now here's where a lot of financial advisers would try and tell you where to cut your spending. I'm not going to do that because you are an adult, and just by glancing at your expenses you should be able to easily identify areas where you're throwing money away. I'm not going to tell you to cut back on your beer, lattés, manicures, golf, or whatever. You can take a look at the expenses you came up with and the places where you can reasonably cut back should just about jump off the page at you.

The one thing I will tell you is that whatever you may have to cut, *leave the 10 percent for savings and investments alone.* This is a vital element that must be preserved if you are to win the Cash Flow War!

Step Five: Staying within Your Limits

So, now you know just what you earn and what you need to spend every month. Congratulations, you have a budget! Put a cap number on each spending category, and make sure you don't exceed that figure for the month, and you'll do just fine. (Don't worry—this is not our only plan. In the third and fourth sections of this book we'll be looking at ways to for you to make a lot more money. But first, let's put a stop to what is happening to most people out there—they're losing ground!). But you need to maintain good records: Now that you know your own personal cash flow, keep close track of your spending each month so that you can begin to see seasonal trends and adjust to these trends in the future. Keep records on your spending and periodically do a checkup. Ask yourself whether you

Action Items

stayed within your budget and if you are making progress toward your goals. When you hit the cap figure for a particular monthly expense, discipline yourself not to spend money for that category until the next month.

Do your best to live within those limits, and continue to adjust the numbers according to your honest assessment of what you can live on comfortably. The hardest part of a budget is learning how to stay within your means. I personally found that there were things I did not want to give up in my life. I decided if I wanted to keep those things I had to increase my means (make more money) by using some of the strategies in this book. Remember you're a soldier in the Cash Flow War now, and discipline will help you to achieve the financial freedom we're all fighting for!

The 10 Percent Savings Rule

Savings could be the most important expense in your budget. This is known as *paying yourself first*. Before you pay off anyone else, make sure that you're paying yourself 10 percent of what you make. If you don't start doing this immediately, you may be destined to live from paycheck to paycheck. However, once you get that 10 percent figure worked into your budget, you will see the quality of your life begin to improve dramatically. Simply put, you should always put 10 percent of the money you bring home into some sort of a savings account. But before we focus on whether to save in a CD, IRA, and so on, let's focus on the main thing first.

You absolutely need to make sure that you *save the money*. Make sure you pay yourself first and that you save 10 percent! Remember Chris and Mary from the last chapter? This was one of the biggest reasons their net worth was so high.

Often we find ourselves with such a tough budget that we don't know where to start looking for that 10 percent. A mountain climber once told me that when a climber looks up at some tall mountain for the first time, there is the thought in the back of his mind that "this thing is just going to be insurmountable." And if you are approaching an issue like saving 10 percent from that angle, *it will be an insurmountable task*. He told me that you can't just take one big step and be at the top of the mountain. You need to take one step at a time and slowly make your way towards to the top. The good news is, given enough time and steps, you will make it to the top. So, cut some of your other expenses here and there and you'll be able to find that 10 percent figure on your budget.

Building wealth is really no different than climbing a mountain or going to the top of the stairs. Each step, no matter how small and seemingly insignificant, takes you closer to your goal. In the beginning you feel like you are not making progress—the top is just too far away. But if you stick to it, soon you can look back and see how far you have come. The harder it is to put away 10 percent, the more important it is for you to do it. Let's say that 10 percent for you is $100 per month based on a net income of $1,000 per month. After a year that is $1,200, which, if that is all you could afford to put away, should be a pretty good sum for you.

> **Think of it this way: For every 10 months you save your 10 percent, you will have an entire extra month of income in the bank!**

> **There is another big benefit to saving. As you begin to save, your mindset begins to shift. When you have money, whether you spend it or not is irrelevant; just the fact that you *could* spend it is enough to make you feel pretty darn good. Just *having* the money makes you feel wealthier and once you start down that road, you won't look back.**

Now that we've covered why you need to be saving money, let's focus on the variety of methods available to you for making your savings count. The most common are:

- **Savings Accounts:** A bank account that usually offers low-yield, but highly protected interest rates. The safety and ease of acquiring such accounts has led to their immense popularity.

- **Money Market:** A mutual fund that invests in very short-term, high-liquidity investments. This is similar to a savings account, though it usually offers better interest rates. Money market accounts can often provide the best of both worlds, higher—yields and quick access to money.

- **CDs:** Certificate of deposits (CDs) are an insured, interest-bearing deposit at a bank, requiring the depositor to keep the money invested for a specific length of time. You will probably not use CDs until you have enough money in your savings account for quick access and emergencies.

- **IRAs:** These can be your best friend and the key to your retirement. A tax-deferred retirement account set up with a financial institution such as a bank, broker, or mutual fund in which contributions may be invested in many types of securities such as stocks, bonds, money market funds, CDs, etc. The Individual Retirement Account (IRA) brings together two tremendously powerful forces, both of which benefit you: compound interest and tax savings. We will learn more about these in Chapter 15.

- **Mutual Funds:** These are typically a "group" of stocks that a professional investment company has put together. They provide great diversification and are often the starting place for the novice investor.

- **401(k)s, 403(b)s, and 457s:** These are employer-sponsored retirement plans named after the respective Internal Revenue Code sections in which they appear. Given their tax advantages and the possibility of employer matching, these plans are well worth considering.

Allies

> If your employer has a 401(k) plan you should be a part of it. It is one of the most powerful savings plans out there. Not only does it provide you pre-tax savings, employers often match a portion of your contributions—giving you an instant return on your money.

Some other forms of savings are:

- **Bonds:** An interest- bearing or discounted debt security issued by corporations and governments. Bonds are essentially loans by the investor to the issuer in return for interest payments.

- **Annuities:** A contract between an insurance company and a person that provides for periodic payments to the individual or designated beneficiary in return for an investment. Typically, an annuity agrees to provide payments to the purchaser of the contract (annuitant) beginning at some point in the future. Annuities are typically very poor investments, and seasoned investors generally avoid purchasing them. Insurance companies typically push selling them very hard since they usually have high fees.

- **Municipal Bonds:** A debt instrument issued by a state or local government. The advantage of investing in municipal bonds (or "munis") is their exemption from federal, and sometimes state and local, taxes.

Remember that some types of savings methods come with risk. At this point we are certainly not interested in risk. Just remember that the goal here is that you simply must save 10 percent of your monthly income regardless of the method you choose. Once you have a handle on your cash flow we can look at putting it to good use.

Marching Orders for Understanding the Importance of Budgeting

- ✔ **Create a budget.**
- ✔ **Make sure your budget is one you can reasonably live with.**
- ✔ **Track your spending and keep within your preset limits.**
- ✔ **Ten percent of your total monthly income should go to savings and investments.**

Part Two

Understanding the Battlefield

No one can possibly achieve any real and lasting
success or "get rich" in business by being a conformist.

J. Paul Getty, author, *How to Be Rich*

Understanding the Battlefield

> *Our main business is not to see what lies ahead dimly at a distance but to do what lies clearly at hand.*
> —Thomas Carlyle, author, *Past and Present*

By now you have a good understanding of where you are in the scheme of the Cash Flow War. You should have some long- and short-term goals and have fully evaluated your situation. If you are like I was, you probably are not happy with it and you are ready to do something about it. Good. It is time to start learning about your adversaries.

The information you read in this part—Understanding the Battlefield—will catapult you into an elite group of people that understand the Cash Flow War and how it works. Most of us are content to keep our noses to the grindstone, working hard every day to make a better life—but surprisingly few of us have the knowledge to really take control. *Learning* about the system helps us *beat* the system.

With the type of information we'll deal with in this section, you can virtually assure yourself of a good financial life. We'll tackle seemingly confusing subjects like credit, banking, loans of all sorts, and insurance—and have them all make sense. All you will need to do is to implement what you've learned, and stay the course.

Let's learn about our adversaries...

Chapter 5: Understanding Credit

I'll walk you through the biggest land mine that the average American will ever have to negotiate: credit cards. We'll look at how to get the best deals on cards, and how to most efficiently pay down credit card debt. We'll move from simply servicing our debt to attacking our debt.

Chapter 6: Understanding Banking

This is a basic primer on everything you need to know about banking. I'll give you the information you need to figure out just what sort of banking institution best fits your needs, and I'll give you some pointers on how to get the best service possible.

Chapter 7: Understanding Mortgages

This chapter will help you to get a better handle on what will probably be the biggest debt you ever incur in your life. I'll walk you through the various types of mortgages and help you decide which is the best type for your situation. I'll also give you some pointers on how and when to refinance, or pay off your mortgage.

Chapter 8: Understanding Personal Loans

This chapter examines those situations we might find ourselves in where we need to borrow a little money. I'll help you avoid the land mines and offer some strategies to help you through what might otherwise be a low point in your personal Cash Flow War.

Chapter 9: Cars and Car Loans

I'll show you just the sort of financial mistakes to avoid when buying a new or used car, offer strategies on how to get the best deal possible, and show you just how to pick the right car for your needs and your financial situation.

Chapter 10: Understanding Insurance

This chapter will help you to determine just what levels of coverage you should have, and how to acquire that insurance most cost-effectively.

Let's Get Started!

Understanding Credit

> *The only man that sticks closer to you in adversity than a friend is a creditor.*
>
> —author unknown

Mail Call

Credit is one of the greatest sources of financial confusion, trapping millions of people in bad debt every month. I will be the first to tell you that credit cards were my biggest source of problems when I was young—and I am going to bet that you are not surprised. I just didn't know how to use them properly. Sometimes the Cash Flow War can be won or lost simply based on this battle alone. Few things are as dangerous to your chances of victory in the Cash Flow War as the easy credit system we have in the United States today. Whether people are abusing credit cards, lack an understanding of how credit card companies make their profits, or simply don't realize the sort of downward spiral that credit card debt can cause, credit card debt has become a major problem. However, as one who has seen the bottom of the credit card barrel and climbed back out, I can help you sort out a few things.

One thing to remember about credit cards is that while you're watching your use of them, you also need to keep an eye on the provider. My friend Nick responded to a credit card promising a zero-percent interest rate; he fully understood that after the interim, the rate would go up to 18 percent. He never exceeded his limit and his payments were always on time. However, he got a notice that his annual percentage rate was being bumped up to almost 22 percent! He asked why, and they said his credit reports showed that his debt-to-income ratio was getting high. It was, in truth, but Nick was paying his bills on time. Luckily, he had the money available to pay off the card and close the account, but it just goes to show that you have to watch these companies very closely.

The Rules of Engagement

Credit cards are probably the most used—yet least understood—weapon in the Cash Flow Game. We are given credit card applications when we are in high school and we continue to get tempting offers until the day we leave this world.

Let's start by looking at exactly what credit cards are: Put simply, they provide immediate access to cash. With a credit card, if you need to make a purchase, you don't need cash on hand, or to call a bank and get a loan (and go through the hassle of all that paperwork). You have immediate access to whatever your credit limit is. It sounds easy enough. Well, with this luxury and ease of usage come more hidden dangers than you would ever have thought possible.

Let's take a look at the game the credit card companies play, and the role we have been assigned in it. For the most part, credit cards are not designed to be paid off at any great speed. Minimum payments are pretty much decided by determining the lowest amount credit card companies can charge us on a monthly basis (to still make interest on their money), and still have the balance slowly paid down. Most credit card companies are in no hurry for you to pay down the balance; they want to charge you the most amount of interest (for the longest time) possible.

A credit card carrying a balance of $5,200 may require a minimum payment starting at $88.00 to $114.00. As your balance decreases, so will your required payment amount. With an average rate card (say, 18 percent) it could take you as long as *twelve years* to pay off your debt. If you pay according to the enemies' plan, you may have paid as much as $12,000 for the $5,200 purchases. Unless the $5,200 item has gone up in value, paying another $3,000, $4,000, $5,000, or more (in interest) to borrow the money doesn't seem worth it in the long run. And that assumes you never charge again during those twelve years.

Welcome to the credit card battle! It's no mystery that the credit companies are trying to charge you as much interest for as long as possible. It is not a mistake that it occurs this way. Remember: Credit card issuers aren't in business to make your life more convenient. They are in business to make money—and they specifically want your money.

Before we learn how to win this battle we'll need to discuss the special rules and language used on this battlefield.

> **Grace period: This is an amount of time in which you can pay off a debt (usually about 25 days) without incurring finance charges. Most credit cards will allow you to pay off purchases without being charged interest by taking advantage of their grace period. To take advantage of the grace period, you must pay your credit cards bills in full each month by the payment due date. If you owe any money on your previous statement (an outstanding or previous balance), you will not be able to take advantage of the grace period on new purchases for the current month.**

Allies

> **Not all credit cards have a grace period. When you use a card with no grace period, the bank begins charging you interest on the day the purchase is made or the day it is recorded on your account, depending on the bank's policy. When a credit card does not have a grace period, there is no way to avoid paying interest on your purchases. Avoid these cards at all costs.**

Land Mines

Interest or percentage rate: The APR, or annual percentage rate, is the finance charge which is always shown as an annual figure, such as 21 percent. This is what it costs you to borrow money from the credit card company.

Cash advance: A cash advance is just a loan billed to your credit card. It's very easy to obtain this loan—you can get a cash advance with your credit card at a bank or an automated teller machine (ATM) or by using checks linked to your credit card account. Of course, most cards charge a special fee when a cash advance is taken out. The fee is based on a percentage of the amount borrowed, usually about 2 percent or 3 percent. Most cards also charge a minimum cash advance fee. Most cards *do not have a grace period on cash advances.* So this means you have to pay the interest every day until you repay the cash advance, even if you do not have an outstanding balance from the previous statement! On most cards, the interest rate on cash advances is higher than the rate on purchases. You should only use this option as a last resort, and before you do make sure you check the details on the contract sent to you by the credit card company.

By the Numbers

Here is an example of charges that could be imposed for a $1000 cash advance that you pay off when the bill arrives:

Cash Advance Fee = $20 (2% of $1000)

Interest for one month = $15 (18% APR)

Total cost for one month = $35

In comparison, a $1000 purchase on a card with a grace period could cost $0 in interest if paid off promptly in full.

The bottom line is that it is usually much more expensive to take out a cash advance than to charge a purchase to your credit card. Use cash advances only for real emergencies.

Fees: Most of us look for a card with no annual fee, and we end up getting cards with fees that will cost us a lot more in the long run. Most cards charge a late fee when payments arrive after the due date. Some banks wait a few days before assessing this fee, but many impose it *the day after the payment was due.* Some companies have a set fee, while others charge a percentage, such as 5 percent, of the minimum payment due. If you end up paying late fees twice in one year it can cost you more than an annual fee!

When you go over your credit limit, most companies will hammer you. These fees are charged every single time you exceed your limit, so you could be hit with several of them during one billing period. Most cards have a set fee, such as $10 or $15, while others charge a percentage, such as 5 percent, of the amount you are over your limit. If you charge $500 over your limit, with a 5 percent penalty, you will pay a fee of $25. This is on top of your regular interest charges. This can really add up fast!

> **Lost card replacement fees: Some companies even charge people whose cards have been lost or stolen more than once or twice. These fees are usually $5 or $10. All though this may appear to be small stuff (and it is), keep an eye out for these types of fees—they tend to travel in packs!**

Minimum payment: This is the smallest amount you can pay monthly and still be a cardholder in good standing. Credit card companies encourage you to make the minimum payment by referring to the minimum as the "Cardholder Amount Due." In reality it's nowhere near the amount you really owe! If you only pay the minimum, it can take years to pay off the debt, and you can pay double or triple what you spent when you figure in the interest. If you owe $2,000 on a card with 19 percent interest, with a $40 minimum payment, and pay just the minimum every month, it will take you 100 months—more than eight years—to pay off the balance, and it will cost you nearly $2,000 in interest payments. If you just double the amount paid each month to $80 you would shorten the payment time to 33 months, or a little less than three years, and save about $1,427!

> **If you just skip paying your bill one month, or if you pay less than the minimum, you'll pay a late fee, lose the use of your credit card, or have your rate increased. In addition, it may generate a negative report to credit bureaus, which could affect your ability to obtain credit in the future. Some cards allow you to skip a payment without penalty. While this sounds like the company is doing you a favor, don't you believe it! You will be charged interest during this period and will actually owe more in interest than you did before.**

Allies

Making the minimum payment is the most expensive way to pay off your balance. The more you pay each month, the quicker you will pay your debt and you will incur fewer interest penalties along the way. Incidentally, the same advice works wonders on your mortgage, but we'll look at that in Chapter 13.

Allies

This is something that helped me after my bankruptcy in the early stages of the Cash Flow War. "Secured cards" can help you better manage and rebuild your credit. Secured cards work just like a typical major credit card with one major difference—your balance is determined by the amount of money you put in a savings account. The money is therefore "secured." Typically, after a period of making good payments the credit issuer will increase your limit without requesting any more money. In some cases they will even refund your savings and you will then have an "unsecured" card.

Mail Call

Here's a quick key to reading your credit card statement from our friends at Consumer Action:

- **Amount Due:** Some cards use this term to describe the minimum monthly payment. This is not the total you owe on the card.
- **Annual Percentage Rate (APR):** This is the finance charge, expressed as an annual figure, such as 16 percent.
- **Cash Advance:** A loan in the form of cash (as opposed to purchases of goods or services) made through a credit card.
- **Due Date:** The date by which your payment must be received by the company for you to remain in good standing.
- **Finance Charge:** The interest charge on your outstanding credit card balance.
- **Grace Period:** A period in which you can make new purchases without paying interest. (Not all cards have a grace period.)
- **Late Fee:** A charge assessed if your payment is received after the due date.

- **Minimum Monthly Payment:** The smallest amount you can pay to avoid being delinquent. Paying the minimum is the most expensive way to handle your credit card bills.
- **Monthly Periodic Rate:** A fraction of the APR ($\frac{1}{12}$), of the APR the rate at which interest is assessed during the billing period.
- **New Balance:** The total owed after new charges and credits have been added up.
- **Over-Credit-Limit Fee:** A charge assessed if you put charges on your credit card that exceed your approved credit limit.
- **Previous (or Outstanding) Balance:** The amount you owed last month after that month's payments and charges were added up.
- **Transaction Fee:** A charge for making a purchase or receiving a cash advance.

Now that you understand some of the rules, let's learn how to take control of this critical battlefield. For starters, let's play a little war game that I call the "Credit Card Game."

War Games: Credit Cards

As I have mentioned, your annual percentage rate (interest) can play a critical part in how long it takes for you to pay off your credit card and how much you pay for the privilege of using the banks' money.

This next part is fun and can have immediate results. I go over this almost every week in a seminar with my graduates. Using Table 5.1, I want you to write down each of your credit cards, their balance, their limit, and the interest rate you are being charged. Once you've done this, you are going to get on the phone and see what you can do to help yourself.

This is a good time to mention to the customer service representative that you are getting other offers that are very competitive in rate and limits. You would like to find out if you have the best rate and limit available on that particular card.

Allies

What you need to do is to call each of them and tell them that you are looking at your current credit card situation: You are looking to pay off some cards and you are only going to be keeping a couple of cards.

The big winners in this war game may have their limits doubled and the interest rate cut in half. Obviously, it is the lower interest rates that will help you pay down your cards faster. With higher limits you will not only have access to more cash, you will be able to cancel a few cards as well by transferring balances to your lower interest rate cards. Keep this in mind: You need to be in good standing with the card company to play this war game. If you are not, wait until you have been paying on time for at least six months.

Action Items for War Games: Credit Cards

1. Assuming you are in good standing with the credit card companies, call each of the companies on your list. Start with the card that has the highest interest rate. Explain that you have several cards (or offers) and you are looking to consolidate. Ask if you have been given the best interest rate and limit.

2. Once you have completed Step 1, rewrite your list—again, with the highest interest rate at the top.

3. Mail minimum payments to all the cards except the one at the top of your list. For the top card, increase your payments to quickly pay off your balance. Say you pay $100/month to the top card. Once this card is paid off, go to the next one down and mail the minimum payment you have been making, plus $100.

Continue this process with each card in series. This process goes slowly at first, but it will eventually pick up speed. You may save money immediately if you have success with Step 1 and lower your rate. But no matter what happens with the rates, you will save a great deal of interest by attacking your credit cards in order.

Priority Payoff Chart

Credit Card	Balance	Credit Limit	Interest Rate	New Limit	New Rate
XYZ Visa					
John Doe M/C					
Bank of FL Visa					
Totals					

The Best Way to Get Credit Card Debt Under Control: Pay Cash!

Credit cards can be a blessing or a curse—and usually, they are the latter. They are certainly convenient but, except in rare occurances, credit cards should only be used *due to the absence of cash*. In other words, if you want to buy something but don't have the money with you (or if it is too much money to carry), then you have a good reason to use a credit card. And it might be a good reason only if you know full well that you will pay off the balance when you get the bill because you have the money available.

Let's make sure you understand the two reasons I think that paying cash is an important strategy. Credit cards, by their very nature, enable us to simply spend money we do not have. This is not exactly news to most Americans. Most of us have credit limits that well exceed weekly, monthly, or even yearly income. This gives us access to a ridiculous amount of cash, but it also helps us to create a ridiculous amount of debt—and with the interest piling up every month, that debt can be very hard to eliminate. The interest penalties are the first reason I suggest you use cash whenever possible.

We all know the problems with credit cards. I've been there and back with credit cards and I *know* that some real-life situations require the use of credit cards. So, in that sense, we are fortunate to have access to them. However, once used, your number one priority should be paying them off.

By the Numbers

> Credit cards are so easy to use because most people don't think of them as real money. It's the same reason that the folks in Las Vegas use chips instead of cash at their tables. Without cold cash in their hands, people are much less inhibited in their spending. It is the same for us in stores. Would you really make a trip to the bank, take out $700 cash, and return to the store to buy that stereo, television, or gadget? Probably not.

Mail Call

The second reason to spend cash is that you will find yourself spending less. You will find that if it requires taking time to go to the bank to get cash, and then returning to the store to pay for the "got-to-have" item, you will likely lose interest in the item. What you are doing here is removing the *impulse* from the impulse-item buy! It's easy to get all worked up and buy something on the spot, but when you remove yourself from the situation, physically access the cash, and then hand over cold hard cash to a salesperson, you'll find yourself buying fewer impulse items.

The second you take out a credit card you're paying with what seems to be play money. But if you take out $100 or $500 or more in real cash you may find your "need" for that item has changed. Or just as beneficial to you, you may find that you can live with a less expensive model.

Allies

> **I can understand if you don't want to be walking around with a wad of cash on your person. Here's one good solution: A recent technology—and it's a free service offered by most major banks—has given us a new method to bypass the traps of credit cards. Debit cards. Debit cards give you the same comfort, security, and convenience offered by credit cards with one major difference. Instead of drawing on a line of credit that incurs more debt, debit cards deduct directly from your checking and/or savings account. They are essentially the same as accessing ATMs, and can be used anywhere most credit cards can. Best of all, since you know that you are dealing with real money, you will be less likely to abuse a debit card. *Be sure to save the receipts to enter in to your checkbook!***

Allies

I mentioned earlier that there are some instances where it is worth spending money you do not have. The test of that spending is really one simple question: "Will this help me in the long run to be more financially secure?" In other words, is it an item, business, seminar, or course that will increase your income at a later date? I actually took advances on every one of my credit cards to start my investment business. Those advances paid for a computer, fax machine, training, and office supplies. It was the best decision I made because—unlike my prior spending habits—this one was entered into with the sole objective of making more money. This is the same basic premise as taking out a college loan in order to build a better career path.

How to Improve Your Credit Rating

As we all know, one of the great paradoxes of life is that it is easier to borrow money when you have a lot of it. And it follows that those who handle credit wisely will be awarded with the best interest rates and credit limits. Let's take a look at what it takes to improve your credit rating.

Here's the "meat" right here: The best way to improve your credit rating is to pay all of your debts! In the absence of the funds to do something like that, the best way is to play the credit card war game we talked about before, and reduce your debt slowly but surely. You should also periodically check with the three main credit-reporting companies (Trans Union, Equifax, and Experian) to make sure that they are actually circulating up-to-date credit information about you.

> **Avoid companies that advertise "repairing" your credit or "wiping out all poor credit." It simply cannot be done legally and the only thing that will happen is that you will lose money to that service. Anything that is legal can first be done by you and then by submitting the proper forms to the credit bureaus—at *no* cost!**

Enemies

Credit Ratings and Scores: Then and Now

The old days of knowing your banker and getting a loan from him or her based on the strength of that relationship are gone. I still get a kick out of my bank card that says "member since 1984"—it gets me no more than someone who just signed up. As a matter of fact, I don't even know who my banker is—I just know the tellers. Your being a member of the same bank for ten years will have little effect on your getting a loan.

Creditors used to look at an individual's credit in order to rate it. This was typically done on a grade level—A, B, C, or D.

A = Great credit. Unlikely to have any problems; no bankruptcy or collections. You pay your bills all on time.

B = Good credit with a few late payments to some accounts; old bankruptcy (more than four or five years ago) and perhaps some small collections that have been paid.

C = Poor credit. Late accounts, some past due or behind; bankruptcy or collections.

D = Not enough info. People with new, few, or very small accounts. These people were usually treated as a "C" or "B–" person at best.

The ability to read credit and determine the grade was almost an art. While one person would give a person's credit a B, someone else would view it and determine it was a C. Then somehow minuses and pluses (as in B+, A–, C+) came into the picture to make it even more confusing. Also items such as age, race, income level, and marital status were often taken into consideration—although they were not supposed to! Needless to say, consistency was thrown out the window given the multitude of different ways to evaluate and rate someone's credit.

How Credit Scoring Works Today

Fortunately, things are a lot different today. Several years ago "scoring" came into the picture. The lending and crediting agencies were skeptical at first. How could something automate what a human had done so "efficiently?" While a human review is still important, scoring provides a nonbiased judgment of someone's credit that is certainly consistent for the consumer. Human intervention is still important and in most cases it also helps the consumer.

Although there are several methods of scoring as people attempt to tweak the system even more, the most common systems are based on a system developed by Fair Isaac. Together these are called FICO scores. Scoring is based on six main areas accounting for the total score:

1. Length of credit history

2. Amount owed

3. Total available credit

4. Types of credit

5. New Accounts

6. Payment History

Each of the three main credit-reporting companies provides the credit report but they now also add the credit score. Trans Union calls it Empirica, Equifax calls it Beacon, and Experian calls it Experian or FICO (Fair Isaac). In the end, the model is the same; the companies can only give different scores based on different information reported to them.

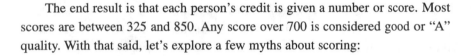

It is not uncommon for one agency to have information about a specific account but not another. If a bad or delinquent loan is reported to Empirica, but not to the other two credit agencies, Empirica's score (correctly so) will be slightly lower. Numerous steps have been taken to avoid this. If a creditor wants an accurate, "complete" picture of someone's credit, they do what is called a "tri-merge" which is a report that merges all three reporting bureaus.

The end result is that each person's credit is given a number or score. Most scores are between 325 and 850. Any score over 700 is considered good or "A" quality. With that said, let's explore a few myths about scoring:

Does scoring affect my privacy?
No more than credit card companies already reporting your information. Scoring is simply taking that existing information and creating a score associated with it.

Will the score alone determine whether I get a loan or credit?
Scoring itself will not determine whether you get the loan or not. At least not any more than your credit does. In other words, if you have good credit, the existence of scoring will not change that; it will only report that good credit as a number. Also, it is important to remember that a lender or creditor can use other factors in its consideration that are not part of the scoring, such as income. You could have a low credit rating and still receive a loan or credit depending on the lender or credit issuer's requirements. Lenders typically have a minimum score requirement for different types of transactions.

Can scoring discriminate?

No. Scoring only takes into account items that are on your credit. The Equal Credit Opportunity Act (ECOA) prohibits lenders from considering some items when determining giving credit. As such, scoring does not factor in race, gender, nationality, religion, or marital status.

Does my score drop if I get a new loan or apply for one?

It may, but not much. The new loan, if paid on time, may help your score go up. Simply "applying" for a loan (in which a creditor "pulls" your credit) may lower your score slightly and will not have a significant effect unless you apply for several different kinds of loans in a short period of time.

What about poor accounts?

A poor account will negatively affect your score. However, the good news is that the older that information gets as you reestablish credit, the less of an impact it has on your score. This is vastly better than the human approach where the person may not be happy with an account you had five years ago and treats it as though it happened yesterday. Scoring keeps things in perspective.

Can someone "repair" or "increase" my score?

Not likely—no one can legally fix something that is accurate. In other words, if you didn't pay someone or you were indeed late, that cannot be removed prematurely. Mistakes can be removed or inaccuracies corrected, but let's learn to do these ourselves and not pay someone.

If I have too many accounts, will that affect my score?

It can. If you have several accounts that you no longer use, you may want to consider closing them. When you play the credit card game and one of the cards doubles your limit, you should consider closing the higher-rate, lower-limit cards.

Do my spouse's accounts affect my score?

Only the accounts you hold jointly. If you have a joint account with someone and they do not make the payment, it will negatively affect your credit. It is also why I do not recommend cosigning for loans or credit cards. With that said, someone once did it for me and it certainly helped me get back on track—and although I will always be grateful, I don't know that I would cosign for someone else.

Your credit history and score not only play a part in your loan approval but can also impact the interest rates and fees you will be charged. Borrowers with better credit and the resulting higher scores typically qualify for lower interest rates and fewer fees. Additionally, other companies such as auto insurers use scoring to determine eligibility and risk, which also has monetary implications.

Marching Orders for Understanding Credit

✔ **Play the Credit Card War Game.**

✔ **Pay in cash or use a debit card whenever possible.**

✔ **Check your credit rating.**

Understanding Banking

> *A bank is a place where they lend you an umbrella in fair weather and ask for it back again when it begins to rain.*
> —Robert Frost, American Poet Laureate

Most people have a bank account, but you should take a few minutes to sit down and figure out if, it's the *right* bank account, and if you're giving your business to the right bank. Always remember that banks should compete for your business—if you find a bank that meets your personal criteria better than the one you're using now, then by all means switch your accounts. It's important that you don't let the hassle of switching your accounts to a new bank keep you from saving money on fees, or from accessing services that will better fit your long term goals and objectives in the Cash Flow War.

Let me tell you flat out that this will not be the most exciting chapter in the book. Here's a little friendly advice—if you're reading this chapter in bed, get up. Pour yourself a cup of coffee. Banks can be boring. When I was researching this chapter, I went online and searched for "banking humor." The first site to come up on Google was a blank page! The second site had this as the featured story:

The young woman who entered our bank to cash a check looked so hesitant that I went to help her. "Please sign the back of the check," I told her, "as you'd sign a letter." She looked at me gratefully, scribbled on the check and passed it to me. Signed on the back was: "Yours affectionately, Pamela."

So you can see that this stuff is pretty dry. But—and there's always a but—this is definitely material you need to know to properly prepare your Cash Flow War strategy. Pour that cup of coffee and work through this with me!

Mail Call

How Do Banks Make Money?

Banks earn money in three ways:

1. They make money from what they call the spread, or the difference between the interest rate they pay for deposits and the interest rate they receive on the loans they make.

2. They earn interest on the securities they hold.

3. They earn fees for customer services, such as checking accounts, financial counseling, loan servicing, and the sales of other financial products (e.g., insurance and mutual funds).

Source: *ABCs of Banking*, Connecticut, Department of Banking

Now that you're armed with the knowledge of how banks actually turn a profit, let us take a look at the different types of banks. You'll have to make a decision on which type best meets your needs.

Three of a Kind

There are three major types of depository institutions (or banks) in the United States. Although there are some variations within the major categories, the basic kinds are commercial banks, thrifts (which include savings and loan associations and savings banks), and credit unions. These three types of institutions are different in their areas of specialization and emphasis, as well as in their regulatory and supervisory structures.

Let's take a closer look.

Commercial Banks

The purpose of commercial banks is to make a profit for their shareholders, just like any other for-profit business. Commercial banks receive deposits, and extend credit through loans, credit cards, and other instruments. They specialize in extending short-term business credit, but they also make consumer loans and mortgages, and have a broad range of financial powers. Commercial banks receive deposit insurance from the Federal Deposit Insurance Corporation (FDIC) through the Bank Insurance Fund (BIF). All national banks, and some state-chartered banks, are members of the Federal Reserve System.

Savings and Loans and Savings Banks

Savings and loan associations and savings banks specialize in real estate lending, or mortgages, particularly loans for single-family homes and other residential properties. They can be owned by shareholders or by their depositors and borrowers. These banks are sometimes referred to as "thrifts" because they originally offered only savings accounts, or time deposits. Over the past two decades, however, they have acquired a wide range of financial powers, and now offer checking accounts and make business and consumer loans as well as mortgages. Generally, savings and loan associations are insured by the Savings Association Insurance Fund (SAIF), and savings banks are insured by the Bank Insurance Fund (BIF).

Credit Unions

Credit unions are cooperative financial institutions, formed by groups of people with some sort of common bond. These groups of people put their money together to form the bank's deposit base; the group owns and controls the institution together. Membership in a credit union is not open to the general public, but is restricted to people who share the common bond of the group that created the credit union. A common bond may be people working for the same company, belonging to the same church or social group, or living in the same community. Credit unions are nonprofit institutions that were originally created to encourage savings and make loans within the common bond community available at lower interest rate to their members.

All credit unions offer savings accounts and the larger ones also offer checking and money market accounts. Most credit unions can offer almost anything a bank or savings association can, including home loans, credit cards, and even some commercial loans. However, credit unions are exempt from federal taxation and sometimes receive subsidies, in the form of free space or supplies, from their sponsoring organizations.

Although there used to be major differences between the three types of institutions, you can see that the lines have blurred somewhat in recent years. You don't necessarily have to choose one sort over the other based on what service you require—you can make your choice based on what you feel you need from a bank, which we'll look at next.

Allies

So, you'd like to know who watches over the banks? You say you can't spend all your time watching your bank? The government agrees with you—federal, state, and local agencies regulate banks. State-chartered banks that are members of the Federal Reserve System are covered by the Federal Reserve System. State-chartered banks that are not members of the Federal Reserve System are regulated by the Federal Deposit Insurance Corporation. State-chartered banks are also regulated by state banking authorities. Banks with "National" in the name or "N.A." after the name are regulated by the Comptroller of the Currency, U.S. Department of the Treasury. Federal savings and loans and federal savings banks are regulated by the Office of Thrift Supervision. Federally chartered credit unions are regulated by the National Credit Union Administration.

What Do I Want or Need from a Bank?

The first question you need to ask yourself is, "What do I want or need from a bank?" Here are the types of things you should be looking at when you choose a bank:

Bank fees: Check the fine print! Look very closely at the fees associated with bank accounts. This is where banks make a lot of money these days. Obviously, one of your goals is to eliminate as many fees as possible. Fees you should look out for are ATM fees, balance inquiries, flat monthly fees, per check fees, overdraft protection fees, fees for going below the minimum balance, bounced check fees, fees for using ATMs that aren't associated with you bank, fees for placing stop payments on checks, fees for providing canceled checks with monthly statements, and fees for closing your account.

Try to avoid fees whenever you can. You may think you have a good checking account until you check the fine print and come up with hidden charges that allow the bank to charge you for:

- Monthly maintenance

- Balances below the required minimum

- Bounced checks

- Stop payments

- ATM or teller use: It better be free to use your own bank's ATM!

- Foreign ATM charges: Check what your bank charges to use an ATM from a competitor. This varies widely from bank to bank.

- Debit card use

- Photocopies of checks

- Canceled check receipts

Locations: Unless you have direct deposit and you do most of your banking online, you obviously want to make sure that your bank has one location that is convenient to your house and one that is convenient to your job.

Online banking: We'll look into the pros and cons of this later in the chapter, but if your bank doesn't offer the ability to pay bills online, check balances, and transfer funds, then you might conclude that customer service is not a priority at that institution.

Types of accounts: You'll want a bank that offers several types of checking accounts and several types of savings accounts. If you write a lot of checks, find a bank that offers either low or no fees to write checks. If you are a saver, find a bank with a high-yield savings account. Choose the bank that offers accounts that fill your current needs, along with the flexibility to upgrade your account as your Cash Flow War victories start piling up.

> **If your bank doesn't offer at least the variety of accounts below, walk away!**

Checking accounts: This account allows you to write checks against the balance you hold in your account. It also allows access to your money through an automatic teller machine (ATM) and is often attached to a debit card.

Savings accounts: Savings accounts are generally used for short-term savings needs. Interest rates vary and are generally less than other savings vehicles available. *Be sure to make sure that the savings account that you choose is insured by the Federal Deposit Insurance Company (FDIC).*

Money market accounts: Money market accounts earn a higher rate of return than most savings accounts. There is usually a minimum balance that generally ranges from $500 to $2,500. There are usually withdrawal restrictions associated with these money market accounts. Be careful to keep above the minimum or be prepared to earn a lower rate or pay more fees for associated services.

Certificates of deposit (CDs): CDs generally offer higher interest rates than general checking, savings, and money market accounts. CDs have higher minimum balances and generally have strict withdraw restrictions whereby you will be locked in for a certain period of time such as 6, 12, or 24 months. Many CD holders will stagger or ladder several CDs so money can be accessed at a variety of times. For example, instead of putting $10,000 in a 24-month CD, put $3,000 in a six-month CD, $3,000 in a 12-month CD, and $4,000 in a 24-month CD to take advantage of better rates with increased access to the money without early withdrawal penalties.

Debit cards: I spoke about these in Chapter 5. Today, most banks offer debit cards that can be used just like credit cards. The big difference is that when you use these cards, you're spending money out of your account, not borrowing money from the credit card company. Using these cards to control credit card debt is key, so if your bank doesn't offer these cards, walk away!

Contrasting and comparing different banks has gotten much easier to do in recent years. With the Internet, you can now compare local bank services and credit offers with those from banks around the nation. Go to *www.bankrate.com* and look for up-to-date interest rate reports on mortgages, auto loans, credit cards, home equity loans, savings, and other banking products

You can also check out your bank through your state's banking commission. Here's where to go to find the banking commission for all 50 states: *www. consumeraction.gov.*

> **Remember, even if you don't have an Internet connection, all you have to do is go to your local library. They have a connection, and they'll show you how to get online, too.**

Allies

Should I Be Doing My Banking Online?

Banking online is becoming increasingly popular, and it may be something you should look into. If you're uncomfortable online, then the answer to this is simple: Don't do it! However, if you're an Internet user, this could be the right move for you.

> **If you do all of your banking online, you should be saving your transaction records either on hardcopy or in a removable storage unit like a CD or diskette. Computers crash and files get inadvertently erased, so keep a back up of everything you do.**

Land Mines

Mail Call

Consumer Action conducted a survey of online banking costumers and came up with some pros and cons for you to consider when making the move to online banking.

Pros

Better interest rates: Online-only banks pay up to five times as much interest for checking and savings accounts as regular banks. At traditional banks, surveyors found that interest-bearing checking accounts are a pretty bad deal overall, with rates ranging from 0.10 percent to 1.35 percent. On the other hand, the interest paid by online banks on checking accounts ranges from the 0.50 percent that Bank A pays on checking accounts with a balance of less than $2,500 to the 2.85 percent that Bank B pays on all balances above $10,000.

Competitive CD rates, some with low minimum deposit requirements: Three Internet banks surveyed require a minimum deposit of $500: American Bank, USABancShares, and USAccess Internet Bank. The 10 traditional banks surveyed require deposits of $1,000 to $5,000.

Free accounts: Many accounts have no or low minimum balance requirements and no monthly fees. American Bank, USABankShares, and offer interest-bearing checking accounts with no monthly fees, whatever the balance.

ATM fee credits: Because virtual banks do not have ATMs, many will reimburse customers for other banks' ATM surcharges a few times each month. All but four of the 19 Internet banks offer monthly credits for other banks' ATM fees. (Security First National Bank, NetBank, Millennium Bank, and USAccess Bank do not.)

Free online bill payment: Sixteen of the Internet banks offer free online bill payment, with 13 including unlimited payments in the deal. When the number of monthly payments is limited, the charge for each additional payment ranges from 32¢ at nBank to 75¢ at Millennium Bank.

Cons

Basic account information: It is not always easy to get basic account information at Web sites or by phone. Representatives typically are trained in one area and callers frequently are told to call another number when asking multiple questions about bank accounts, loans, or investments. Most Internet banks offer customer service by e-mail, but surveyors found that option to be the most inconvenient, because of the time it took the banks to reply and their frequent misinterpretation of questions.

ATM deposits: Virtual banks cannot accept ATM deposits. You must use direct deposit or send a check in the mail.

ATM fees: Customers of virtual banks probably cannot avoid some other banks' ATM charges unless they have an account at a brick-and-mortar bank. After using up their allotted ATM fee reimbursements, virtual bank customers often have to pay a surcharge to withdraw money from another bank's ATM.

Lack of local branches: With an online-only bank, you can't go to a local branch to make deposits and withdrawals or straighten out problems in person.

> **All the banks that Consumer Action checked out were insured through the Federal Deposit Insurance Corporation (FDIC). Before doing any banking online, check out the bank and make sure they are insured!**

Allies

You'll need to weigh these pros and cons carefully. Maybe an online bank is for you, or maybe you prefer to know there's a local branch of your bank right down the street. Increasingly, people are choosing banks that have both local branches and online resources, accessing the best of both worlds—and this may be the best option. You might also consider using a local bank for your most active accounts such as checking and use online banks for CDs or savings accounts to take advantage of higher interest rates.

Marching Orders for Understanding Banking

✔ **Check out the fees you are currently paying.**

✔ **Compare and contrast competitive banks.**

✔ **Consider looking into some online banks.**

✔ **Consider a traditional bank that has a strong online element.**

7

Understanding Mortgages

> *The best way to realize the pleasure of feeling rich is to live in a smaller house than your means would entitle you to have.*
> —Edward Clarke, from *Moncur's Quotations*

Home ownership is just about the most obvious manifestation of the American dream. Whether you're looking for the house in the suburbs with the picket fence or a hipster's loft in some downtown hot spot, sooner or later we all give in to that nesting urge and settle down in our own place. The only problem is it generally takes quite a bit of money to achieve this dream.

It's pretty obvious that a home mortgage will likely be the largest loan most of us will take in our lives, so it should be equally obvious that we need to clearly understand the process. It's almost a given in American society that at one point you will take a mortgage and buy a house. But is that always the right way to go? Maybe you'd be better off renting, or with a lease option?

Sometimes we make decisions simply based on lack of options or understanding. Why should we buy a house? Why should we do a 30-year loan? Should we go with a fixed-rate or variable mortgage? Oftentimes, we turn to the very people who are making money on our mortgages to provide us with the answers. Does that seem right to you? Of course not—but by the end of this book you will not only know the right questions to ask, but you will also know some of the answers yourself.

The number one question you need to answer for yourself is whether you should buy a home or rent one.

Buying versus Renting a Home

Renting has definite advantages for most people at some point in their lives, especially young, single adults. Renting involves little or no responsibility for repairs, maintenance, and yard work. Some rental complexes provide all sorts of extras, such as swimming pools, tennis courts, and laundry facilities. Renting also provides more mobility—young singles are more likely to move due to job and family changes, and it's easier to move quickly when you are renting.

Another major advantage of renting is that it doesn't require a large outlay of cash. Most rentals require a security deposit, but that's nothing compared to a down payment when buying a home. Monthly cash costs may also be reduced, as utilities may be included in your rent payment.

The major disadvantage of renting is lack of control over the property. This ranges from waiting for landlords to fix unpleasant living conditions (from leaking faucets to broken windows), to landlords raising the rent (hopefully with proper notice), making your costs higher. They can also put restrictions on the property, such as not allowing children or pets, and not permitting you to do redecorating. Renting also provides no significant tax or equity benefits for you. The owner is gaining equity, but you are not.

When you buy a home, you have control over the situation. Things get fixed (or not) at your own schedule. And instead of throwing away your rent every month, you're building equity.

The biggest advantages of home ownership are financial, including equity: tax deduction for mortgage, interest, and property tax deductions. And since most homes increase in value over time, the owner's equity increases. As you pay off your mortgage, you gain even more equity. However, owning your own home does have some traps that you want to avoid and will learn about in the next couple pages.

Allies

The bottom line is that if your life is settled enough to make buying a house a viable option, then you should do it. Why waste your money paying off somebody else's bills? However, let's make sure youe avoid some of the "home phrasing" traps that most people fall into. Instead, let's enter into the situation with our eyes wide open and with full knowledge of the rules to this particular war game.

Got Debt?

I always ask my students if they think buying a home is good debt or bad debt. Good debt can be seen as a rental property, or investing in something like this book or a class that can educate you to make more money later. Bad debt is spending extra money on miscellaneous items that give you nothing in return, or on items you could have lived without. But what about the house you buy for yourself? Is that good debt or bad debt?

There are two good arguments that a house mortgage is good debt. One is that the property will appreciate in value and two is that you will get a tax deduction on the interest you pay on your mortgage. But are these really both good arguments? Let's look at this a little closer.

Let's say you have a $100,000 mortgage loan at 10 percent interest for 30 years. That would give you payments of $877.57 per month. Over the life of the loan you will pay $315,925.20 for the privilege of borrowing the $100,000 or, in other words, you will pay $215,925.20 in interest for using the bank's money.

Remember that you only get to deduct the *interest* portion that you paid from your taxes. And, it is not a dollar for dollar deduction. So, as far as real money that you kept in your pocket and didn't pay Uncle Sam because you had a mortgage interest deduction, it works out to about $60,000 (give or take allowing for deductions or limitations). You just paid $215,925.20 for the right to keep about $64,000. This doesn't exactly sound like a cash flow winner does it?

Enemies

> **Would you pay me $100,000 so you would not have to pay someone else $30,000? I didn't think so. So why pay the Bank $100,000 (in interest) to avoid paying the IRS $30,000? Earn your money, pay the IRS their money, and keep the $70,000 in your pocket!**

Secondly, is your $100,000 house going to be worth $300,000 at the end of the loan? It might be, but it's pretty unlikely—not to mention we haven't even spoken about the expenses of property taxes or repairs to the house!

What I will tell you is that your house payment is neither good debt nor bad debt. We will call it "necessary" debt. You have to live somewhere so you might as well have that monthly expense build you equity. But we don't have to play this War Game the way the banks want us to. We're out to win the Cash Flow War—we'll return to this scenario and I'll show you how in Chapter 11.

Most of us enter into a traditional mortgage but let's be aware of a few other options that will come up from time to time in our financial lives.

Lease Options

Suppose you feel you're ready to buy a house, but your bank account and your credit history say no. If you're not financially ready for a mortgage, or you just don't want to be tied to one, maybe you should look into lease options.

For many of us, the traditional way of buying a home won't work. That's because buying a home the traditional way involves putting a lump sum of cash down, getting a loan for the balance, and paying off the balance over the next 30 years. Many of us lack one or more of the following traditional requirements to get a home this way:

- A large down payment
- Good credit
- A regular and predictable monthly income
- Geographic stability

If you fit in here, then a lease-option may be the perfect way to go!

The Benefit of a Lease Option

What is a lease option? A lease option is like a down payment that shows that you're serious and will take good care of the property. When you sign a lease option, you become a tenant-buyer and you'll have to put down three to five percent of the value of the house as an up-front option payment.

This is how it works: A lease option starts with a normal lease agreement, signed for a home for a set period of time. The tenant makes monthly rent payments and the landlord provides the tenant a place to live.

With a lease option, we add an additional step, an option agreement, which gives the tenant the privilege (but not the obligation) of purchasing the house within a given time period for a price agreed upon in advance.

Here are some of the benefits of buying a house with a lease option agreement:

- **Faster Equity Growth:** Equity can accumulate exponentially faster than with conventional financing.

- **Rent Money Is Working Toward the Purchase of the Home:** Each month that you pay rent, all or a portion of that payment should be credited towards your down payment or off of the sales price.

- **Option Consideration Is Credited Towards the Purchase of the Home:** When you sign a lease purchase contract, you must pay the landlord/seller an option deposit. This money is your vested interest in the home and will be fully credited (100 percent) to either your down payment or the sales price.

- **Minimum Cash Out of Pocket:** When you purchase a home conventionally, you must pay closing costs, prepaid interest/reserves, and a down payment. With a lease purchase, you pay only first month's rent and an option deposit. This will save you between 10 and 25 percent.

Allies

- **Frequently No Down Payment at Closing:** Since you have given the landlord/seller an option deposit plus you have been receiving large monthly rent credits, there will frequently be very little or nothing left to come up with for a down payment at closing.

- **Increased Buying Power:** Your buying power is dramatically increased. You can get into a lease purchase home for as little as first month's rent and a $1 option deposit. Compare that to a lender who requires 5 to 20 percent down plus closing costs and prepaid interest/reserves.

- **Credit Problems Are Okay:** Qualification restrictions are not as strict as conventional financing. You will be approved at the sole discretion of the landlord/seller.

- **Maximum Leverage:** You are spending very little money to control a very expensive and potentially very profitable investment.

- **Immediate Profit Potential:** Assume that you have the right to buy a property for $100,000 at the end of the lease and the house is now worth $125,000. You can actually sell your option, which means you can sell your right to buy the property to someone else for as much as $25,000. You get the benefit of appreciation and never owned the home!

- **Time:** Before you actually buy the home, you will have time to repair your credit, find the best financing available, investigate the home, and research the neighborhood.

This all sounds pretty good, doesn't it? There are however, some disadvantages:

Enemies

- If you don't exercise your option by the pre-agreed date, you'll lose the option deposit.

- With a traditional mortgage, every penny you pay in housing costs goes to paying interest and principal. With lease-option, usually only a portion of your rent is applied to the cost of the house.

- You *can* get a mortgage with only a 5 percent down payment, so don't think this is the only way to go.

- These are not common-place agreements in better neighborhoods. You'll have to look very hard to find a landlord willing to do a lease option in a desirable neighborhood.

- You typically receive no tax benefits from a lease-option.

Lease-options can be a fine choice for investment properties or if you have some serious obstacles in your way when applying for a mortgage, and should be considered under certain circumstances.

Different Types of Mortgages

If you decide to take the big leap and sign a mortgage, there are many options available to you. (If you run into a term here that you don't understand, check the glossary in the back of this book or online at sites like *www.loanshoppers.com* or *www.quickenloans.com.*) Let's investigate some of these:

30-Year Fixed-Rate Mortgages

A 30-year fixed mortgage is repaid by the borrower making 360 equal monthly payments over a period of 30 years. Since your payments are fixed, you can expect to make the same monthly payment for the entire term of the loan, regardless of any changes in the housing market (except for any increase in reserves for taxes and insurance). This is a popular loan used to buy a private house and is available for conventional, jumbo, FHA and VA loans. You can also get a 15-year fixed rate mortgage, which is basically the same except your monthly payment is 25 percent to 50 percent more, and you pay it off in half the time. With a 15-year program, you'll also be paying a lot less interest. We will talk more about this in Chapter 11.

Adjustable Rate Mortgages

Adjustable Rate Mortgages (ARMs) are nice because of their low beginning interest rate (when compared to the 30- and 15-year mortgage loans). This low introductory rate is used to calculate the mortgage payment for a specified period of time. Once this introductory period is over, the interest rate is adjusted periodically based on a preselected index. So, with ARMs, you're rolling the dice a little bit and betting that your rate won't increase too much. Be aware that there are caps on how high your rate can go, and this is negotiated at closing time. The most commonly used index is the yield on the one-year Treasury bill. The new interest rate is determined by adding this index to a set margin (which is determined by the lender). The most common program is the one-year Adjustable Rate Mortgage (one-year ARM). The interest rate on the one-year ARM is adjusted once each year, for 30 years, and so on for 3-, 5-, 7-, and 10-year ARMs.

Jumbo Mortgages

A jumbo mortgage is a mortgage loan that is larger than the limits set by Fannie Mae and Freddie Mac ($333,700 as of January 1, 2004, with a higher limit in some states). Since these two agencies will not purchase these types of loans on the secondary market, they usually carry a higher interest rate.

FHA Loan Programs

An FHA mortgage loan is insured by the Federal Housing Administration. Although mortgage lenders provide the mortgage funds, the FHA sets underwriting standards for approving applicants. In many cases, FHA underwriting guidelines are more lenient than conventional underwriting guidelines. This makes it easier for borrowers to qualify for a mortgage loan (low down payment requirements and a higher monthly debt allowance). Applicable loan limits differ by county, so contact your local HUD office for specifics.

VA Mortgages

A VA mortgage loan is a mortgage loan that is guaranteed by the Department of Veterans Affairs (DVA). One of the biggest advantages of using a VA loan is that the borrower can finance the purchase of a property with no money down. However, VA loans are restricted to individuals qualified by military service or occasionally to the public for resale in the event of foreclosure.

5/25, 7/23 Balloon Programs

A balloon mortgage loan is a type of mortgage loan that has a short term (typically five or seven years), but the monthly payment is computed using a 30-year term. When you use a balloon loan, you make a regular monthly payment for the scheduled term (five or seven years). When this loan term is over, you must pay off the remaining balance in one lump sum. If you are buying a house in the belief that the market will skyrocket in the next few years, and you're planning to sell it, you could make a killing here! If you decide not to sell the property after the loan term is over, you have the option to refinance the mortgage with a new one. With a 7/23 balloon mortgage you have the option to convert to a fixed rate (for a nominal fee) after the initial term is over. The interest rate for the remaining term of the loan (23 years) will be adjusted once to reflect market conditions, and then remain fixed for the remainder of the loan term.

Just like with the lease-option program, you'll have to determine for yourself which mortgage program best fits your need. However, whichever program you choose, you should always keep an eye on accelerating your payments—this is one of your pieces of heavy artillery in the Cash Flow War, and we'll explore that more fully in Chapter 11.

Which Mortgage Program Is Right for Me?

I've prepared a little chart (shown on the following page) that you might want to think about as you examine your mortgage options. Remember, these are just generalizations, and not all these statements will apply to you. Also, remember that these are just the tip of the iceberg in these categories; each of these programs can be customized as to term and so on:

> **Just like any other industry, the people in the mortgage business have their own special jargon. However, unlike other industries, these folks are going to loan most of us the largest amounts we'll ever borrow in our lives. An important weapon in your Cash Flow War arsenal is the ability to understand these people when they dive into their jargon, so I've adapted a glossary from a few different sources to give you an intro into mortgage-speak. Don't read this now! It would be pretty boring to read a glossary—but just know you have this weapon in your armory for the next time you enter into mortgage negotiations. For more info turn to the Appendices for a Glossary.**

Allies

A Mortgage for Me

Program	Mortgage Characteristics	Appropriate for borrowers who:
Fixed-Rate Mortgage	• Interest rate and monthly payment remain the same for the entire term of the loan.	• Plan to live in property for a longer time. • Like total payment stability. • Have a low interest rate available to lock in for 30 years.
Adjustable Rate Mortgage	• Interest rate adjusted every year (or less, depending on term), so payment is subject to change every year for remainder of loan.	• Plan to live in property for a shorter time. • Like initial payment stability, can accept later changes. • Need lower initial interest rate and lower payment to qualify.
5/25, 7/23 Balloon Programs	• Interest rate and monthly payment remain the same for five or seven years. • At the end of five or seven years, loan is due in full. Borrower must refinance into new loan at prevailing interest rates.	• Plan to sell or refinance home within five or seven years. • Willing to refinance at prevailing market rates and can tolerate one payment adjustment.

Marching Orders for Understanding Mortgages

✔ Determine whether renting or buying is right for you.

✔ Look into lease options.

✔ Explore the possibilities of different mortgage programs.

Understanding Personal Loans

> *Lack of money is no obstacle. Lack of an idea is an obstacle.*
> —Ken Hakuta, author, *How to Create
> Your Own Fad and Make a Million Dollars*

There are some old sayings that go something like this: "You can't get something for nothing" or "There's no such thing as a free lunch." I think they really mean "Beware of people offering you easy money." Now that you have a better understanding about money that is going out (your car payments, mortgage, etc.), let's move on to gaining a better understanding about money that may be coming in. Oftentimes we can borrow money to help us out of a difficult situation—but you need to remember that nothing is ever free! When I drive around any American city and see building after building dedicated to banking, I can't help but think to myself that *we* are the ones paying for all that prime real estate!

With the exception of some leverage strategies that we will talk about later in the book, borrowing money will *always* work against you in your Cash Flow War strategy. The question we need to really look at is, just how badly will it work against you? If we are going to borrow money, we need to understand how to minimize the damage. Some battles in the Cash Flow War are about minimizing casualties! There are several ways to borrow money. Let's take a look and see which ones will do you the least damage.

Credit versus Loans

Not so long ago, it wasn't that unusual for someone to walk into his or her local bank and borrow a few hundred bucks to get through some unexpected expenses, such as borrowing $500 to get the car fixed or to buy a new washing machine. And banks would commonly grant unsecured loans to people whose good name in the community was enough of a guarantee of being paid back. However, if you tried this today your banker, once he stopped laughing, would probably hand you a credit card application and send you on your way. It's just not that common a way of lending money anymore and there are three main reasons why:

- Credit cards, which are a form of unsecured loan, are everywhere, everyone has them, and most offer cash advance services.

- Changes in the IRS code in the mid-1980s eliminated tax deductions for many consumer interest payments. Those tax changes drove people to home equity loans to buy consumer goods because, in most cases, you can still get a tax break on the interest.

- Banks look at credit a new way, and loans are sadly no longer based on personal relationships. Applications are evaluated by computers and being an upstanding member of a community or a patron of a bank for years means relatively nothing.

The big reason why a bank would rather give you a credit card than a personal loan is that they stand to make more money off the credit card—a lot more money. If you take a cash advance against your credit card, and then just make the minimum payments, the bank will make a killing on the interest before you finally pay it off. With a personal loan, however, you are paying the money back within a specified time and the bank—while it still makes its money—will only make the pre-agreed amount on the interest.

What Is a Personal Loan?

A personal loan is when a bank or another lender advances you a certain amount of cash and you don't put any collateral against the loan. When you take out a mortgage, your collateral is the house; when you take a car loan, the collateral is the car. The collateral is what the bank will take back if you stop paying on the loan. So it serves as security for timely repayment. When you take a personal loan, there is no collateral, so the loan is "unsecured." Because the loan is unsecured, the interest rate is typically higher. This is justified because the bank is assuming more risk when making this sort of loan.

Because personal loans are more expensive they may not be such a good idea for you. The average interest rate on a personal loan is considerably higher than that of a home equity loan. And unlike home equity loans and lines of credit, unsecured loans are not tax-deductible. Also, besides interest, you will commonly have to pay an annual service or maintenance fee on the loan that is either a flat fee or a percentage of the lump sum. Even some credit cards can be cheaper than unsecured loans; you need to be very careful when accessing a personal loan.

> **To see what current rates on personal loans are in your area, log onto the Internet and search for current national surveys of nationwide loan rates. Use search terms like "loan rates" or "personal loans." Make sure you do your due diligence: Once you find a good site, you must double back and check current credit card rate information before you decide to take the plunge either way.**

Allies

Why Would You Consider Applying for a Personal Loan?

I took out numerous personal loans when I was younger. I usually needed the money because I was still fighting the Cash Flow War and had limited income. I used them for things such as car repairs, or when a big appliance would break, or I'd get an unexpected bill and my credit cards were already overextended (or I didn't have any). These loans are usually a one-time shot—or they *should* be. However, some people use these loans over and over again. Once you have implemented some of the budgeting strategies we discussed in Chapter 4, you will find that you won't need these loans and that you will have the money on hand for most common emergencies.

One misconception about personal loans is that the only people who apply for them are those who can't get a loan anyplace else. This is not necessarily the case. Some people who take personal loans already have a big mortgage, and simply don't have enough equity in their house yet to take a loan against it. However, it is true that these loans may be the easiest to get for people whose income and savings are at lower levels. In many cases they may be the only sort of loan that they have a shot at from mainstream sources. And when I say mainstream sources, I am consciously omitting payday loans (which we'll look at later in this chapter).

But it isn't only people who don't have a lot of money in the bank or equity in their house who take out personal loans. Lots of people in upper income brackets are heavy users of unsecured personal loan privileges, too. They just call it something different—they refer to it as a large line of credit attached to their checking accounts. Why would they do this? People with large deposits and investments know they might forget to move money around before they make a large purchase or take a trip, for example. A personal loan or line of credit can be used to fill in the holes that would otherwise appear in their account balance.

Mail Call

My friends Jim and Beth were very big on using personal loans. The strange thing was that they didn't need to! They just thought it was the cheapest way to leverage their money. They were surprised to find out the real "cost" of this borrowed money and quickly found other ways to handle these unexpected expenses.

When it comes to personal loans, people with money take out credit lines and lower income people take out lump sum personal loans. There are some differences between the two, as we'll see.

The Difference between Lump Sums and Credit Lines

Okay, let's make sure we're clear on one point: Personal loans are unsecured loans that come in either a lump sum or a revolving line of credit. Whatever type of unsecured loan you take, you can expect to be able to borrow between about $1,000 and $35,000 on a personal loan. Bankers get a little nervous about loaning larger amounts than that to the average customer without collateral.

Lump Sums

Lump sums, which are also called closed-end loans, usually carry a fixed interest rate, while lines of credit carry an adjustable rate. A line of credit may end up costing more or less than a closed-end loan because it moves with fluctuating interest rates. So, you're rolling the dice a little bit that interest rates will either remain flat or drop over the time you spend paying down your line of credit

The terms of a lump sum closed-end loan depend on your credit report and how much you borrow. The better your credit score, the longer the bank will give you to pay it off—which is not necessarily a good thing. Obviously, the shorter the term on your loan, the less the bank can whack you with interest fees. To pay back lump sums, banks usually issue coupon books. Check with your banker but automatic payments deducted from your checking or savings account might cut your interest fees.

> **It's always, always, always, better to pay off a loan quickly. For example, if you borrow $10,000 at 15 percent interest and pay it back in 48 months, you'll pay $278.31 a month, or a grand total of $13,358.88. But if the bank decides you're a good credit risk and extends you longer terms _they are not doing you a favor!_ If you pay the same loan back in 72 months, your monthly payments may be less—$211.45—but you will pay a total of $15,224.40. With the 72-month loan, you'll end up paying the bank $1,865.53 more (almost 15 percent!) over the course of those extra 24 months. It is hard to get ahead when you are paying fees like that!**

Line of Credit Loans

Line-of-credit personal unsecured loans work kind of like credit cards with a time limit. For example, your bank may approve you to borrow $10,000 on a line of credit for three years. So, your credit revolves as you pay off portions of the available credit—if you borrow $3,000 and pay that loan off, you can still borrow up to $10,000. If, however, it's not paid off you can only borrow $7,000. No matter what you borrow on your line of credit, you must pay off _everything_ when the pre-agreed time limit comes up.

Before You Take Out a Personal Loan

You should really make sure that you've exhausted all your other means of raising cash before you take out a personal loan. Even if you get the best terms you can, they really aren't a good move to make when you consider the effects of such a move on the goals and objectives you've laid out in your plan for your Personal Cash Flow War.

Here are a few other avenues for raising some quick cash you might want to explore:

Allies

Action Items

Have a garage sale: I am constantly amazed at how much money you can make having a garage sale. It may sound kind of funny, and maybe it's a long shot, but you never know what you may find when you look around your house. This is a great excuse to do a little spring cleaning in an effort to raise a little quick cash. The general rule of thumb here is, "Do I really need it?" So many of us can find items around the house that were bad gifts, impulse buys that we never used, or things that our kids have or that they no longer use.

Online auctions: An extension of the garage sale is to use online auctions to get rid of unused items around the house. I know several people who have made good full- and part-time income selling items on eBay (the ultimate flea market). I have even sold items via online auction and can't believe the amount of money I got for some items. The great advantage of an online auction like eBay is that it exponentially expands your marketplace—instead of selling just to people who happen to drive by your house, you're selling to millions of people online. It is not hard to do and with just a little computer knowledge you may find yourself a new part-time job!

Ask for a raise: This may not be the easiest thing to do, but sometimes the only way to get a raise is to actually ask for one. And since you're reading this book, and looking for ways to improve your station, I'd have to assume that you're a hard worker and you probably deserve a raise. An additional bonus to receiving a raise is that after you've met the unusual expense that caused you to think about a personal loan in the first place, you then can use the extra salary increase to add to the 10 percent savings goal or pay down other bills we talked about in the budgeting chapter.

Refinance and reinvest: If interest rates are more favorable than the current interest rate on your mortgage, you can refinance and free up a little liquid capital. You don't even need a lot of equity to refinance because mortgage lenders aggressively seek new customers. You may also be able to pay off some of those high-interest credit cards in the process (this is referred to as a "Cash out Re-fi"). Check with banks about how to use the equity for liquid capital through refinancing.

Utilize your talents: While this is a vague category, you may have a talent that can give you fast, small boosts of income. For instance, if you are a computer whiz, you could help someone who is computer illiterate set up their system for some quick cash. Whatever your talents, perhaps there is a way to use them—not as a way to make large sums of ongoing money, but merely as a way to get your savings started. Think about this one a little bit.

Take boarders/rent rooms: This will only apply to some people. Many of my friends have children who have grown up and moved away. They have spare rooms available that are completely unused. They have found that if they rent out their rooms during part of the year to college students, they can make quite a good deal of extra money—money that they use towards their savings.

Government grants: One last place to look is into government grants and other assistance programs. If you are going to utilize your talents to effectively start a new business, you could qualify for a variety of free government grants. I've included a variety of the resources available to you online in the Appendix.

What to Look for in a Personal Loan

If you've exhausted all your options, and you really think you need to go for a personal loan, here are some things to look out for before you sign on the dotted line:

- Look at the total cost of the credit and not just the monthly payments. As we saw earlier, a lower monthly payment is not necessarily always better.

- Make sure you read all the fine print and look out for hidden charges. Take a hard look at all of the associated fees. The sort of things that bankers will try to sneak in on you are fees for credit insurance, buying clubs, and other extra fees.

- If you don't understand the contract, a fee, or something else in the document, make sure that you have the loan officer explain the charge. You have nobody but yourself to blame if you end up paying for a fee you don't understand. Sometimes when a loan officer is confronted and questioned in this manner, they can find a way to make the fee disappear.

- If what you're being told by the loan officer is different from the actual wording in your contract, and they tell you not to worry about it, it's time for you to get up and walk away. Once you put your John Hancock on that piece of paper, you are bound to the terms. Verbal explanations and promises from a loan officer don't mean a thing in the long run. Zero! The contract is the contract. Remember, the loan officer works for the enemy. Although they may be nice and helpful they are not part of your Cash Flow Team. That particular loan officer may not even be working in the bank next week. The only things that count at this point are whatever is in the contract you're signing!

Here are a few more tips on things to do before you sign a personal loan, adapted from our friends at *Bankrate.com*. If you have a better option—home equity, a credit card, 401(k) loan, a rich relative—think twice before borrowing without collateral. But if you have no other way to go—or are hell-bent on it— take these tips:

Mail Call

- Do your homework. Find the best interest rates in your area or call up a handful of local banks and compare prices.

- Ask if the interest rate is fixed or variable and what the rate cap is. Also inquire about annual fees.

- If you belong to a credit union, forget about all these tips and just go there. Interest rates on unsecured loans can run as much as one or two percentage points lower than major banks.

- If you do business with a community bank, take advantage of the human factor. Being a familiar face can earn you some slack if your credit background is smudged. Small banks might offer lower interest, too.

- Be honest about why you want the loan. Your bank may be able to offer you a loan option you hadn't thought of, or perhaps that jet-ski you're eyeing can be used as collateral, thereby securing your loan and trimming interest.

- Don't fill out applications at several banks and have all of them check into your credit history. This can make you look desperate and lower your credit score.

"Payday" and "Cash Advance" Loans Are Never a Good Option!

The best thing I can say about payday loans is...nothing much at all. These loans may be the quickest way I can possibly think of to guarantee a resounding defeat in the Cash Flow War. I suppose if you are in need of emergency cash and have *no other* alternatives, a payday loan used *once* could help a very dire situation. The problem is that they are typically not used once. People use them over and over again. Let me be very clear about this: It will be *very* difficult to win the Cash Flow War if you are using these loans on a regular basis. There is absolutely no such thing as a good deal on a payday loan. In fact, if you don't know what these are, I'm almost hesitant to introduce the idea into your head! But you really do need to know how bad these are so that you can avoid them at all costs.

> **Let me tell you in no uncertain terms why these are so dangerous. Consider this: A recent report by the Consumer Federation of America (CFA) found that "payday lenders continue to make short term consumer loans of $100 to $400 at legal interest rates of 390 to 871 percent in states where payday lending is allowed." More disturbingly, the report finds that payday lenders are exploiting new partnerships with national banks to make payday loans in states where the loans are otherwise prohibited by usury ceilings or other regulations.**

How Payday Loans Work

Some of us find ourselves in the "fringe" financial market due to errors on our credit reports, or just plain bad credit, that cause denial of traditional credit. So people feel that they must turn to payday lenders. And even if they appear to be "ma and pa" stores such as local pawn shops, increasingly these are part of national chains, or may be partnered with banks, or may even be "sub-prime" affiliates of a bank. The interest rates they get away with are simply unbelievable. And how do they get away with it? They don't call it interest. Payday lenders charge a "fee" and just by a little sleight of hand, changing one word, they can claim themselves exempt from the standard usury laws that cap interest rates.

Here's how these lenders actually "loan" desperate people the money they need: Payday lenders make small advances based on personal checks held for future deposit at interest rates approximating 300 percent APR or higher. In some respects, I don't blame the people running the stores. Remember, people with money make money off the people who don't have money. But understand the situation for what it is. For example, you write a check for $230 and receive $200, and the lender agrees not to cash your check until your next payday. The actual cost of that loan for two weeks is $30, which works out to great return for the lenders. If you can't afford to pay it back, in many states you can simply pay the finance charge, or $30, to "roll it over," still owing $230 at the end of the month, ballooning your total finance charges up to $60 for a $200 one-month loan.

Hopefully, you'll have this stuff all figured out in a few months after you implement the budgeting strategies you learned in Chapter 4. I know that when I was taking personal loans to bridge the gap between paychecks, it was one of the things that eventually led me to bankruptcy. Use this sort of funding only when strictly necessary—try to avoid them by making use of some of the other options we discussed in this chapter.

Marching Orders for Personal Loans

✔ **Examine all your options before taking a personal loan.**

✔ **Make sure that you read all the fine print, and understand all the fees before you sign off on a loan.**

✔ **Only use a payday loan in the direst of emergencies, and if you have absolutely no other options.**

Cars and Car Loans

> *There is more to life than increasing its speed.*
> —Mahatma Gandhi, author
> *The Story of My Experiments with Truth*, autobiography

Defensive Buying

I will be the first to admit that America is a car-crazy culture and some of us get a little crazy when we're buying a car. Car companies spend millions of dollars in advertising to make us want to pick cars that match what we perceive as our personalities. We're the only country that is like this! One quick visit to other parts of the world and you'll quickly see how their cars (if they have them) are much, much older—and it often looks like they only have a car to serve as transportation. What are *they* thinking? Obviously, they are not wasting money on new cars.

For some people there is an undeniable allure to driving a cool, modern, match-your-personality car, and for most of us that fascination we had with having a nice car when we were teenagers doesn't ever go away. For a good portion of Americans, there's something very satisfying about knowing you have a nice vehicle—but that monthly car payment can be a Cash Flow killer!

Back when I got into trouble with my credit cards and subsequent bankruptcy, I had a car payment on a car that I probably shouldn't have been driving. It was a great car, but definitely a car I could not afford at the time. It's important when you're looking into buying a new (or new-to-you) car that you keep yourself grounded and buy the car you really *need* instead of the car you really *want*. I don't want to be a killjoy here; remember, after you achieve your victory in the Cash Flow War you'll be able to buy *any* car you want, along with a lot of the other finer things in life. I'm just saying that, at this point, you probably need to be a little more hard-headed and realistic when you're looking at cars.

Allies

> **One thing that I found surprising when I first started learning Cash Flow secrets from successful people was that very few of them ever bought new cars. They would always buy a car that was a year or two old—and their cars were still mint, still under warranty, and much, much cheaper than brand new cars.**

How Much Car Do You Really Need?

If you sit down and examine exactly what your needs are rather than your wants, you'll be able to figure out fairly quickly what the right car is for you. Take a few minutes and figure out objectively what you really use your car to do. If you live in a big city, you may find that you don't even need a car! All too often we choose a car because we like the way it looks, or because it is the new "hot" car. Just think about how many SUVs you see in the parking lot at the supermarket. Now think about how many of those ever actually go any deeper off-road than parking on the grass at a soccer game!

Mail Call

> **Thousands and thousands of new, gas-guzzling 4x4s and SUVs are sold in Florida every year. There are no hills in Florida, let alone snow!**

Unfortunately, if you're basing the second largest expenditure you will probably make (after housing) on the way a car looks, or the perceived prestige it brings while you're driving it, you'll probably bust your budget or end up going car shopping again real soon. It's vitally important to let your *needs*, not your *wants*, drive your car purchasing decisions.

Here are things you need to consider when buying a car:

- How many people do you need to fit in the car on a regular basis?
- What kind of driving do you most often do? Highway, around town?
- How long is your commute?
- Is good gas mileage important to you? (Consider the ever-rising cost of gas.)
- Do you want a manual or automatic transmission?
- Do you really need four-wheel drive, or all-wheel drive?
- What extra safety features do you need? (Anti-lock brakes, extra airbags.)
- How much cargo space do you need?
- Do you do any towing?
- Does the car fit in your garage or parking spot? (Don't laugh, I know several people who brought a car home only to discover this problem.)
- Will it be a hassle to park on the street?
- What will it cost to insure?

Remember, before you start working on the checklist, you need to remove all emotion from this whole process. Most people get a real rush from buying a new car (myself included), but you really need to go through this list and figure out what type of car you need before you end up in a showroom getting bowled over by all the new bells and whistles they've added to the new cars.

Allies

> **Pick a car that you really wanted 7 to 10 years ago but didn't buy. Go look and see how much that car is selling for now. I think you will be surprised how much even the most expensive car has come down in price. In the end, if you forgo that five-year loan and put that money away instead, in about 10 years you could purchase at least two of those cars!**

Mail Call

Allies

> Take a deep breath and remember: Nobody really *needs* a car like a BMW, Porsche, or Hummer. They are all certainly nice cars, but unless you're a Formula One driver or a polar explorer, it's just about impossible to make the argument that you actually need one of these cars! These cars are typically purchased for ego purposes, and not for efficiency. Again, once you have won the Cash Flow War, buy whatever you want and enjoy it. Till then, let's not waste our money on a big depreciating asset when we could put that money to good use.

Once you've completed your list of needs, you should be able to see at a glance whether you need a compact, a sedan, a mini-van, or a pickup truck. Really evaluate your lifestyle and work off the previous list to see just how you're going to use this vehicle. Be reasonable: You don't want to buy a big, tricked-out Ford F150 to haul four kids around just like you're not going to buy an Audi TT convertible to carry plumbing supplies. Or if you have three kids, you probably won't be getting a Corvette. You need to figure out what type of car best fits your lifestyle, and then you need to determine which car of that type best fits your budget.

What Type of Car Should I Be Looking At?

You have several choices of car types to choose from: sedan, compact, SUV, mini-van, pickup truck and these new pseudo-SUV/mini-van crosses that I'm not even sure what to call. After you narrow your car choices down to a type of car, then you should start shopping right? Wrong! First you need to figure out how much money you can realistically afford to spend on a car.

Start out with a sharp pencil and the budget you created in Chapter 4. How much room do you realistically have in there? Could you, for example, fit an extra $200 a month in your budget without blowing the whole deal, and especially without touching the all-important 10 percent you're supposed to be saving? If so, can you fit an extra $300 a month in your budget? Maybe $250? You get the idea. You need to get a general idea of how much you extra room you have in your budget. Now you know how much you can afford to pay for a car every month.

> While you know your finances better than anyone, especially after the self-examination you conducted in earlier chapters, remember that the cost of a car isn't just what you end up paying the dealer. There's also maintenance and the inevitable repair. Non-U.S. and premium brands typically command higher prices for parts and labor, so keep that in mind. Leave yourself some wiggle room in your numbers for increased costs down the road while you're computing just how much you can afford to spend on a car.

> You know what type of car you need. You know how much money you can spend. But car dealers know that most car purchases are made based on emotion. You *must* remove the emotional factor when you walk into a showroom or onto a used car lot. You know your needs and you know your budget. Don't let a slick salesman get you all excited and into a car that you can't afford or don't need!

Before you get too crazed and excited about how much you can afford and start looking at top-of-the-line cars in your type, remember that the expenses on a car will include not only your car payment, but also your insurance, gas, maintenance, and other miscellaneous costs associated with operating a vehicle. General operating expenses can run you as much as one-third to one-half of the monthly cost of a car. What you need to do is to take the amount that you have determined fits in your budget and multiply it by .66. This number is absolutely the top figure that you should consider spending on monthly payments for your car.

> As a general rule, the more expensive the car, the more it costs to insure and maintain it.

Now we've got a few key steps down. We've identified the kind of car you need, and the kind of money you can spend. The third step is to stay out of the showroom!

You need to figure out what cars you're going to be looking at long before you talk to a professional car salesman; remember, their agenda is different from yours. They're looking to push you into a car of their choosing, and there might be a few different reasons they will steer you that way. The company they work for might be promoting one car heavily; there might be an added financial incentive for them to sell a particular model, or they may genuinely and honestly believe that they know which car is right for you. Well, forget what the salesman says—he doesn't know you, and you've already done your homework and figured out what you need. For you, the salesman is just there to facilitate a test ride, help you compare and contrast similar brands, and to hammer out the most favorable payment for you.

Allies

> The Internet has become an invaluable tool for you as a car buyer. You can check prices of similar models using the NADA Official Used Car Guide (*www.nadaguides.com*) published by the National Automobile Dealer Association or the Kelley Blue Book (*www.kbb.com*). These guides are usually available at local libraries. For used cars, *www.carfax.com* and *www.autocheck.com* sell information on the history of vehicles gathered from state motor vehicle departments and other sources.

Mail Call

One thing you will notice is that people who have won the Cash War often will not purchase new cars. Cars are a depreciating asset. In other words, the second you drive it off the lot, it will decrease in value about 20 percent. Then, after the first year, another 15 to 20 percent. Most savvy car shoppers will buy a used car that is 12 to 24 months old. In addition to getting a great price, they often come with low mileage and the manufacturer's warranty! Not only do Cash Flow Veterans buy used vehicles, they tend to keep their cars longer. A study conducted for the book *The Millionaire Next Door* showed that over 53 percent of millionaires surveyed owned a car two years old or older. In fact, 12.3 percent owned a car six years old or older.

Should I Buy or Should I Lease?

I tend to like leases for two situations: 1) If I am not going to keep the car long term; or 2) I am concerned about rapid deprecation if I buy it (such as a high-end sports car). With that said, none of my cars are currently leased.

To get a loan for a car, and often for a lease, you'll probably need to make a down payment of around 10 percent of the total price of the vehicle. The larger your down payment, the smaller your monthly payment will be and the less you will pay in total for the car in the long run. But make sure you don't cripple yourself or deplete your savings account with too large a down payment. Find a comfortable balance.

A lease requires little or no money up front and offers lower monthly payments. But when the lease ends you are left without a car and a need to replace it. Buying a car is more expensive initially and the monthly payments are higher. But at the end of the loan, you will own a car you can still drive or sell.

The advantages of leasing are:

- You can drive a better car for less money.
- You can drive a new car every few years.
- No trade-in hassles at the end of the lease.

The advantages of buying are:

- When interest rates are low, it makes more financial sense to own a car rather than lease it.
- No mileage penalty.
- Increased flexibility—you can sell the car whenever you want provided you are not "upside down" in the loan.

Allies

A Few Reasons *Not* to Use the Car Dealer When Financing a Car Loan

When I was recovering from my bankruptcy, I still needed a car. I worked with a dealer who could help get me a car loan and get me that new car I wanted. I say worked "with" very loosely. Because in the end, *we* were doing anything but working *together* to help me. Since I was not very knowledgeable about the Cash

War at the time, this mistake cost me an additional $4,900 in finance fees. That was about an additional year in payments!

That all happened because I didn't have good credit and not a lot of people were willing to work with me. However, even with good credit there are still some things you need to be aware of. One thing you need to remember is that cash is king, and that you can get great deals if you have cash or have negotiated your financing elsewhere. With that said, let's take a look at dealer financing.

Although the financing options you see on TV look pretty attractive, there are several major drawbacks. The low APRs dealers advertise usually come with bigger down payments. And it usually means you are limited to the on-site stock the dealership needs to move, which means you may not get the car you need with the options you need. You'll get a car loaded with a factory option package, which may indeed include some neat stuff, but not items you need or want.

Some low APR deals have prepayment penalties that come along with them. Imagine that! Someone loaning you money that wants you to make payments for a long time and build up interest costs—it seems we've seen that tactic before. Since dealers want to get rid of the car, you might think they'd give you a good financing deal in order to profit on the sale itself. While this may be the case, consider that the auto dealership's finance manager's sole purpose is to see to it that you walk out of that dealership with the *highest* monthly payment possible. If you are paying cash, (or have arranged your own financing), the finance manager will still try to talk you out of it by telling you all the so-called advantages of letting them arrange the car loan for you.

Why would they do this? Because car dealerships are masters in the Cash Flow War, and they know they can make a great deal of money off you by offering financing. Why else would they do it?

Car dealers make money off car loans in four ways:

1. The financing itself: The banks will pay a certain percentage of the amount financed to the dealership. The higher the interest rate the dealer can talk you into, the higher the kickback to the dealer. Remember that the dealer is normally outsourcing these loans, so he will be adding a bit on top of what the bank charges to pay for his time.

2. Extended warranties: There are many different warranty companies and many different levels of coverage available. Most dealers mark up the price anywhere from $400 to $2,000.

3. Credit insurance: Dealers earn about 50 percent of the insurance premium on your coverage.

4. The finance manager will try to sell you a variety of products: everything from rust-proofing and paint sealant to window etching and alarm systems. All of these basically useless items carry a huge markup.

How to Get the Best Deal on Your Car Payment

One good rule to follow when financing a car is never to finance for more than three years. Banks and dealers offer financing as long as 72 months. In addition to the horrible cost you will pay by financing that long, you will also not be able to sell your car for several years—this is what people are talking about when they say you are "upside down" in a loan. If you cannot afford the payments of a three-year loan, you should either be looking at another less expensive car or putting down a bigger down payment.

Allies

> When you walk you into a dealership always remember that they will treat you with more respect if you appear well prepared. If you're looking at used cars, know the Blue Book value. If you're looking at new cars, know which cars compete against it in price and value. If you appear to know what you're doing, it will go a long way towards keeping the dealers honest.

Land Mines

Here are twelve things that will help you win this particular battle in the Cash Flow War. Follow these guidelines and you'll get your best deal, regardless of whether you're buying or leasing, or getting a new or used car:

1. **Line up your financing first.** Credit unions are your best bet, banks are your second best, and auto dealers may be an option if they're running a great deal that month. But you should always have an alternative to dealer financing

before you walk into the showroom or onto the lot. With that behind you, you can give the dealer a shot at making you a better deal. Sometimes they actually can make you a better loan. But be careful: What the car dealers don't want you to know is that they make as much money, and often more, from arranging the car loan then they do on the car deal itself!

2. **Do your due diligence** on the cars you're looking at before you ever walk into a showroom. Check out *www.carprice.com* and *www.kbb.com* (Kelly Blue Book) for pricing information, and check out *www. Edmunds.com*, *www.Intellichoice.com*, and *www.Leasesource.com* for online information on leases including current lease deals.

3. **It's not just money** you're looking at here—you need to be safe too! The National Highway Traffic Safety Administration (*www.nhtsa.dot.gov*) lists Vehicle Indentification Numbers (VINs) of its crash-test vehicles and will let you search an online database of manufacturer service bulletins. The Center for Auto Safety (*www.autosafety.org*) provides information on safety defects, recalls, and lemons, as well as service bulletins.

4. **Find out if the manufacturer** is offering rebates that will lower the cost. Two Web sites that offer this information are *www.carsdirect.com* and *www.autopedia.com*. Find out if the amounts quoted are the prices before or after the rebates are deducted.

5. **Avoid the items** that bring a high-profit to dealers and low value to you as a consumer and possible reseller. I'm talking about things like credit insurance, extended service contracts, auto club memberships, rust proofing and upholstery finishes. Always remember: *You do not have to purchase credit insurance in order to get a loan.* If they tell you that you do, then walk out! The car dealer usually earns 50 percent of the price of this coverage, and that money is buried in *your* car payment.

6. **Carefully choose your options.** If the better stereo is worth the extra money to you, go for it. Remember, though, that it will not raise the resale value of the car. Two things that will lower the resale value of the car if you don't have them are air conditioning and an automatic transmission.

7. **Kick the dealer to the curb!** You need to take a long *solo* test drive. You need to get to know the car, not listen to even more high-octane salesmanship. Before you drop a wad of cash on car costs, you want to be sure you are buying the right car for you. Drive it on the freeway, on side streets, and in regular traffic and turn off that *stereo*—you already know what music sounds like. Listen to the car.

8. **Be assertive!** Make the salesman earn his money: Ask a lot of questions. Ask some questions that you already know the answers to, just to determine if he's being honest with you. Later, make the sales manager earn his money, too. There are a lot of things that can be negotiated: price, features, financing, terms, trade-in value, and warranties. Nail them down on every single negotiable aspect.

9. **Don't be afraid to walk out.** In fact, do it often! When you find a car you love, get the best deal you can from that dealership. Make sure you get it in writing! And then leave, and go to another dealership and see if there isn't a better deal out there. Show the second dealer the terms you've negotiated and tell him you want him to beat it. Don't worry, no matter what kind of pressure the first dealer put on you, the first car will almost always wait for you. And if it doesn't, so what? They make a few thousand of those cars every month—and they need to sell every one of them.

10. **Before you sign** the deal, take a copy of the contract home and review it carefully away from any dealer pressure. Make sure you are getting credit for any trade-in. Look for any charges that were not disclosed at the dealership, like conveyance, disposition, and preparation fees. Get all the terms in writing. For a lease, make sure that every item of equipment is listed on the lease to avoid being charged for missing equipment at the end of the lease.

11. **Check out the seller.** This is an area that a lot of shady people make their living in. I apologize to the vast majority of honest and hard-working car salespeople out there, but there are a few of your brethren that have made it necessary for us to keep a wary eye out. For car dealers, consult your state or local consumer protection office. If it's a private seller, check the title to make sure you're dealing with the vehicle owner. Also, browse the classifieds for other auto ads with the same phone number—this is a sure

sign of an unlicensed broker who sells used cars by posing as the owner, and definitely a shady character you want nothing to do with.

12. **Take a break.** This can be a stressful and tough process, unless you're like me and you love the art of the deal. But remember: If you're not having fun, go home. When you get tired or overly stressed about shopping, you're more likely to make a decision you will regret later. Take a break and come back another day, when that new car smell will be enticing again.

Follow these guidelines and once you're actually driving off the lot in your new or slightly used car, you can be confident that you've done everything you could to make the best deal possible. Congratulations on your new ride!

Marching Orders for Cars and Car Loans

✔ **Figure out the kind of car you need—not the kind of car you want.**

✔ **Make sure the car fits comfortably into your budget (and your garage!).**

✔ **Do your due diligence on the car before you ever walk into a dealership.**

Understanding Insurance

> *There are worse things in life than death. Have you ever spent an evening with an insurance salesman?*
> —Woody Allen, playwright, actor, and director

Most people feel the same way Woody Allen does about insurance and insurance agents; if you would prefer not to think about insurance, I'm here to tell you that you need to think again. Insurance agents get a bad rap! As you continue to win battles and build up assets in the Cash Flow War, you need to deploy an insurance agent to make sure that your assets are protected.

The topic of insurance can be boring and sometimes unnerving. I know I don't want to think about dying, or even about being sick a long time. But, unfortunately, you need to have your reserves protected when you venture forth into the Cash Flow War, and a good insurance agent can be one of your best allies.

The first question to answer here is: "Do I need insurance?" And the answer is that if you own anything valuable, or if you have children, you need insurance. It's that simple. Probably, at the least, you'll need auto, home, and life insurance. Health insurance should be supplied by your employer; if you're self-employed, we'll cover the best ways to obtain health insurance. In addition to the big three listed above, you may also need an umbrella policy, which we'll get into later in this chapter.

Allies

Home and auto insurance are usually mandatory. Besides being required to have them due to state laws and mortgage rules, they can help you out with repair costs and liability in the case of damage to your home or your car. Both essentially cover damages to you and your property; however a large portion of auto insurance covers third party damage and injuries in the form of liability coverage. In the case of auto insurance, in most states it's mandatory to have at least the minimum coverage.

Lenders always require homeowners with mortgages to buy home insurance. You may think that the policy terms required by your lender are enough, but that might not be the case. Remember, lenders are only concerned that you cover the risks to your property they have financed. This most likely does not include your full exposure to loss were your home and all your personal property to be destroyed. It is important that you assess your property, determine its value, and get the full coverage you need in the case of a loss.

Life insurance is actually pretty simple to figure out. If you were to die tomorrow, what kind of money would those dependent on you need to make it through until they could provide for themselves?

Just how much insurance you will need and what sorts of insurance you will need is where you might have a different opinion from your insurance agent. In this chapter, we'll take a look at different kinds of insurance and give you some tools that will help you figure out just *how much of what kind* of insurance coverage you really need.

Do I Really Need Life Insurance?

Let's start with life insurance. We'll examine how much you need and the different kinds available.

The first question to ask is, "Would my death leave anyone in a financial bind?" Once you become a parent, any adult in your house earning income should have life insurance coverage that will last until your youngest child gets through college. And in a family without a lot of money saved, a stay-at-home parent may need a small policy to cover child care costs that would be created by that parent's absence. Even if you belong to the dual-income, no-kids crowd, you may need life insurance to cover large shared financial obligations, such as a mortgage. For older empty-nesters, though, life insurance is often an expense you don't need—as long as your retirement nest egg is big enough to support your surviving spouse. If you're single with no kids you don't need life insurance yet.

How much life insurance you need is a pretty simple calculation. Take out the budget you created back in Chapter 4, and use this as a basis to figure out your family's yearly expenses. Figure out how many years you'll need to cover those expenses, and add in the cost of college for all of your kids. Now, add up all of your pension and 401(k) type accounts. Subtract that number from the total expenses you figure out above, and the figure you come up with is the amount of life insurance you'll need.

Different Kinds of Life Insurance

There are four basic kinds of life insurance, and you'll need to figure out which one best fills your needs in the Cash Flow War.

Term

This kind of life insurance covers policyholders for a fixed time span; this is the basic, no-frills version. It always costs less for everyone except the very advanced in age. There are two types of premiums: level term and annual renewable. Level-term premiums remain constant throughout the life of the policy and can be bought in increments of up to 30 years, while premiums for annual renewable increase as you age. Ordinarily, level premiums are higher than renewable premiums in the early years of the policy and lower in the later years. These days the best bargains are found in level-term policies of 10 years and more. Many term policies have a conversion feature that allows you to convert the policy to a whole life product later on without having to submit to a medical exam.

Whole

Whole life combines term insurance with an investment component. A whole life policy has two parts: the mortality charge, the part of your premium that pays for the insurance coverage, and a reserve, the part that pays for the investment component that earns interest. As you age, the portion that goes into the reserve decreases while the portion that pays for the mortality charge increases. The cash surrender value (which is also called the cash value) is what you'd get if you cashed in your policy. If you decide to give up your policy, your cash surrender value can be paid in cash or paid-up insurance.

Land Mines

> **Although one of the benefits an insurance agent will use to sell you whole life coverage is that it is a savings vehicle, there are several problems with using whole life for savings purpose. One is that the policy's advertised rate of return is just an estimate. In fact, the policy's returns will fluctuate with the markets—and will usually trail returns available from other investments such as equity mutual funds. Another problem is that whole life is expensive, and you may not be able to afford all the insurance coverage you actually need.**

Allies

Wealthy people winning big in the Cash Flow War can use whole life policies as estate-planning vehicles. You can set up an insurance trust, which applies the proceeds of the policy to estate taxes when you die, thus saving your heirs the expense of settling the estate with the government. However, until you have significant assets and income, whole life is likely not for you.

Universal

Universal, like whole, combines insurance with savings. The savings component, called an accumulation fund, earns interest monthly and is used to pay the mortality charge. The sales pitch for universal is that premiums are flexible:

Enemies

> **I have a few problems with universal policies. If you skimp on premiums in the policy's early years, you'll get rocked with higher charges later on when you expected to be paying little or nothing. The alternative is to drop the policy and withdraw the savings you may have built up. If you drop the policy, you'll have to pay a surrender charge.**

As long as you pay enough to maintain the mortality charge, you can skip adding to the accumulation fund if money is tight. And if you contribute enough to the accumulation fund in the policy's early years, you can actually earn enough income to pay your premium in later years.

Variable

Variable-life insurance is the best of the combined term and savings-type policies. They combine a mortality charge with a savings vehicle that you choose from among a number of alternatives offered by your insurer. With variable life, the savings component is usually one of several investment portfolios that are structured like mutual funds. On average, most companies offer 10 different portfolios, including stock, bond, and money market funds. There are two basic types of variable life. One demands a fixed premium payment. The other, variable-universal life, has a flexible premium like universal life. Remember that variable returns fluctuate with the financial markets. If the stock market takes a hefty dive, you may find the cash-value portion of your policy in the tank.

Make sure you check out the fees your insurance company charges you on the savings component. The insurers often manage these funds themselves, collecting fees for administering the insurance and managing the portfolios.

> **When checking the fees you're paying, make sure you cross out the "waiver of premium" rider. Under this rider, which can cost as much as 10 percent of your annual premium, your insurer will continue your coverage in case you're disabled. But you should already have enough disability insurance from work to cover living expenses, and if you do, you don't need a waiver of premium. Some companies offer spousal or dependent riders that add a term-insurance element to your whole life policy that will cover your spouse or your children. Chances are, if your spouse needs term insurance, you can find a cheaper policy. And unless your child is supporting the family, he doesn't need insurance.**

My take on the entire spectrum of life insurance products is that most of us who purchase life insurance are better off buying basic term insurance and then making our own separate investments into mutual funds. You're already saving the 10 percent we talked about in Chapter 4, so just add a little bit to it when thinking about life insurance. Why let some insurance company charge you additional fees on something that you should already be doing?

Do I Need Home Insurance?

If you don't own a home yet, skip this part (or read it for future reference). If you already have a mortgage, you already have home insurance—or you should. What we need to figure out is if that insurance is adequate. Most people think that you only need to buy enough insurance to cover 80 percent of the costs of rebuilding your home, since it is unlikely that a home will be completely destroyed. But if you live in an area that experiences events like fires and hurricanes, your best bet is to buy insurance to cover 100 percent of rebuilding.

You can come up with a rough estimate for how much coverage you'll need just by multiplying the square footage of your home by the local building costs. You can ask your agent or an appraiser or builders' association for local construction costs per square foot for your kind of home. Then, you'll need to figure out how much it would cost to replace any extras like central air or a jacuzzi.

Allies

> **With replacement policies, make sure you have an accurate estimate of the cost of replacing your home. Construction and labor costs, as well as the cost of materials, will increase over the years, so you'll need to update your cost estimate regularly. Your best bet is to check annually with local contractors—not just your insurance agent—to see how much it would cost to rebuild your home. And if you have something extraordinary, like a fireplace made of Italian marble, make sure you get a rider. Your 120 percent cap is not going to cover expenses like international shipping.**

Once you arrive at a figure, you have another decision to make. Typically you have two choices. The cheaper policy is called "cash value" insurance. It pays you cash for what the destroyed property was worth at the time of destruction, including depreciation. The more expensive option is "replacement cost" insurance, which covers what it would take to rebuild your house with similar quality materials.

Remember that you are insuring the contents of your house as well as the house itself. That means everything, not just the big stuff. If you have a fire and lose everything, you will need to show an insurance company proof of what was inside if you want it replaced. Here are three things you can do that will help you win that battle.

Allies

1. Write down the model and serial number of every major appliance in your house (TV, refrigerator, stereo, etc.).
2. Grab a video camera and walk through your house room by room. Don't forget the kitchen cabinets and closets. Film everything!
3. Store the above information *offsite* or in a fireproof safe.

Some companies still offer guaranteed replacement policies that cover the full amount needed to replace your home and its contents no matter how high the bill. This is becoming increasingly rare, however, and you're more likely to find that the maximum insurance available to you is replacement coverage with a 120 percent limit.

Which sort of coverage you choose depends on what makes you comfortable and how much you can afford. Guaranteed replacement is obviously the best kind of coverage to have but it can cost as much 10 percent to 15 percent more than cash value. (The cost of guaranteed is usually much closer to the average cost of standard replacement value coverage.)

Here are the top five ways to save a few bucks on your home insurance:

Action Items

1. **Stay with the right crowd.** In almost any market, one company wants your business more than its rivals do. For example, you're highly desirable to some companies if you own a home in New York, Minnesota, Arizona, Illinois, and Connecticut where historical loss rates are low. Other insurers go after groups of customers they judge to be affluent and responsible, such as university alumni or membership organizations. Call your alumni association or any clubs you belong to see if it has a deal with an insurance company. If all else fails, check with a local agent.
2. **Increase your home security.** Inform your insurance company when you install burglar alarms and deadbolt locks. Home security measures can earn you discounts ranging from 5 percent to 20 percent. Do you have a

live-in housekeeper or nanny? Since the presence of a live-in employee can reduce the chance of break-ins, you can also get a break. Your central alarm system could save you hundreds on your annual premiums. Insurers will routinely give 15 percent to 20 percent off for a fire and burglar alarm system hooked up to a third-party monitoring company.

3. **Combine your coverage.** Many companies give discounts of 5 percent to 15 percent off your homeowner's policy if you combine it with your auto policy. The only time it may be cheaper to keep them separate is if you have a bad driving record. You also may be able to get a discount if you have a policy for your boat, a package of riders, or an umbrella policy (more on that later) with the same carrier.

4. **Raise your deductible.** You probably have a standard deductible of $250, but if you're willing to roll the dice a little bit and take a higher deductible, the savings can be substantial. At most companies, raising your deductible from $250 to $500 brings your annual premium down 10 percent. If you're willing to go from $500 to $1,000, you might be able to save another 10 percent.

5. **Rural problems:** If you live out in the sticks, be prepared to pay higher rates than folks who live in town. In most cases, you'll be bumped to a higher rate class if you live more than five miles from the nearest firehouse or more than 1,000 feet from the nearest fire hydrant. If you live in the country, don't count on finding a policy with a direct writer. Instead, work with a local insurance agent to price-shop among small mutual insurers that specialize in insuring dairy farms and rural homes—you'll do much better.

Renter's Insurance

Even if you're not a homeowner you may still need insurance protection. Renter's insurance covers you against fire, theft, and vandalism. Additionally, you can be held responsible for injury to another person or for damage to another person's property if an incident occurs within your rented residence. Don't assume that your landlord's insurance covers you—because it doesn't. Your landlord's insurance covers his or her property, not yours.

Renter's insurance is normally pretty cheap, and if you get it from the same company that insures your car you may receive a bargain. To figure out if you need renter's insurance, look back at the net worth exercise we did in Chapter 3. What would it cost you to replace all your stuff if you got burned out, or if somebody broke into your home? Is it worth paying $30 or $40 a month to insure it?

How Much Car Insurance Do I Need?

Most states require you to have a minimum amount of car insurance, and if you have a car loan or a lease, the lender will require you to have insurance as well. Basically, you have to have car insurance and there's almost no way to get around it. But, it's important that you don't just take whatever policy the lender lays in front of you. Here are some tips on ways to shop around and reduce your car insurance costs.

Shop around: When looking for a new policy, get at least three quotes. And if you *really* want to save, gather several more than that. According to a recent survey of more than 100,000 consumers in 26 states, rates for comparable coverage can vary by more than $500 for six months' worth of coverage.

Source: Progressive Insurance

Allies

Assuming you have a decent driving history, you should get the best deals from direct writers like Geico or Amica, since they remove the agent or intermediary (who often receives a commission of 15 percent). But these folks can be picky. If you've got a bad driving record, your best bet is to check with the major providers, such as State Farm and Allstate, and then head to an independent agent to see if they can beat your best quote. You also can comparison shop at Web sites such as *www.insweb.com,* which operates as an independent agent and a lead generator.

Don't always assume that the big guys don't have good rates; they can be very competitive, especially when you have multiple policies with them.

Allies

Don't stray too far from established companies when searching for a cheaper rate. You could find yourself with worthless insurance. Make sure you go with a company that has a good credit rating with a rating service such as Standard & Poor's at www.spglobal.com or Moody's at *www.moodys.com*. You might also want to check with your state department of insurance to see if a particular company has a high number of consumer complaints. (Go to *www.naic.org* to find the Web site of your state's department.)

Get All Available Discounts

You can save money by combining your coverage, which we talked about in the home insurance segment of this chapter, and knock off 10 percent to 20 percent from your premiums if you insure both your home and your car with the same company, or by insuring more than one car with the same company. More commonly available discounts are:

- **Defensive-Driving Classes:** This can often merit a 10 percent discount on premiums.

- **Good-Student Discounts:** Students with GPAs of 3.0 or higher can be eligible for discounts of as much as 25 percent.

- **Retirement Discounts:** Be sure to let your insurer know when you retire—particularly if you retire at a relatively young age. Since you're likely to be driving less once your working days are over, this can often earn you a break on premiums.

- **Association and Group Discounts:** Discounts may be available for affiliation with all sorts of associations—your alma matter, a military group, or a professional organization. If you work for a large employer, that could earn you a discount as well.

- **Safety Discounts:** In some states, including New York and Florida, drivers must be rewarded for having certain safety features on their car, such as antilock breaks, airbags, and automatic seat belts. Certain antitheft devices could be eligible for a discount as well.

- **Loyalty Discounts:** Stick with the same company for more than one year, and you could earn a break of 10 percent or more on your premiums.

The most important thing with car insurance is to look around a little bit, because you can really save a bundle by comparison shopping.

Do I Need an Umbrella Policy?

Umbrella policies supplement the liability coverage you already have through your home and auto insurance and provide an extra layer of protection. If you don't have enough liability coverage to resolve a claim or a lawsuit, the person bringing the action might go after your home or your other assets to pay for damage. Umbrella policies cover damage claims that you, your dependents, or even your pets may cause.

How Umbrella Policies Work

This information about umbrella policies is likely something you should file away until after you've won a few Cash Flow War battles. The extra protection this sort of insurance provides really isn't necessary until you start accumulating a nice pile of assets—but once you declare victory in the Cash Flow Wars, an umbrella policy is a must.

Umbrella policies kick in after the liability insurance in your homeowners and auto policy runs out. If you have a home insurance policy with liability coverage of $300,000, the umbrella policy will pay claims above that amount up to the limit selected. For example, if your liability limit on your auto insurance policy is $250,000 of bodily injury protection per person and $500,000 per accident, your umbrella coverage would kick in after you have exhausted your auto liability coverage. Most of the risk is assumed under the primary auto or home policy, which is why a personal liability umbrella policy is so inexpensive. You can buy a $1-million-or-larger umbrella policy for less than $200 a year.

Allies

To figure out if you need an umbrella policy, you have to add all your assets and then subtract the total of your liability coverage. If your assets are worth more than your coverage, you may need an umbrella policy.

Umbrella policies are usually sold with a deductible that might run anywhere from $250 to $1,000. If you're on the hook for a multimillion-dollar lawsuit, that's a small price to pay. Umbrella policies also offer coverage not found in your auto and homeowners policy. They cover false arrest, false imprisonment, malicious prosecution, defamation, invasion of privacy, wrongful entry, or eviction. Most primary policies cover bodily injury and property damage, but not personal injury. Certain umbrella policies also provide coverage if you face liability arising from your service on the board of a civic, charitable, or religious organization.

Land Mines

Even if you buy a top-of-the-line personal liability umbrella policy, you can't protect yourself against every possible claim or lawsuit. There will be exclusions in the umbrella policy just as there are exclusions in every insurance policy. Just cover yourself enough to cover all your assets and that should be fine.

Marching Orders

Marching Orders for Understanding Insurance

✔ Figure out how much coverage you need

✔ Shop around! You can save a ton of money on the right policy

✔ Consider an umbrella policy

Part Three

Mastering the Rules of War

All our dreams can come true—
if we have the courage to pursue them.

Walt Disney, creator of Mickey Mouse

Mastering the Rules of War

> *The vision must be followed by the venture. It is not enough to stare up the steps—we must step up the stairs.*
>
> —Vance Havne, author

We know ourselves. We know our enemies. Now we must fight. With self-evaluation, savings, and cost-cutting out of the way, we are about to make a quantum leap in the Cash Flow War. You can think of it as having completed Boot Camp and now you're ready to advance—you're ready to take the next steps towards your eventual objective of financial freedom.

In Part Three, *Mastering the Rules of War,* we'll move forward. We all know there's more to life than living from paycheck to paycheck, so this part of the book will deal with how you can start making your money *work for you.* This is where we get to use some of the strategies and concepts we have learned in the first two sections. It is also where you are going to learn a few things that 99.9 percent of all people *don't know.* These weapons, if used properly, will be among the most powerful in your Cash Flow War arsenal.

I'll help you along with my personal strategies, philosophies, and even my own personal mindset on building the kind of financial freedom most people only dream about. These are the techniques I use every day to continue to build (as well as retain) my own wealth. More importantly, these simple-to-use strategies can be applied to your life to achieve the same results I have seen time and time again.

I firmly believe that you can easily put these strategies to work for you. I know that if you do then you will more easily find the success you've been working toward. You're ready to take the next steps—you're ready to get proactive! To do that, you'll need a deeper understanding of the rules of the Cash Flow War. You'll need to start doing the things that people who can already claim victory and financial freedom have done.

Mail Call

> **Millionaires do have some secrets. But the secrets are anyone's for the asking! There is an old saying, a favorite of mine, which says: "The difference between winners and losers is that winners do what losers don't want to." In reality, the difference is really just the willingness to learn (and execute) what others won't.**

Get Ready to Take the Next Step

As you can see, ultimate victory in the Cash Flow War is built by meeting one challenge at a time, and then combining all those small battlefield victories into one grand campaign. You've won the battle on the homefront by virtue of incorporating the knowledge you gained in Parts One and Two into your daily life, and you've solidified your borders and you're ready to begin your expansion!

Part Three is all about expanding your personal financial borders by carefully winning battles. It is this stage that begins to catapult you well above those around you. If you're just getting started in investing, picking your first property can be intimidating. It's hard to keep your emotions out of the equation. If you recognize that your emotions have taken over and you're on the verge of investing with your heart rather than your head, don't fret. It's easy to figure out why emotions come into play—you're scared of losing your money.

There is no shame in a bit of emotion. There are steps you can take, however, to minimize the risk and alleviate your fear. The best way is to educate yourself about investing. In Part Three, in addition to reinforcing some of the concepts we discussed in Parts One and Two, I'll give you some rock-solid advice and tips on how to plan for your future so you can go into investing without the fear of losing your shirt.

Before we get started I want to make sure you have a solid base camp. Here is what you can expect in Part Three: Mastering the Rules of War.

Chapter 11: Accelerating Payments

We'll explore how and why you should accelerate payments on your credit cards, car payments, and other loans, and especially on your mortgages. I'll tell you why the banks don't want you to do this and debunk the myth of tax benefits on interest paid.

> **Giving away our hand early? By accelerating payments for credit cards, mortgages, auto loans, and student loans, you can become completely debt-free in just a few short years rather than the lifetime it would otherwise take. Another added bonus of accelerating your payment is that you're actually *paying off the money you borrowed,* not just paying off the interest that the original purchase incurs over time.**

Allies

Chapter 12: Financial Calculator

This chapter will change the way you look at money forever, and will open the door to the secrets that the wealthy have been holding out on for years. My graduates often say that the calculator is often one of the most valuable tools they have ever mastered. Not only can you use a simple financial calculator to find out what sort of automobile you can buy based on your monthly payment, or find out your mortgage loan payment based on your purchase price, you will use this simple tool to perform a quantum leap in your financial future—in just about every category!

Chapter 13: Taking Control of Your Retirement Accounts

We'll explore different kinds of accounts and how you can get the biggest bang for your buck. Here's a reality check: Most people are planning to depend on Social Security—by now, you know that is not *really* planning.

Chapter 14: In Preparing to Pay for College

For those of us with children, we'll take a look at how you can prepare to pay for the biggest fixed cost you will ever meet as a parent: college! We'll take a hard look at Coverdell's and the 529 plans that are designed to help you meet these costs, offer tips on how to figure out just how much cash you'll need, and explore various prepay options floating around out there in the world of academic financials.

As most Americans are realizing, some experts predict that Social Security will begin running cash deficits by 2015, and by 2037—the year the so-called trust fund runs out of IOUs—those deficits will top $1 trillion. Some say the program's long-term liabilities are a whopping $22 trillion! As bad as this may be, Social Security also is becoming a bad deal for younger workers. Younger workers are likely to get a paltry one to two percent return on their FICA tax contributions. Many minority workers will actually get *less* back from the system than the amount of taxes they paid into it.

Chapter 15: Playing the Market: Stocks, Options, and Mutual Funds

Although they call it playing, it's not a game! This chapter shows you how you should carefully consider your investment options before deciding to invest. Once you dive into the stock market and start dealing with stock brokers (or not), you need to be prepared and have the knowledge necessary to be appropriately skeptical when it comes to miracle stocks and investments that promise large sums of money to be earned securely in a short period of time.

This chapter will help you carefully weigh the advantages and disadvantages of investing in certain securities. It will also help you to define your investment objectives in terms of returns and decide on a limit for losses over a given period of time.

Chapter 16: How to Avoid Bankruptcy

According to the Federal Reserve, the typical family that files for bankruptcy owes more than one and a half times its annual income in short-term, high-interest debt. A family earning $24,000 had an average of $36,000 in credit card and similar debt. If you find yourself in this situation (or even getting close), this chapter will offer you some valuable information about the differences between different types of bankruptcy and—more importantly—how to avoid bankruptcy all together.

Base Camp for Mastering the Rules of War

Setting Up Your Home Office

At this point I suggest that you take a little time now and really put together a home office, a place where you can sit down and really think about your finances. My first home office was my kitchen table in a studio apartment. All you need is a little nook somewhere that you can set up as a work area. You just need a little space in your dwelling that says to you, "When I sit down here, I'm sitting down to work!"

Quick Tips for Setting Up a Home Office

- Set aside a special space for your office, especially if you hope to claim a home-office deduction on your taxes.

- If you have a door, close it.

- Try to minimize the number of distractions in your immediate work space (TV, GameBoy, Nintendo, children).

- If you have small children at home, don't look at those magazine photos of the home-based working mom talking on the phone and studying a spreadsheet while a delightful nine-month-old plays at her feet. That's a fantasy world. It really doesn't work that way. Get an in-home caregiver or family member—anyone—to help out. Your nerves, and your children, will thank you.

- Make your workstation as comfortable as possible—you may be spending a lot of time there.

- Get organized. This means buying file cabinets, file folders, and labels— then putting them to use. If money is tight at the beginning of this process, use cardboard boxes.

- Try to set a work schedule that suits your own high-productivity cycles. Most people have a time of day that they work at their best. Find yours and make that your prime working time.

Set some rules for yourself, like a break every hour, a set time every day that you *leave* your home (even if it's just to walk around the block)—and no surfing the net, except for business-related surfing. Your rules should address your own weaknesses.

What's This Going to Cost Me?

Well, it can cost you nothing at all—or up to several thousand dollars (depending on the type of business you want). Remember, all you really need is a place to sit and think and a flat surface to write on. If you want something a little fancier than that, you can follow the guidelines I recommend.

The good news is that the price of computers and other office automation equipment has come down dramatically over the past 10 years. Prices for phone service vary from place to place, but new, all-inclusive packages from providers like AT&T, MCI, and Verizon provide unlimited local, regional, and long-distance calls for less than $40 a month. Likewise, high-speed Internet access (broadband or DSL) is available for $25 to $100 per month.

Computer

You can get a top-of-the line computer with a 17-inch monitor, a CD-ROM drive, and all the software you need already installed for less than $1,000. If you don't need a lightning-fast computer, you can really get just about everything you need in a computer for less than $500. You just need to shop around at consumer electronics stores and warehouse clubs, and check those prices against the big boys like Dell. Somebody always has a good computer on sale.

Two-line Cordless Phone

Today's top-of-the-line cordless phones start at less than $200, offering home offices the same clarity as a corporate boardroom with a microphone optimized for hands-free, one-to-one phone conversations. If you are planning on spending a lot of time on the phone, consider a lightweight cordless headset—I don't know what I would do without mine.

Office Furniture

Depending on how fancy you want to get, you can spend anywhere from a few hundred to a few thousand dollars to equip yourself with a desk, chair, and filing cabinets. Spend the big bucks after you've racked up a few Cash Flow War victories! For now, you can do very nicely with what you already have or by buying what's on sale at your local office supply store.

Okay, Soldiers, Mount Up!

Enough of this briefing room pep talk. The big push is on. It's time to take our **Understanding of the Rules of the Cash Flow War** and go out and start winning some battles!

11

Accelerating Payments

> *Creditors have better memories than debtors.*
> —Ben Franklin, inventor

One of the most important things to understand when winning the Cash Flow War is knowing which side of the cash register you are on. Money changes hands back and forth all the time: Sometimes we are the ones borrowing money, sometimes we are the ones lending it. Even once you have won the Cash Flow War, you will occasionally find yourself in a situation where you will borrow money. In Chapter 7, I mentioned briefly how important it is to accelerate your payments on your credit card debt. In this chapter I'll explain why this is a vital strategy to pursue on all your debt when leading your troops in the Cash Flow War.

We're going to look into accelerating payments on both mortgages and credit cards. First, we'll look at home mortgages.

Let's go back to our example from Chapter 7 on mortgages. Imagine that you take a $100,000 mortgage out on a house. Just like most people do, you take a 30-year mortgage. If, to keep it simple, we say the interest on the mortgage is 10 percent, you would be paying $877.57 a month (not counting taxes and insurance), making your total payments $315,925.20 over the life of the loan. And that all seems normal. Your parents did it that way, and your friends did too. Even the banker and probably your real estate agent told you that was the way to go. We *expect* to pay to borrow money—but how much should we be paying?

Nobody ever told you that if you just cut back on a few things and paid the bank $1,000 a month (instead of $877.57) you would pay the mortgage off in 18 years instead of 30. Your total payments would be just under $216,000! Just by coming up with an extra $122.43 a month, you'd be saving almost $100,000 of real money in your pocket! But of course, the bank doesn't tell you that. Why should they? They're in this thing to make money, and you should never forget that.

Before I go any further let me say that your friends and family will come up with two arguments against accelerating your mortgage. I hear these same objections every time I speak.

1. **If I pay off my mortgage sooner, I won't be able to use my tax deduction.**

   That is correct but please, please, please understand that the tax deduction is not as good as millions of people have been taught. You only get to deduct the *interest* that you are paying. In the first scenario, you are going to pay $215,925 in interest but only a portion of that (after deduction) will be real money that stays in your pocket (roughly 25 to 33 percent depending on your tax situation). Remember: Would you give me $100,000 for the right to not give someone else $30,000? Of course not—so why pay the bank $100,000 in interest just so you don't have to give the IRS $30,000? It doesn't make sense!

2. **If I can invest my money (in this case the extra $122.43 per month) in something greater than 10 percent wouldn't I come out ahead?**

   This is an unlikely occurrence. Keep in mind that accelerating a mortgage is a *guaranteed* investment/savings. Remember Ben Franklin's advice: "A penny saved is a penny earned." Every time you pay extra money (accelerate), you are *saving* 10 percent. I don't know of too many investments that guarantee you that return. Secondly, whatever you invest in you will have to pay tax on. Every dollar you earn will be taxed. So, you better earn more than at least 13 to 14 percent to even think about this strategy.

The only truth you really need to remember about anyone that extends you credit or "allows" you to make a purchase on time payments is that they are all in it to *make money*. And the longer you take to pay off that purchase, the more money the seller or lender stands to make. It's a simple concept: The longer you owe someone money, the more interest you'll pay on that money. However, if you pay the money back more quickly than is asked for, you'll end up paying less interest and keeping more of your own money.

Should You Accelerate Payments on Your Mortgage?

This sounds like a great idea right off the bat, and as a matter of fact, you were probably already sold on the big savings, but there are few things you need to look at before you make the leap and start accelerating your payments on this big-ticket item. The example I used to begin this chapter is attractive, but there are some things to consider first. Answer these questions before deciding whether an accelerated payment schedule is right for you:

Do you have debt other than your mortgage? Like higher interest credit cards? If so, pay off the cards first, and then work on the mortgage. The cards are more than likely at a higher interest rate and the interest you pay on them is not deductible.

Are you contributing the maximum to your tax-deferred retirement plans? You need to look at this closely to determine whether the interest you would make on your 401(k) (for example) would be more beneficial to you than paying your mortgage off earlier. If you have recently refinanced at the historically low levels we saw in 2003, then maybe accelerating your mortgage payment may not be the best move for you right now. Maybe that money should go into a 401(k) or a 529 college tuition plan. This is definitely a judgment call—one guiding principle is that if you're saving 10 percent of your salary already, then it's time to accelerate mortgage. If you're saving less than that, you should bump up your savings first.

Have you refinanced lately? If you bought your house more than 24 months or so ago, it may be time to refinance. As of late 2004, mortgage rates are pretty low—but because I'm not sure when you will be buying this book and reading, mortgage rates may not be as low. You need to check what the mortgage rates are and determine if now is a good time for you to refinance. One good rule of thumb is that if you can drop your interest rate by two or more points, then go for it. Another advantage of refinancing is that you can take some cash out and obliterate all of your really high-interest debt like credit cards, and consolidate your debt into one payment a month. Debt consolidation at lower rates can be a great deal provided you don't run out and charge up your credit cards again.

Does your current mortgage have prepayment penalties that effectively nullify the advantage of satisfying the loan early? I don't believe in prepayment penalties but nonetheless, they are out there in some mortgages. Will it cost you more than it's worth to pay off the mortgage? You need to sit down and sharpen up a pencil and figure this out.

Now, if you can clear those four hurdles, you need to start thinking about accelerating your mortgage.

Accelerating Payments on Your Mortgage

Your mortgage company has all sorts of plans for you when you want to accelerate your payments. But first make sure that you don't have a prepayment penalty; if you do, call your mortgage company and see if you can get it waived. As far as the accelerated payment plans your bank offers, my advice is that if it costs you one single dime in fees, forget it. You can do it yourself for free—there is no reason to pay fees just for the privilege of paying back a loan faster!

You don't even have to pay more money per month to accelerate your mortgage payments. Simply by making the same payment in weekly increments instead of monthly increments you can cut time off of your mortgage loan provided the mortgage company will apply partial payments rather than holding funds until it equals the required monthly payment.

Biweekly Accelerated Mortgage Payment Program

Your mortgage company probably has an "equity accelerator program," where you can make 26 payments a year, or one payment every two weeks. Essentially, you're making one extra payment a year and avoiding a lot of interest by paying every two weeks. Sounds fine, right? Wrong! They may hit you with fees—you should just do it yourself.

This is called a biweekly mortgage, and is one where half of your regular mortgage payment is made every other week, rather than monthly. This method simply adds one more principal and interest payment each year so that you end up making 26 half payments or 13 full mortgage payments in a year instead of 12; it greatly accelerates the attack on your mortgage debt. It works well for some people, especially those who receive a paycheck every other week.

Let's assume you have an $80,000 mortgage at 8 percent interest. If you have 30 years left on your mortgage, you'd be paying $587.01 per month. But if you just split that in half and sent in $293.51 every two weeks, you could save yourself over $37,000 in interest and knock almost seven years off your loan.

You can do this yourself if you wish. Just take your regular monthly mortgage payment and divide it by 12 ($48.92 in this example); add that amount to your monthly payment, and show it as an additional "principal" payment. You're done, and you still get the benefit of paying your loan off faster and you've avoided paying fees. Just be sure to clearly indicate the additional amount to be applied to principal so the mortgage company applies correctly.

Mortgage Acceleration Chart

Payment	Amount	Amortization (years)	Total Interest Cost
Monthly	$587.01	30.0	$131,326.07
Accelerated biweekly (½ payment every 2 weeks)	$293.51	23.3	$94,280.21
Accelerated weekly (extra ½ payment each month)	$635.93	22.9	$94,597.39

Land Mines

Most lenders require an enrollment or setup fee for the biweekly mortgage accelerator program, some require a transaction fee, and others call for a mandatory automatic payment authorization. An average national mortgage lender charges a one-time enrollment fee of $375 for its equity accelerator program plus a transaction fee of 75¢ for each biweekly draft. Why should you pay this fee? Just divide your monthly payment by 12 and pay that extra amount each month.

Credit Card War Games

Here's a simple example of the benefits of accelerating your debt payments. This time I'll use credit card debt as an example.

The interesting thing about credit cards is that they make all the rules. Have you ever looked at the fine print on the back of your statement? The following is a direct quote from one credit card statement on my desk regarding how they will allocate your payments. "We will allocate your payments in the manner we determine."

I think that says it all.

The best advice I can give you is to pay them off as quickly as possible and do whatever you can to mail more than the minimum payment. Minimum payments are just that—the *minimum* amount you can pay, resulting in the *maximum* amount of time and money you will owe them.

Since credit card companies all make different rules, it is difficult to provide one definitive example of what they all do. But let's take a look at credit cards in general and what we can do to improve the situation.

Let's suppose you have four credit cards at the various interest rates as listed in chart on the next page. The debt on the four cards adds up to only $8,500—not a staggering amount, but certainly not chicken feed. But here's the shocker: If you make only the minimum payments requested by the credit card companies, it will take you between 7 to 12 years to pay off these credit cards! And that assumes that you never charge on them again.

Credit Acceleration Chart

Card	Balance	Payment	Interest
Store Card	$3,000.00	$55.00	21.0%
Master Card	$2,000.00	$40.00	19.8%
Discovery	$1,500.00	$30.00	15.0%
Visa	$2,000.00	$35.00	12.0%

At this rate of payment, you're "servicing" your debt at $160 a month. You're just paying enough to keep it hanging around. But always remember that you have several options when servicing this debt.

Option One: Minimum Payments

Credit cards give you the option of making minimum payments only. This is the worst possible way to go, and should be avoided at all costs. The credit card companies even get a little sneaky here, so always remember as you keep making the minimum payment, your balance gets smaller and the amount of the required minimum payment also gets smaller. But the interest on your debt remains the same. The $40.00 minimum payment you're making now will eventually drop down to the card's lowest payment (usually around $12.00 to $15.00), and it will take you a long time to pay off your debt.

✔ In addition to taking longer to become debt-free, paying only the minimum amount will cost you hundreds (if not thousands) of dollars more in interest.

Option Two: Maintain Same Payment

As your balance gets lower and lower, most companies will allow you to make smaller minimum payments. Skip this. Just by maintaining the same constant debt service (in this case $160.00 a month), you can vastly reduce the amount of money you're paying in interest. Imagine that you continue making the combined $160.00 payment a month no matter what the minimum on the monthly bills say. As the minimum payment required by the card goes down as the balance gets

Allies

smaller, you continue to make the same payment on each card. This will accelerate your debt and pay it off faster.

✔ Maintaining the same payment is a step in the right direction and will begin to save you money as the credit card company lowers your payment.

Option Three: Increase All Payments

Here's where we switch from servicing your debt and gear up for attack mode! If you can find an extra $80 a month, you can accelerate, or increase, the payment on each card by $20.00. Your total debt attack is now $240.00 a month. Instead of paying the minimum on each card every month and sticking to that, you find an extra $20.00 payment and maintain that level.

Allies

✔ By increasing each payment by only $20 you will save (in our example) over $6,000 in interest payments and you will be debt free in *half the time!*

Option Four: Increase Payment on the Credit Card with the Highest Interest Rate

Let's imagine that you found the extra $80 a month we talked about in the previous example, and you're using it to accelerate payments. The first mistake people make is going after the lowest *balance* card to get it paid off quickly. Although it may be a great psychological win, it does not add up to the most amount of money staying in *your* pocket (and out of the enemy's hands).

Start with the *highest rate* card. Pay the other three cards the minimum payment amount and pay all the remaining money to, in this case, the 21 percent store card. You would mail $35, $30, and $40 to the lower rate cards and the rest ($135) to the highest rate card.

After the store card is paid off, you would mail $175 per month to the highest rate card (the $135 plus the $40 minimum you were previously paying). The other two would continue to get the minimum payment. Keep repeating this "payment rollover" every time you pay off a card, and move those amounts (plus the minimum) to the card on your list with the next highest interest rate.

✔ By attacking the highest rate cards first, you are focusing your money at the heart of the problem. This strategy will allow you to become debt-free in the quickest manner possible.

Allies

Credit Card War Games: When you're thinking about accelerating payments, go back Chapter 5 and reread the sections about getting better interest rates on your cards. You can usually push your debt to a card with lower interest rates, and then when you accelerate your payments you'll be that much further ahead of the game.

Allies

Marching Orders for Accelerating Payments

Marching Orders

✔ Always make more than your minimum payment.

✔ Pay back your higher-interest loans first.

✔ Never pay fees to increase your payments.

✔ Review Chapter 5 to see if you can lower your interest rates on your cards, as this will result in an instant savings.

Calculator Clarity

> *Someone doesn't need a gun to rob people, they just need a HP12C [financial calculator].*
> —Jon Richards, mentor, real estate investor

As my friend Jon taught me years ago, don't be taken advantage of financially simply because you do not know the rules or how to figure out the numbers for yourself. The rules are not that hard to learn, and I'll teach you how to run the numbers in this chapter.

I've been teasing you with this chapter throughout the beginning of this book, and for good reason. By the time you're done with this chapter and you've done the exercises you'll never again sign a deal on a car, house, or any other major purchase without understanding fully what you're getting into. You'll never experience "buyer's remorse" again because you'll never have to sign any sort of financial transaction without knowing, to the penny, how much it will eventually cost you and to the penny, how much you will be paying in interest.

And it doesn't stop there. Once you master the financial calculator—and you will be a master by the end of this chapter—you'll be able to invest more intelligently, structure better business deals, and figure yields on all of your financial transactions. Numerical problems that were once almost impossible for the average Cash Flow Warrior to figure out can be solved within seconds with a little $30 calculator.

Allies

> You'll never have to fear that the finance manager or the loan officer is practicing some sort of arcane voodoo when they're working out the terms of a major purchase—you'll now have access to the same tools that they have, and you'll be able to keep them honest!

This is a pretty powerful weapon you'll be adding to your Cash Flow War arsenal, and here's the best part: it's really not that hard to learn how to use.

Most people walk into their local car dealer with just enough information to hurt themselves. Our schools (such as they are) have only taught us a small amount about budgeting. So, the average person walks into a dealership and declares how much they can afford per month according to their budget. These seemingly savvy people (and I have been one of them in the past) have just given the fox the keys to the henhouse.

Once you say something like, "I can afford $400 per month," the salesperson will run off to go converse with the "wizard" behind the curtain (and we never actually get to meet the wizard). And then guess what happens? Lo and behold, the payment magically comes back at $398.27 or something like that. How did they do it?

The person still purchases the car because they think they must have worked out the best deal possible. In reality, they most likely left a lot on the table. Next time, as a Cash Flow Warrior, you will pull out your calculator (which will confuse the salesperson because only "wizards" know how to operate one of those) and you will do the math. I can guarantee that you will find that you can get your payments lower, or that they are charging you too much for the car, or that your interest rate is too high. All of these things may help you save money and possibly shave years off your car loan.

Let's get started.

Financial Calculator Boot Camp

Please understand that I am not talking about regular calculators here. They won't do what we need to do. You need to buy a financial calculator. There are some very good yet inexpensive calculators on the market. The Hewlett Packard HP 10B and the Texas Instruments BA 35 are both excellent choices. The Texas Instruments (Financial Investment Analyst) is the one that sits on my desk—they don't make them anymore so you may have to use one of the others. Most cost around $40 and do everything you will need to do.

Most financial calculators are basically the same. They all have the primary five keys that you will be using to input most of your Cash Flow War calculations. These five keys are normally in the first or second row of your calculator, and here's what they look like and what they mean:

N = Number of payments

I = Interest, or yield/return

PV = Present value, or loan amount

PMT = Payment

FV = Future value

I'm going to use a table in this chapter to represent how these keys will be used. The top row of the table represents the keys used to solve the calculations. The next row will be the figures used in our calculation examples.

N	I	PV	PMT	FV

Get familiar with this format, and it will be much easier to plug the appropriate numbers into the appropriate boxes to solve your calculations. You need to start thinking in terms of N, I, PV, PMT, and FV.

Let's Start Crunching Numbers!

Yes, I know, it's hardly a blood-stirring rallying cry like "Remember the Alamo!" But, bear with me, you'll find that the results will be pretty darn exciting. Watch how simple this is. In most of your Cash Flow War calculations, you will only be using four key strokes: N, I, PV, and PMT. Anytime you know any three of these four functions, you can easily solve for the fourth. In the following example our unknown function is N (number).

Figuring Out a Future Value

Okay, let's try a basic calculation like a savings account. Let's say that you want to save $100 per month for the next 10 years. The bank is offering a four percent rate of return (compounded monthly) and, for the purpose of this exercise, let's say it will stay that way for the whole 10 years. We are also going to open the account with $200. So what do we know?

N	I	PV	PMT	FV
120	4	−200	−100	?

We know that we are opening the account with $200 (PV); we know that we are going to put in $100 per month (PMT); we know that the bank will pay us four percent (I) and we know that we will do this for 10 years (120 months). With that said, and entered in the calculator, we only need to solve for FV (what will the value be in 120 months?).

N	I	PV	PMT	FV
120	4	−200	−100	15,023.15

Note that for the savings example we made both PV and PMT negative (−) numbers. That is money going out (to the savings).

Figuring Out the Number of Payments

Action Items

Let's imagine you borrowed $5,000 in seed money to get a business venture off the ground. The terms you agreed to were to pay off the lender in 36 months, or three years at 10 percent interest, until the loan is paid off.

So, what do we know? We know the amount (PV) of the loan ($5,000), we know the interest rate (I/Y) is 10 percent, and we know the number of payments is 36. But what we don't know is how much we need to pay each month in order to have it completely paid off in 36 months.

Look at the table below. The FV (future value) key isn't needed in this calculation, so it won't have a number related to it

N	I	PV	PMT	FV
36	10	−5,000	?	0

So, basically all you have to do is input the numbers in the right places. Simply enter the three known functions (figures) in any order, and your calculator will solve for the unknown function.

Since you're borrowing $5,000, this is the present value (PV), and that figure would go in the PV box. This must be a *negative* number.

The interest rate is 10 percent, but that's an annual rate. Depending on the type of calculator you purchased, you will either enter "10" for I or you may have to divide by 12 and put that number in I (in this case it would be 10 divided by 12 to give you .83) Some calculators will do it for you, so you only have to put in the "10."

The number of payments is 36, so that number goes in the N (number of payments) box.

So we now have the loan amount ($5,000) in the PV box, the interest rate (10 percent) in the I box, and the number of payments (36) in the N box, zero in FV, but we still have a question mark in the PMT box. All you need to do is calculate the PMT key—you come up with 161.34.

N	I	PV	PMT	FV
36	10	−5.000	**161.34**	0

Your calculator will let us know it will take 36 payments of $161.34 each at 10 percent interest to pay off your $5,000 loan.

> Guess who the good guys are here? Well, it's you and your calculator. Your ability to figure out your own "loan amounts" will help you from being taken by some less reputable people out there. Just think of the applications—you can take this calculation and figure out to the penny just how much it will take to pay off your credit card debt, for example. You can juggle numbers and see how much faster you can pay it off if you just increase the payment a few bucks a month. Same thing with your mortgage!

Allies

Figuring the Balance on Your Mortgage

Let's do another calculation. But before we do it, take a quick look at a couple of Land Mines and Allies. These are the most common mistakes people make that lead to a wrong answer.

Common Calculator Mistakes

1. PV was not entered as a negative number. The calculator needs to know "money out" and "money in." That is how it can figure out a yield or interest rate. So, for purposes of keeping it simple, we always use the investor's side and make PV the negative money going out and PMT the positive (money coming in).

2. Old number still in the wrong category (was there a number left in FV by mistake?)

3. Wrong payments per year. Most of what you do will be 12 payments per year. That is something we have to tell the calculator. If for some reason you want to change your calculator to quarterly payments or annual payments (see your calculator manual), then you have to make sure you switch it back when you are done).

Things that Can Help You Out

1. Write the problem on paper first.

2. When you make a mistake, use the "recall" key. Every calculator has a "recall" key. This allows you to check the answers in each category without changing them. When you make a mistake you may feel as though you should clear everything and start over—but it is often easier if you use the "recall" key, find the error and just change that category.

If this hasn't happened to you yet, it's going to happen to you someday. You'll be figuring out how to make some masterful advance in the Cash Flow War, and while you're marshaling your forces, you'll want to know your net worth down to the penny and you'll have to know the balance on your mortgage.

Before you were the master of the financial calculator, you would have had to take the word of your mortgage company. Now that you're practically a rocket scientist with this marvelous little tool, you'll be able to make several key strokes on your calculator and have your answer instantly.

Here's how to do it: Suppose you find a house for $100,000. You got a good deal. After shopping around for a loan, you find a friendly banker willing to loan you 85 percent of the purchase price. You need to put up $15,000 for the down payment, and your will bank loan you $85,000 at eight percent fixed rate, for 30 years (360 payments).

Let's make a table and see what your payments will be.

Solving for Monthly Payments

N	I	PV	PMT	FV
360	8	**−85,000**	?	0

If we solve for PMT we get

N	I	PV	PMT	FV
360	8	−85,000	**623.70**	0

We see that your payments will be $623.70 per month, P&I (principal and interest). This payment represents both the principal and interest on your loan which will amortize (pay your loan off) in 30 years (360 payments).

Now, let's suppose that a few years down the road, after you implement everything you read in this book, you decide that you want to pay this thing off, just to get this mortgage monkey off your back. Let's imagine that after making 51 payments you want to know what your loan balance is so you can cut a big check. Your loan was structured for 360 payments and you've made 51, so that leaves 309 payments to go. So enter 309 for N, 8 for I, $623.70 for PMT, and solve for PV (loan balance).

We see that your loan balance, after making 51 payments, is $81,549.25.

Solving for Loan Balance

N	I	PV	PMT	FV
309	8	?	**623.70**	0

Solve for PV and you will get

N	I	PV	PMT	FV
309	8	**−81,549.25**	623.70	0

Let's say that you didn't realize it would be that much to pay off the loan and you decide to "accelerate" your payments. Now what you want to know, if you would like to own this house free and clear 15 years from that moment, is how much would you need to pay each month?

First off, what do we know? We know we want to pay it off in 15 years (or 180 months). We know that we are paying eight percent interest, and we know (from above) that after 51 months, we owe $81,549.23. What we don't know is how much to mail every month to pay off the loan in 15 years. Here is what we do know:

N	I	PV	PMT	FV
180	8	−81,549.23	?	0

So, now that we have our numbers in the calculor, let's just calculate for Payment.

N	I	PV	PMT	FV
309	8	-81,549.23	**779.33**	0

Wow! For a mere $155.63 more a month, you will pay off your house in 15 years instead of 309 months (25.75 years). That does not even get into the interest savings you have (real money in your pocket) that we discussed in Chapter 5. You will find this very helpful on everything you are paying on. Oftentimes, for a little more money, you can have a considerable positive impact on your own cash flow. If for some reason my wife and I take on any debt (typically a property investment) we always accelerate the debt and pay it off as quickly as possible.

Credit Cards

Action Items

Let's say that you have a balance of $6,500 on your credit card. The interest rate is 21 percent and they want you to mail a minimum payment of $125.00. Sounds fair enough, right? Let us just check how long it will take to pay off that debt at the "minimum payment."

Here is what we know:

N	I	PV	PMT	FV
?	21	−6,500	125.00	0

Once we let the calculator figure out the number of months is will take to pay off:

N	I	PV	PMT	FV
138	21	−6,500	125.00	0

Excuse me? 138 months to pay off my credit card? Actually, 138.80 months comes to 11½ years. Not only that, the minimum payment may even lower as you pay your balance down—taking an even longer time to pay off. You and I are in the wrong business!

We learned in Chapter 5 that credit card companies just don't want us to pay them off. This is probably the *first* area where you should be paying as much you can afford.

21 percent? This will seriously wound even the best Cash Flow Warrior if it goes on too long. Accelerate it and get rid of it first! Once you do, it will be all downhill from there.

Investing and Your Return

Now I want to explore something that will become very important to you, particularly in the final portion of this book. In the case of our investments, we want to know the return on our investment. As we will get into later in the book, yield is everything—not the dollars.

Let's take a basic investment that you buy and resell later (hopefully for a higher price).

When I was young I used to buy cars that ran well but didn't look so great. People buy things based on how they look. It was not that hard to find cars that were mechanically very sound but were not very pretty on the outside.

One example was an old Volkswagen Karman Ghia that I bought for $2,500. It had a new engine but, unless rust and primer are colors people were looking for, the outside was not pretty. I took the car down to my local paint shop that used to paint any car for $99.95. It cost me another $75 to fill in a few dings. When all was said and done, I put in about $450 into cleaning up this car. After three months, I sold the car for $4,600. So what was my return?

What I know is that it took four months (N), I had a total investment of $2,950 (PV)—$2,500 for the car and $450 to clean it up, and that I sold it for $4,600. When in the calculator worksheet, it looks like this:

N	I	PV	PMT	FV
4	?	−2,950	0	4,600

And the answer is:

N	I	PV	PMT	FV
4	**140.96**	−2,950	0	4,600

That's a 140 percent return on my money! Keep in mind, that is a four-month return, not annual. If it had taken me 12 months to sell the car, I still would have had a 45 percent return! But you can bet that I didn't wait until the end of the year to get that money reinvested.

Now that you know how to work a financial calculator you're fully equipped to figure out just about any financial transaction you might engage in. You are now armed and dangerous: You're fully checked out on one of the most powerful weapons available to the Cash Flow Warrior!

Marching Orders for Calculator Clarity

✔ **Buy a financial calculator.**

✔ **Practice with the examples in this book.**

✔ **Apply your newly earned knowledge to your situation.**

✔ **Use blank calculator worksheets for practice; they are provided for your use on pages 341 and 342.**

Taking Control of Your Retirement Accounts

I have enough money to last me the rest of my life, unless I buy something.

—Jackie Mason, comedian

While you're out there on the front lines of the Cash Flow War, you need to remember that there's a day coming in the future when you'll no longer want to be an active warrior. With that in mind, everybody needs to create for themselves a little nest egg, something that you can contribute dollars to now that will keep you in a comfortable lifestyle in your golden years. If you're thinking that Social Security will carry you through then you haven't been paying attention to the news over the last few years. This is a rock-solid fact: Social Security will give you just about enough money to live out your retirement years somewhere around the poverty level. Accept the fact that you need a retirement account and move on to learning how to fund it!

Joining a 401(k) plan (or a similar tax-deferred plan) is one of the best weapons you've got in your Cash Flow War arsenal. But not only do you need a retirement account, you need some significant funds in there—the major obstacle to a secure retirement is the impact of inflation on the buying power of your money. Most people who retire at age 65 can expect to live another 20 years or more. That's a very long time to support the ordinary comforts of life without a paycheck, let alone pay for the travel, recreation, and hobbies you'll have time to enjoy when you aren't working—and two decades of inflation is a serious threat to the buying power of your savings.

Let's take a look at some of the various defined contribution retirement plans out there. We won't even discuss the defined benefits plans—if you're one of the few who works in a place that still offers an old-style pension plan that is entirely funded by your employer, your human resources person can tell you all you need about that plan. But I'm betting that even if you have an old-style pension plan, you'll still need a retirement account on the side to live out your old age in comfort.

Even though you probably already know this, allow me to show you a quickie example of why it's good to be in one of these pretax retirement accounts. If your employer offers a 401(k) plan or other retirement savings plan, there are many reasons to join. (See table below.)

- It's easy. The money is automatically deducted from your paycheck.
- Your contributions come out of your paycheck pretax, and you don't get taxed on any of the interest you're earning until you withdraw the money, and you will most likely be in a much lower tax bracket by then.
- You'll pay Uncle Sam less in taxes—your taxable income will be reduced by the amount you contribute.
- You'll have more money left over in your paycheck if you invest in a retirement account pretax, as opposed to after-tax investing. Check out the following table and you can see what I'm talking about.

401(k) Retirement Comparison

	Pretax Investment	After-tax Investment
Gross Monthly Income	$2,000	$2,000
Pretax 401(k) contribution	$160	—
Taxable Income	$1,840	$2,000
Income tax (using 28%)	−$515	−$560
Net Monthly Income	$1,325	$1,440
After-tax investment	—	$160
Usable Income	$1,325	$1,280

The bottom line here should be obvious: If you have the opportunity to save some money away for retirement, and you can do so before the government gets to tax it, then you definitely should!

> If you ever get a chance to talk to Ted Benna, the man who created the 401(k), he'll tell you flat out that God showed him this way to help ordinary people. Benna was working as a benefits consultant to the banking industry and had been investigating tax loopholes in section 401(k) of the tax code, which had been part of the 1978 Tax Reform Act, and stumbled across the clause in federal tax laws that allowed pre-tax investments for normal citizens. However it was that he found this loophole, I'm just thankful that he did!

Mail Call

Retirement Accounts

Allies

Generally, retirement accounts fit under one of two basic IRS categories—Individual Retirement Accounts for individual benefit or Qualified Plans (see Table 13.2) available to employers for the benefit of their employees under ERISA. Let's take a look at the different plans, and then we'll take a look at how they actually make money for you.

Individual Retirement Accounts (IRAs) are trusts or custodial accounts opened for your individual benefit or the benefit of your beneficiaries. These plans offer tax advantages for setting aside money for your retirement, or in some plans, certain educations expenses. You may be able to deduct your contributions for income tax purposes, in whole or part, and earnings accumulate on either a tax-deferred or tax-free basis, depending on the type of plan. There are five types of IRAs:

Tax-deferred

1. Traditional
2. Spousal IRA
3. Simplified Employee Pension (SEP IRA)
4. Savings Incentive Match Plan for Employees of Small Employers (SIMPLE)

Tax-Free

    5. Roth (including Spousal IRA)

Traditional IRA (Tax-Deferred)

A traditional IRA may be opened by an individual who has earned income and wishes to defer taxes on funds set aside for retirement. Contributions are voluntary from year to year and can be made annually up to age 70½. The annual contribution limit for 2004 is $3,000 ($4,000 in 2005–2007) with an additional $500 allowed for individuals 50 years or older for a total contribution of $3,500 (or $4,500 in 2005).

    Contributions are deductible (or pretax) up to certain income and participant limitations. However, you can still contribute to an IRA to take advantage of tax-deferred gains even if the contribution itself is not tax-deductible in that year by filing a specific IRS Form. Distributions can be taken penalty-free at age 59½ with minimum distributions commencing at age 70½. There is generally a 10 percent early withdrawal penalty prior to age 59½. Distributions are taxed at your income tax rate in effect at that time.

Roth IRA (Tax-Free)

A Roth IRA may be opened by an individual who has earned income under certain limits. The annual contributions are the same as for the Traditional IRA ($3,000 for 2004 and $4,000 for 2005–2007 with the additional $500 catch-up contribution for ages 50 and older).

    While contributions are made post-tax (no tax deduction for contributions), the earnings accumulate tax-free. This means distributions *are never* taxed! There are also no minimum distributions required at any age. The catch? Your income can't be more than $160,000 adjusted gross income (AGI) for a married couple ($110,000 for single person). Income limits apply for the year in which a Roth IRA is opened but an account can be kept open even if you exceed the income limits in subsequent years. However, contributions will be limited in subsequent years if the income limits are exceeded for that year.

Spousal IRA

The Spousal IRA may allow contributions to either a traditional or a Roth IRA for a nonworking spouse, a spouse without an employer plan, or a spouse with little or no compensation. Certain restrictions apply that can be discussed with your accountant or investment advisor.

SEP-IRA (Simplified Employee Pension)

The funds for this plan are contributed solely by the employer for the employee's benefit. There is not an option for employee salary deferral contributions. Any size employer may adopt a SEP-IRA including governmental, tax-exempt, and for-profit employers. The employer may contribute whatever is less: up to 25 percent of compensation or $40,000 per employee. Money that your company puts into a SEP plan will be presented to you as part of your pay but it gets contributed towards your traditional individual retirement account (SEP-IRA) pretax.

The SEP-IRA is frequently used by small companies or self-employed individuals as a simple way to set up a retirement account with a much higher level of contribution than a traditional or Roth IRA. The contributions made by the employer to the employee's retirement account are an expense to the company. In the case of a self-employed individual they might be both the employer and the employee. This means it is an expense to the company/employer and pretax income to the employee, enabling the self-employed to defer tax on both sides until withdrawals are taken.

SIMPLE (Savings Incentive Match Plan for Employees of Small Employers)

Employees contribute pretax salary and employers must contribute based on one of two formulas. SIMPLE Plans are for companies with 100 or fewer employees earning $5,000 or more. The maximum employee contribution for 2005 is $10,000. Employees 50 years or older may contribute an additional $2,000 as a catch-up contribution for a total of $12,000. Generally, the employer must match the employee contribution provided it does not exceed three percent of the employee's income. The employer can choose to make nonelective contributions, instead of matching contributions, of at least two percent of the employee's compensation. Essentially this plan is a simplified version of the 401(k) plan allowed under Qualified Plans. It has lesser contribution levels than a SEP IRA or a 401(k), so it is not as widely used.

Qualified Plans are available to employers to open for the benefit of their employees. They are qualified by the Internal Revenue Service under the Employee Retirement Income Security Act (ERISA). Qualified Plans have certain benefits and restrictions that are different from Individual Retirement Accounts. At present, Qualified Plans are considered tax-deferred, although there are proposals to make a tax free type account available (similar to a Roth) as early as 2006. While there are simplified plans for employers to use for employees under the

IRA programs (such as the SEP-IRA and the SIMPLE), these plans are not covered under ERISA.

401(k) Plan

Implemented in 1981, the 401(k) plan is one of the most commonly recognized profit sharing retirement plans in use today. Employees defer salary to make pretax contributions to a 401(k) plan and the employer may match part or even all of it. The employee salary deferral limit is $14,000 per year in 2005. For employees 50 years or older, there is a $4,000 catch-up provision, allowing a salary deferral limit of $18,000 (2005). Employers may contribute up to 25 percent of the employee's compensation, with the combined employee and employer contributions not to exceed $40,000 per person each year.

Individual 401(k) Plan

The individual K plan is a simplified version of the 401(k) plan available to business owners without common law employees (which means no W-2 employees). It is available for owners (including spouses or partners), including corporations, partnerships, and sole proprietorships. It allows small companies or the self-employed to take advantage of the higher contribution levels of a 401(k) plan without some of the more complicated compliance testing issues.

403(b) Plan and 457 Plan

These plans are similar to the 401(k) but apply to specific types of employers. Employees contribute pretax salary to the plan and the employer may match part or all of the entire amount. Tax-exempt employers such as educational organizations, churches, tax-exempt hospitals, schools, and charities typically offer 403(b) plans; the 457 plan is restricted to state and municipal government workers. Employees may contribute up to $14,000 in 2005. Employees 50 years or older may contribute an additional $4,000 as catch-up for a total of $18,000. Employers may contribute up to 25 percent of the employee's compensation with the combined employee and employer contributions not to exceed $40,000 per person each year.

Money Purchase/Profit Sharing

The funds for this plan are also contributed by the employer and may allow for employee contributions under certain plan types. Generally, profit sharing contributions are limited to 25 percent of compensation, or up to $40,000. The same

Maximum Allowable Contributions

	2004	2005	2006	2007	2008	2009
Traditional and Roth IRAs						
Up to age 50	$3000	$4000	$4000	$4000	$5000	$5000
Age 50 and above	$3500	$4500	$5000	$5000	$6000	$6000
401(k), 403(b), 457						
Employee Contribution; Employer may also contribute to qualified plans as shown below						
Up to age 50	$13,000	$14,000	$15,000	$15,000*	$15,000*	$15,000*
Age 50 and above	$16,000	$18,000	$20,000	$20,000*	$20,000*	$20,000*
Simple IRAs						
Employee Contribution; Employer may also contribute a matching amount with certain limitations						
Up to age 50	$9,000	$10,000*	$10,000*	$10,000*	$10,000*	$10,000*
Age 50 and above	$10,500	$12,000	$12,500	$12,500*	$12,500*	$12,500*
SEP IRAs Employer Contribution	Whichever is less, $40,000 or 25% of compensation					
Qualified Plans, 401k, Profit Sharing or Keogh Employer Contribution	Whichever is less, $40,000 or 25% of compensation					

*Indicates future increases indexed to inflation in $500 increments.

Source: Entrust Administration Inc.

goes for Money Purchase Plans. The 401(k) plan is the most common type of a Profit Sharing Plan.

Keogh Plans

Keoghs are retirement plans commonly used by the self-employed. Although the term Keogh is no longer used by the IRS or ERISA in their publications, these plans are still in use. They are also referred to as HR10 plans. Contributions are 25 percent of compensation to a maximum of $40,000 on a tax-deferred basis.

Make sure that you understand the difference between taxable accounts, tax-deferred accounts, and tax-free accounts. Taxable accounts are regular investments, using post-tax dollars that give no shelter from taxes, and every transaction's gain or profit is potentially taxable. In a tax-deferred retirement account such as a 401(k) or a traditional IRA, you invest pretax dollars and pay no taxes until you withdraw the money—but at that point everything that comes out of the account is taxed at ordinary rates. Luckily, you're usually in a lower tax bracket by the time you retire. In a tax-free account such as a Roth IRA, you pay taxes on income *before* it goes into the account (post-tax dollars), but all your contributions and earnings are tax-free when they are withdrawn.

What Actually Happens Inside These Retirement Accounts?

When you contribute pretax dollars into a conventional type of retirement account, you're buying stocks, bonds, and mutual funds. For a discussion on more innovative investments available be sure to read about Self-Directed Plans later in this chapter. Because of the combined sizes of these accounts, you can get into funds that might otherwise be too expensive for you to buy.

Every plan offers its own investment options. You'll get to choose which options your money goes into. The selections available to you under a conventional type of plan will consist of investments that typically fall into three asset categories:

1. Cash equivalent investments

2. Fixed-income investments

3. Growth investments

But it's even less complicated than that. When you get right down to it, there are only two ways to invest your money in a retirement account. You can lend it to a borrower—a bank, or a corporation, or the government, for example—that will pay you interest for its use. That's what you do when you buy a corporate or government bond or shares in a bond mutual fund. When you invest in cash equivalents and fixed-income funds, you are a lender. Cash equivalents are an excellent short-term investment.

Alternately, you can buy something whose value may or may not increase over time, or later sell it at a profit. That's what you do when you buy stock in a corporation, or shares in a stock mutual fund. When you put your assets into growth investments, you're an owner. Growth investments have a much higher upside for a long-term investor but a potentially greater risk.

You need to decide which kind of retirement investment is best for you—cash, fixed-income, or growth? That depends entirely on what you are trying to accomplish and how much time you have in which to accomplish it. There is no one-size-fits-all investment. The key to successful investing is matching the different characteristics of these three asset classes to your own goals. The longer you have until you retire the more risk you can afford to take with your investments.

Basically, when you invest in a growth asset, you're buying something that you hope to sell one day at a profit. You don't want stability of principal in this kind of investment. On the contrary, you want your principal to grow. Growth investments include stocks and stock mutual funds, real estate, precious metals, and collectibles.

Growth investments offer the highest potential return of the three asset classes (cash equivalent, fixed-income, and growth investments) and are your best chance to outperform inflation. Here's why: When you invest $1,000 in a stock mutual fund, the best-case scenario is that you'll eventually sell your shares for a lot more than $1,000, perhaps for a very high multiple of $1,000. By contrast, when you lend $1,000 to a bank, a corporation, or a government agency, the best-case scenario is that you'll eventually get back the same $1,000 plus some interest.

Unfortunately, by the time you get the original $1,000 back, it may buy much less than it did when you originally invested it. Over long periods of time, the stock market is the only non–real estate investment that has consistently outpaced inflation. Since 1926, inflation has risen at an annual compound rate of 3.1 percent. Stocks have earned a 10.2 percent compound annual return, as measured by the Standard & Poor's 500 Index, which tracks the average performance of 500 widely held common stocks.

How to Choose Which Assets to Buy in a Conventional Retirement Plan

This is what's called asset allocation, and it will help you choose which parts of your retirement plan to buy into. The biggest secret to successful asset allocation is maintaining your investment mix regardless of what's happening in the financial markets. Remember that this is the part of the Cash Flow War that you're taking the long view on. If you've decided that your best allocation is 60 percent stock investments, 30 percent bond investments, and 10 percent cash investments, stick with that allocation even when the bond market is soaring and the stock market is in a free-fall and all your buddies are dumping their stocks to buy bonds. You can move your other investments around, but the key to retirement planning is maintaining the course you've set.

Fixed-asset allocation is easy to maintain because it relieves you of trying to second-guess what the market is about to do. You don't have to ask "Is this a good time to buy stocks, or is this a good time to buy bonds?" You simply rebalance your plan periodically—once a year is fine—in order to maintain the original allocation percentages. Here's how you rebalance: Let's say you started with 50 percent U.S. stocks, 20 percent foreign stocks, 20 percent bonds, and 10 percent cash. At the end of the year, you add up the total value of your portfolio and discover that because your bonds performed so well, they've risen in value to account for 35 percent of your portfolio. In the meantime, your U.S. stocks holdings have lost value and they now account for only 45 percent of your total portfolio.

To rebalance, you'd transfer enough money out of your high-performing bond fund and into your lower-performing stock fund to return to your original allocation percentages.

Rebalancing actually forces you to sell high and buy low. Very few people manage to buy low and sell high unless they are automatically rebalancing their portfolios. Human instinct naturally rebels at selling an investment that's earning money like crazy in order to buy one that's been losing value for weeks or months. Instead, most investors do what comes naturally: They sell their funds that are doing badly and buy funds that are doing well. That's why they lose money.

There are funds out there that sell themselves as asset allocation funds. Will an asset allocation or lifestyle fund rebalance itself for you? Not necessarily. You have to read the prospectus to find out. Some asset allocation funds do stick with a specified allocation mix and periodically rebalance their portfolios to maintain the mix. But other asset allocation funds keep changing their investment mix to take advantage of current market conditions.

Obviously, you can't stay with one asset allocation mix forever. Whenever your financial situation undergoes a change you should take a look at your original allocation to make sure that its level of risk and return still fits your goals.

It's also very important to reallocate your assets when you're within five years or less of achieving a specific goal or reaching a major anticipated lifetime event. Any money you're planning to use in a couple of years is better kept in a money market or GIC fund than in a stock fund.

Take a Look at How Well Tax-Deferred Retirement Accounts Can Work

You don't have to make a lot of money to save a lot of money for retirement if you get into a tax-deferred plan. (See table on page 168.) You should be contributing some amount of money into your 401(k) plan no matter what your financial situation is, and you really should be contributing as much as possible, particularly if your employer matches your contributions, effectively giving you free money.

Just think that if you contributed just $50 per month (less than $2 a day) to a 401(k) plan and retired in 40 years, and that money earned 10 percent interest compounded monthly in the account, when you retired, your 401(k) account balance would be about $316,203—over a quarter of a million dollars. That is a lot of money, even if you take inflation into account, especially when you consider that you probably spend about that much money on sodas, lattes, gum, and whatnot and get nothing in return.

But suppose you made a modest salary of $36,000 for the rest of your life but decided to contribute 15 percent ($450) of your $3,000-per-month salary? Assume also the money grows at 10 percent compounded monthly. Here is what your account balance would look like over the next 40 years, even if you never got a raise and your employer never contributed a dime.

The end result is not so bad—almost three million bucks for someone who never made more than $36,000! And if you assume a $20 match from your employer for every $100 you contribute, then your balance would be almost $4 million after 40 years. Without ever doing anything else, with a tax-deferred plan, you can take a long view and win the Cash Flow War by the time you retire. And just imagine what that money would look like added to all the other things we've been talking about in this book.

Approximate Amounts Investing $50 per Month versus Investing $450 per Month

Year	Account balance	
	$50 per month	**$450 per month**
1	$628.28	$5,654.51
2	$1,322.35	$11,901.11
3	$2,089.09	$18,801.82
4	$2,936.12	$26,425.12
5	$3,871.85	$34,846.68
10	$10,242.25	$92,180.24
15	$20,723.52	$186,511.66
20	$37,968.44	$341,715.98
30	$113,024.40	$1,017,219.57
40	$316,203.98	$2,845,835.81

Allies

Compound Interest

The reason these plans work so well is the application of compound interest. It's really amazing how the money piles up over a period of years. Your principal (the money you and your employer invest in the plan) earns interest, and that interest earns interest, and that interest earns interest. That's compounding. Its effect is amazing.

The longer your money is invested, the better compounding works for you. Or to put it another way, the earlier you start saving for retirement, the smaller the amount you'll actually have to defer to save to reach your goal. When you take advantage of the compound interest by investing early, you don't have to take as much investment risk to achieve your goal.

Dollar Cost Averaging

Another reason why tax-deferred plans work so well is because you're investing a set amount every few weeks you're actually being forced into the safest investment strategy you can follow: dollar cost averaging.

After you've decided on an investment allocation plan, you may worry about whether this is the right time to begin implementing it. Is this really a good time to buy? What about short-term market fluctuations? Nobody wants to invest precious retirement savings only to see the market plummet like a stone a week later.

Dollar cost averaging is a technique that eliminates this anxiety. You don't have to worry about timing when you're dropping a fixed amount into your retirement plan with every paycheck, and paying no attention whatsoever to whether the market is up or down. Let's say you invest $400 a month. It's a mathematical certainty that your $400 will buy more shares when prices are down and fewer shares when the prices are up.

> **To be a successful market timer, you would have to be right twice: at the market peak, in order to know that it's time to sell your investments, and again at the market bottom, in order to know when it's time to start buying. Let's say you correctly guess when the market has peaked and you sell your holdings before prices start to fall. You still have to figure out when to buy again so that you'll be in a position to take advantage of the market recovery. Market recoveries are easy to miss because the biggest advances tend to be compressed into very short periods of time.**

Dollar cost averaging protects you against one of the worst risks of market timing: the risk that you won't be invested in the market when it surges forward. The very best time to buy is the moment when prices have been falling for weeks or months and the market looks truly awful. The very best time to sell is the moment when the market is performing superbly. Not surprisingly, few people can bring themselves to do either.

The Self-Directed Retirement Account

There are a growing number of Cash Flow Veterans taking advantage of self-direction of retirement plans. This means you decide exactly what type investments you wish to make in your retirement plan. All IRA and Qualified Plans have an investment section in their trust or plan documents that outlines what types of investments are permitted and under what circumstances. Many plan

Allies

administrators limit the types of investments, but in a truly self-directed plan the investment language permits you to direct the trustee or custodian of your plan to make any investment permitted by law. Here are just a few of the investment options available through self-direction:

- Real estate
  - Rental homes
  - Apartment buildings
  - Condominiums
  - Commercial property
- Limited partnership and LLCs
- Real estate notes and mortgages
- Contracts for deed
- Lease options on real estate
- Auto paper
- Unsecured loans
- Tax lien certificates
- Factoring of invoices
- Accounts receivable financing
- Leases
- Like and unlike exchanges
- Securities
- Certificates of deposit
- Stocks, bonds, and mutual funds
- U.S. Treasury gold or silver coins
- Gold bullion
- Palladium

Thousands of investors are fed up with the stock market or relying on someone else to watch their nest egg and have taken the battle into their own hands. If you are successfully investing in real estate, for example, now you can apply that knowledge and the resulting profits to your retirement plan. The key to self-direction is threefold:

1. educating yourself on what is not allowed by the IRS
2. aligning yourself with a reputable plan administrator that truly allows self-direction
3. being knowledgeable in your chosen investment vehicle

The most common questions regarding a self-directed plan relate to what types of transactions or investments are permitted. The IRS tax code answers this question by outlining what is prohibited or not allowed rather than specifically defining what is allowed. Certain investments defined as collectibles are specifically disallowed by statute as follows:

- Any work of art
- Any rug or antique
- Any metal or gem
- Any stamp or coin
- Any alcoholic beverage
- Any other tangible personal property specified by the Secretary for purposes of this IRS subsection

Note: U.S. government minted gold or silver eagle coins along with gold or palladium bullion are not considered collectibles.

Additionally, certain transactions between a plan and you or any other disqualified person are prohibited. Prohibited transactions must be avoided at all costs and deserve a closer look for anyone interested in self-direction of their retirement funds.

Prohibited Transactions and Retirement Accounts

Prohibited transactions generally involve self-dealing wherein a transaction involves you or some other disqualified person. Retirement plans were generally designed to benefit you when you retire and not before. As a rule of thumb, avoid any transaction that appears to provide you or any other disqualified person with a benefit prior to your retirement.

This means your plan may not directly or indirectly sell, exchange, or lease any property to you or a disqualified person. Further, your plan can't lend money, extend credit nor furnish goods, services or facilities to you or a disqualified person. Assets can't be transferred between, or used for the benefit of, you or a disqualified person.

Who is a disqualified person? According to the IRS, you are disqualified along with any members of your family including your spouse, ascendants (parents), descendants (children), and any spouse there of. Also any company in which you own, directly or indirectly, at least half of all stock or voting stock, capital or profit interest, or the beneficial interest of a trust or estate. Disqualified persons also include a fiduciary or person providing services to the plan, an employer whose employees are covered by the plan, and other certain directors, officers, or lesser percentage holders as described in more detail in the code.

What does all this mean in plain English? One of the most common examples is if you currently owned a home or piece of real estate in your name and then attempted to transfer it into your retirement account. This would be a prohibited transaction. So would buying a piece of real estate in your retirement plan and then either living in it yourself or renting to one of your family members. Real estate purchased by the plan can not have been previously owned by you or any other disqualified person. It also can't be occupied by you or any other disqualified persons. If you are truly intrigued by the profits of self-directed retirement plans, we have only covered the tip of the iceberg on the knowledge you need to obtain. It is imperative to understand the full depth of applicable regulations that have been overviewed in this chapter. Start by researching reputable plan administrators. Visit *irs.gov* or visit my Web site at *www.cashflowwar.com* for more information.

Prohibited transactions must be avoided in self-direction of retirement plans as violation and failure to correct can carry hefty penalties—up to 155 percent! Can this be correct? Yes. First, there is a tax of 15 percent for the violation. If there is a failure to correct the violation within a certain time period an additional tax equal to 100 percent can be involved. Further, it might be deemed as a distribution potentially subject to the 10 percent early withdrawal penalty and any ordinary income tax owed thereon (30 percent for this example).

How to Figure Out How Much Money You'll Need for Retirement

Remember that when you're figuring out how much money you'll need for retirement, you have to think about inflation. Inflation risk is by far the biggest land mine for any long-term investor. One dollar doesn't buy as much today as it did five years ago. In another 20 years, you can bet that buck will buy substantially less than it buys today. If you're earning four percent in an FDIC-insured account and inflation is four percent a year, your real return after inflation is zero. Your real return after taxes is negative! For a long-term goal, the last thing you want is stability of principal—if your principal doesn't grow, you can't possibly stay ahead of inflation. Cash equivalent and fixed-income investments have historically provided a very small real return—the return that's left after inflation is subtracted—over long periods of time. When your retirement is more than ten years away, your biggest single risk is inflation. The best way to reduce inflation risk is to invest in growth assets like stocks or appreciating real estate.

For example, assume that you were to retire today and want $30,000 per year (today's dollars), allowing for 7.5 percent earnings and 6 percent inflation. *You will need $636,879.60* ($636,879.60 invested when you retire). (See table below.)

Year	Beginning Balance	Withdraw	Interest	End Balance
1	$636,879.60	$30,000.00	$45,515.97	$652,395.57
2	652,395.57	31,800.00	46,544.67	667,140.24
3	667,140.24	33,708.00	47,507.42	680,939.66
4	680,939.66	35,730.48	48,390.69	693,599.87
5	693,599.87	37,874.31	49,179.42	704,904.98
6	704,904.98	40,146.77	49,856.87	714,615.08
7	714,615.08	42,555.57	50,404.46	722,463.97
8	722,463.97	45,108.91	50,801.63	728,156.69
9	728,156.69	47,815.44	51,025.59	731,366.84
10	731,366.84	50,684.37	51,051.19	731,733.65
11	731,733.65	53,725.43	50,850.62	728,858.84
12	728,858.84	56,948.96	50,393.24	722,303.13
13	722,303.13	60,365.89	49,645.29	711,582.52
14	711,582.52	63,987.85	48,569.60	696,164.28
15	696,164.28	67,827.12	47,125.29	675,462.44
16	675,462.44	71,896.75	45,267.43	648,833.13
17	648,833.13	76,210.55	42,946.69	615,569.27
18	615,569.27	80,783.18	40,108.96	574,895.04
19	574,895.04	85,630.17	36,694.87	525,959.73
20	525,959.73	90,767.99	32,639.38	467,831.13
21	467,831.13	96,214.06	27,871.28	399,488.34
22	399,488.34	101,986.91	22,312.61	319,814.04
23	319,814.04	108,106.12	15,878.09	227,586.01
24	227,586.01	114,592.49	8,474.51	121,468.04
25	121,468.04	121,468.04	0.00	0.00

Retirement Cash Flow Worksheet

Income

Pension   _____

Social Security   _____

Retirement account(s)   _____

Keogh   _____

401(k)   _____

Annuity   _____

Spouse's pension   _____

Spouse's social security   _____

Retirement account(s)   _____

Income from business   _____

Part-time job   _____

Dividends   _____

Interest   _____

Rental income   _____

Income from trusts   _____

Gifts to you   _____

Alimony received   _____

Tax refunds   _____

Other   _____

Total annual retirement income   _____

Home Expenses

Mortgage or rent   _____

Electricity   _____

Gas   _____

Water and sewer   _____

Telephone   _____

Internet access   _____

Property taxes   _____

Homeowner's insurance   _____

Household help   _____

Furniture   _____

Other household items   _____

Home maintenance   _____

Other maintenance costs (appliances, etc.) _____

Other   _____

Total home expenses   ══════════════════════════════

Family Expenses

Food and grocery   _____

Clothing   _____

Laundry and dry cleaning   _____

Birthday, holiday, and other gifts _____

Medical expenses _____

Dental expenses _____

Eye doctor _____

Eye glasses _____

Life insurance _____

Other insurance expenses _____

Other _____

Total family expenses _____

Transportation Expenses

Gasoline _____

Auto insurance _____

Auto maintenance _____

Auto payments _____

Other auto expense   _____

Other travel expense   _____

Boat/RV insurance   _____

Boat/RV maintenance   _____

Boat/RV payments   _____

Other   _____

Total transportation expenses   ═══════════════════════════

Entertainment Expenses

Vacations   _____

Movies   _____

Cable TV   _____

Magazines and books   _____

Dining out   _____

Club memberships   _____

Greens fees   _____

Continuing/adult education expenses   _____

Hobbies   _____

Other   _____

Total entertainment expenses   _____

Taxes

Federal estimated   _____

State estimated   _____

Real estate   _____

Other   _____

Total taxes   _____

Other Expenses

Installment loans   _____

Investment expense   _____

Accountant's fees   _____

Attorney's fees   _____

Charitable contributions   _____

Political contributions   _____

Other   _____

Total other expenses   ======================

Total: Surplus or Shortfall

Total expenses   _____

Total income   _____

Less total expenses   _____

Surplus or shortfall   ======================

If you have a surplus, good for you. You're right on target. And if you have a shortfall, well, don't get all freaked out over it. You're reading this book, so you can eventually win the Cash Flow War. And once you've won, your retirement will be all taken care of anyway.

Marching Orders for Taking Control of Your Retirement Accounts

✔ **If you don't have a retirement account already, open one today.**

✔ **Figure out the ballpark figure for what you'll need in retirement funds.**

✔ **Match your asset allocation within your retirement account to your retirement goals.**

✔ **Consider a self-directed retirement account on a tax-deferred or tax-free basis.**

Preparing to Pay for College

> People keep asking me "Are you saving for his college yet?" I haven't even paid for my college yet...I'm gonna have to walk him up through the financial aid line to the people I still know and say "Hi, I've got a tab going."
>
> —Don Friesen, comedian

You may still be paying for your own college, and now have to worry about how to pay for your kids' education. Maybe you think your child will get a government grant or a scholarship. While I certainly hope they do, you need to have a back-up plan—and the sooner the better.

I often wondered how some people with seemingly few assets to choose from have successfully sent their kids to college (without scholarships). My friend Alice somehow put *three* kids through good schools. She did it with a lot of hard work, but she backed up that hard work by putting her money in the right place at the right time.

Let's talk about sending the kids to college; and before we get too worried about how much it's going to cost, just remind yourself that you have some Allies in the Cash Flow War that can help you meet this necessary expense head on. We'll talk about your Allies a little bit later in this chapter, but let's get a handle on the sort of money this is going to take.

Something all of us who have children need to start thinking about right now, is how much it's going to cost to send them to college. I already know what it's going to cost—*a lot!* Industry analysts who follow college costs are predicting that by 2021 the average cost of one year at a *public* university will be more than $20,000. Add in clothes, books, room and board, and a little pocket money, and you're looking at well over $100,000 for a state university. I'm not even going to talk about private colleges—they will be off the charts by then.

Though college costs are increasing right now, if your savings horizon for college is closer than 20 years, the picture is still scary. In 2003, tuition at four-year public institutions jumped by an average of 9.6 percent, according to the annual survey of college costs released in October 2003 by the College Board.

Let's take a look at how much you can realistically expect to pay to send one child to college.

Estimating College Costs

When you're figuring out how much college will cost you, you can separate the costs into two categories: direct and indirect.

Direct college costs include tuition, fees, room, and board. You can find out these numbers just by contacting any particular college. My advice is to find out what the direct college costs are for the state college nearest where you live, a private college that is well thought of, and then a dream school of the Yale, MIT, or Stanford type. This way you can get familiarized with the range of costs out there *today*.

Indirect college costs include other necessary expenses such as books and supplies, transportation, medical coverage, clothing, recreation, and other personal expenses. These indirect costs will vary considerably among individual students, and are much more difficult to estimate than direct college costs. The best way to get a ballpark figure for indirect costs is to contact the financial aid offices at the colleges you selected above; tell them the institution you're interested in and ask for information concerning typical indirect expenses of students at that particular school. They should have a good idea of current costs.

Once you have the information about the current direct and indirect costs of college, you can project those costs into the appropriate year by using a simple formula that will cover the cost of inflation.

Just add the direct cost to the indirect cost and come up with the current total for one year at the three different colleges you picked. Next, pick the appropriate number from the inflation chart below and multiply your total by that. I don't think inflation will really be at nine percent but it's best to make this estimate high so you don't get caught short. Do it for each of the three colleges. Now you know how much one year will cost. Now multiply that by four, and you'll have a ballpark idea of where you need to be regarding college costs. (See chart below.)

College Cost Chart

	Inflation		
Years to College	6%	7%	9%
4	1.26	1.31	1.41
5	1.34	1.40	1.54
6	1.42	1.50	1.68
7	1.50	1.61	1.83
8	1.59	1.72	1.99
10	1.79	1.97	2.37
12	2.01	2.25	2.81
14	2.26	2.58	3.34
16	2.54	2.95	3.97
18	2.85	3.38	4.72

Pretty scary, huh? Just think what happens when your kid changes majors, and you need to come up with another year's worth! Not to worry, there are several good ways available to start saving for college costs now.

Different Strategies for Saving for College

Once you've realistically estimated the amount of money you'll need to meet college expenses, you need to pick an investment strategy. There are a few ways you can go, and you should consider which of the following criteria are most important to you when you're selecting a college savings program:

- **Investment contribution.** Does the investment require a one-time contribution, irregular contributions, or monthly contributions? Is there a minimum or maximum contribution size?

- **Convenience.** Will it be simple to establish the account, or will it require a lot of paperwork? Will you need to hire an attorney, or will you need an accountant to do your taxes after you begin?

- **Ownership of the fund.** Do you want the money to be in your child's name? This could mean that you'll never have access to the money even if your kid gets a scholarship or decides not to go to college in the event you need the money for an emergency. Do you want your child to have control of the money now, in the future, or ever?

- **Risk.** The younger the child, the greater the investment risk a parent can assume. For example, a parent starting a college fund for a 15-year-old may not feel comfortable investing in higher-risk alternatives such as stocks, while a parent starting a college fund during the baby's first year might be willing to assume such a risk. If your child is young, the best investment might be one that yields long-term growth. However, if your child is older, you may prefer safer investments that are more liquid.

- **Tax Considerations.** Will your investment contributions be with before- or after-tax dollars? Will earnings be tax-exempt, tax-deferred, taxed as ordinary income in your tax bracket or your child's tax bracket? There are some tax savings to be had if investments are made in the child's name. Before age 14, the first $550 of investment income is tax free, and the second $550 is taxed at 15 percent. Any amount above $1,100 is taxed at the parent's rate. Once the child reaches age 14, all income is taxed at the child's rate.

Carefully considering these five criteria can help you determine which savings vehicle is the right one for your situation.

Allies

529 Plans

These plans offer an after-tax investment for college—the main advantages of these plans is that your money grows at compound interest rates (just like a 401(k) plan) and you're not taxed on gain, and the beneficiary is taxed at his or her rate when the money is withdrawn for direct and indirect college costs. So, if the beneficiary is a full-time student, the tax penalty will be very, very small. Programs are administered by a state agency or an organization designated by the state such as a for-profit investment company. These plans differ slightly from state to state. Some states have plans with no specific residency requirements and are available to prospective students from any state. Other state plans are available only to residents. Most states have a 529 plan in place, or are in the process of designing such a plan. My advice is to go with a plan administered by an investment company—you're talking about a lot of money here, and you should go with the pros.

This is how 529 plans work: A contributor establishes an account for the beneficiary for the purpose of paying expected college expenses. Mutual fund companies manage many of these 529 plans. The contributor, based on his or her investment goals (as you determined above), chooses a specific fund portfolio available from the mutual fund company and then makes contributions to the fund according to his or her wishes. Generally, you can start an account for as little as $250 and contribute up to $55,000 per year. These numbers may vary a little bit in your home state, and will probably increase in coming years.

With state plans, the funds in a 529 are usually invested in a family of pre-selected portfolios according to the age of the beneficiary or the years to enrollment in college. The contributor usually has no say in how the funds are invested beyond choosing between possible choices of a balanced, conservative, or all-equity savings option. The portfolios typically hold more stock while the account's beneficiary is young, and as the child ages the funds are automatically moved into portfolios with a larger portion of fixed-income investments. This reduces the risk of stock market volatility on funds needed to pay for college expenses in the near future. The performance of the portfolio depends on market conditions, and there is no guarantee that there will be enough money in the account to cover all education expenses. With an investment company plan you can exercise a lot more of your judgment when shifting investments within the plan.

That said, some state plans are worth looking into. For example, New York's College Savings Program ups the ante by offering state tax incentives. Contributions of up to $5,000 per year, $10,000 for a joint return, are deductible for New York state purposes. In addition, earnings included in qualified withdrawals are completely tax-free for New York state purposes, though they are tax-deferred for federal purposes. You do not need to be a New York resident to set up an account. In addition, the student need not attend a school located in New York. Make sure you check out the plan in your state to see if the deal is as good.

No matter how good a particular state plan may look to you, you've got to investigate the funds these plan offer investment in. State plans will typically offer the lowest-risk investments, and hence offer the lowest rate of return. Investment firms will typically have a larger range of investments across the spectrum of risk. Check out Chapter 15 for advice on picking mutual funds when you're investigating these plans.

The money you put into a 529 plan may be applied to the costs of tuition, fees, books, supplies, and equipment required for attendance at an eligible educational institution. Most accredited institutions of higher education in the United States and some foreign institutions qualify as eligible. This includes most private colleges, public universities, graduate schools, two-year community colleges, and vocational-technical schools. If you use the money for anything else, you'll get pounded by penalty taxes.

With a 529, the contributor always maintains control of the account, regardless of the age of the beneficiary. You can change the beneficiary as long as the beneficiary is a member of the family of the original beneficiary. If the designated beneficiary receives a scholarship or dies or becomes disabled, there is no penalty for withdrawal of funds.

Coverdell Education Savings Account

Allies

If you know how a Roth IRA works (we reviewed them in Chapter 13), then you already have a pretty good idea of how a Coverdell education savings accounts works. They both allow you to make an annual nondeductible contribution to a specially designated investment trust account. Your account will grow free of federal income taxes, and if all goes well, withdrawals from the account will be completely tax-free as well. This is an after-tax investment.

With a Coverdell, you are not able to take an income tax deduction for your contributions. However, the good part is that any portion of future withdrawals will come out tax-free if used to pay the qualified higher education expenses. The Coverdell plan is becoming obsolete, as the 529 plans seem to be the way to go when you compare the two. For example, the contribution limit is way too low: The maximum contribution is only $2,000 annually and contributors must have less than $190,000 in modified adjusted gross income ($95,000 for single filers) in order to qualify. The $2,000 maximum is gradually phased out if your modified adjusted gross income falls between $190,000 and $220,000 ($95,000 and $110,000 for single filers). I'm thinking that $2,000 a year will never meet my goals! It can be effective as an additional college savings vehicle when combined with self direction (see Chapter 15).

Land Mines

I have a few concerns about the Coverdell plan. First off, you can only contribute $2,000 a year. Secondly, your contribution goes into an account that will eventually go to your child if not used for college. You cannot simply refund the account back to yourself like you can with most 529 plans. This means that if your kid decides not to go to college, they'll eventually get all the money for nothing when they turn 30. Now, you might want to do that anyway, but I would prefer to have a choice!

Allies

Prepaid Tuition Plans

This is the least expensive way to go, and often the best, but it will limit your child's choices of schools. Certain states, such as Alabama, Alaska, Colorado, Florida, Massachusetts, Michigan, Ohio, Oklahoma, Pennsylvania, Tennessee, and West Virginia offer various types of prepaid tuition plans, generally for students attending state schools. Residents of these states can buy a contract or bonds at a fixed price, based on the rates of college tuition today. Payments can be made in lump sums or monthly installments. The state, in turn, invests the money to earn the difference between the amount you are paying and the projected cost of tuition at the time your child reaches college age. Those who sign up are fully protected, as the state assumes all the risk of the investments. Check with your state's commission on higher education to see if a prepaid tuition plan is available where you live.

Mail Call

> **The advantage here is that you have guaranteed that you will meet the direct costs of college. The disadvantage is that your child may be limited to state colleges, and you have not covered the indirect costs.**

Prepaid tuition plans are not for everyone. They mostly attract people who tend to be more conservative in their investments (then again, it was the choice my wife and I made for our daughter years ago; even if she changes her mind and wants to go to a different college, we will be able to cover the difference with other investments). However, if you're still interested and a plan is offered in your state, you'll want to know if it covers only the cost of tuition, or room and board, too. Also, check to see if it applies to private schools. Many plans such as Florida's allow the value to be transferred to an out-of-state college with no guarantee it will cover their tuition or actual cost like it is guaranteed to do with a Florida state college. Finally, confirm that your original deposit will be returned if your child attends a private or out-of-state college, is not accepted to a state school, or chooses not to attend college at all. Different states have different rules—if your state offers a plan that can be used at private schools, and you can get your deposit back if things change, prepaid tuition could be the right path for you.

Savings Plan Trusts

Certain states—such as Connecticut, Iowa, Kentucky, Louisiana, Massachusetts, New Hampshire, and New York—offer special college savings accounts known as savings plan trusts. These accounts allow the contributor to save as little or as much as they like on behalf of a designated beneficiary's qualified education expenses. Contributions can be as little as $25. These accounts may guarantee a minimum rate of return and generally provide favorable tax treatment. This might be a good plan to supplement your savings if you opt to go the prepaid tuition route.

The money in these accounts may be used at any qualified institution of higher learning within the United States. If you move to another state, the money in the trust goes with you. Some savings plan trusts allow monies to be used for other family members' qualified education expenses. Check with your state's commission on higher education to see if a savings plan trust is available where you live—again, the rules on these accounts vary from state to state, so this may or may not be a good option.

Marching Orders for Preparing to Pay for College

- ✔ **Figure out the direct and indirect costs for three different schools.**
- ✔ **Decide on an investment goal.**
- ✔ **Review the college savings plans and decide which one is best for your situation—it may be that a combination of a few different plans is the way to go.**

Playing the Market: Stocks, Options, and Mutual Funds

> *It will fluctuate.*
>
> J.P. Morgan, merchant banker, when asked
> what the stock market would do over the coming year.

This chapter is your crash course on stock market investments. No matter what your investment strategies, you will find yourself in some stock-related investments at one time or another.

Although I, like others, call it "playing the market," you already know that this sort of activity is no game—it's a war, and you're in it to win it! And wars are generally decided by some bold action; one side takes a calculated risk and carries the day. So, you should be aware that every kind of investment involves risk. But *not* investing is risky, too—saving your money under your mattress or in a low-yield savings account certainly won't help you win the Cash Flow War. It won't even help you keep up with inflation.

If I had to guess what the biggest weakness most people have when investing, I would have to say it is emotion. Too often people react on a stock "tip" that a friend has or that they overheard on an elevator. That same level of emotion can make someone refuse to sell a stock that is dropping fast. There is no place for emotion in this arena. I don't believe in feelings or hunches. And you should never assume you are the only one that understands how that particular pet stock will run up or down. You can be right many times, but when you are wrong it may cost you big time.

There are many books that can help you. It's easy to trade online and there is a whole new crop of computer programs to aid in your investment decisions. Some are good, some are not. Do your homework first. Although there is no magic bullet, investors have more powerful tools at their disposal than ever.

As a Cash Flow Warrior, the biggest question you face isn't whether you should take risks with your money—it's what kind of risks you should take. The first rule of this aspect of the Cash Flow War is that the higher an investment's potential return, the greater the potential risk involved. Just remember that even if that risk isn't readily apparent at first glance, it's there. There is no such thing as high returns from a low-risk investment. One caveat here: Not all Cash Flow strategies require an initial outlay of cash, but we'll talk about that in Part Four. For the purposes of this chapter, just assume that *any* of the investments we'll be talking about carry their own special risks. You just have to determine how much risk you're comfortable with.

Mail Call

> **Almost all successful people take risks—it is what separates them from the rest of the world. We just need to learn everything we can to minimize risk and increase the payoff.**

For example, a high-yield bond is just a stockbroker's nice way of saying junk bond. Junk bonds always pay more than other bonds because companies with bad credit ratings are not as safe a bet to make their interest payments and repay their loans as companies with good credit. So, companies that issue high-yield bonds have to pay you more interest on the money you're loaning them when you buy their bonds. You might never see a penny of it, or you might make a bundle. This doesn't mean that you shouldn't buy a high-yield fund. After reading this chapter, you may decide that for a particular goal and time horizon, the potential reward on a high-yield investment outweighs the particular risk. But you should never assume risk isn't there—because it is.

Allies

One way to gauge an investment's degree of risk is to compare its yield with the prevailing rate on U.S. Treasury bills, what many people consider the world's safest investment. You can check T-bill rates daily in most newspapers. The higher an investment's yield above the yield for T-Bills, the riskier the investment is—*no matter how that investment is marketed. Remember: If it isn't intrinsically risky, they wouldn't be paying you as much to borrow your money*!

When "playing" the market, it all boils down to what sort of investor you are. One rule of thumb is that if you have a longer time horizon to your goals then you can afford to take more risks—if some of your picks don't pan out, others will. If you have a short investment time horizon, then you need to make relatively mistake-free investments, like T-bills.

By the Numbers

Try and stay focused on your return percentage, not the money. One of my younger graduates invested $1,000 given to him by his parents. In three weeks he successfully grew the stock to $1,200. I asked him what he was doing to protect his gain and he replied "nothing, it is only $200." That was a mistake. The fact that he only made $200 was because he only had $1,000 to start with. But what he did have was a 20 percent gain in three weeks—certainly worth protecting.

We'll look at four different asset classes while we're discussing investments in this chapter—growth investments (stocks), cash equivalents (T-bills), fixed-income investments (bonds), and options.

Different Types of Investments in the Stock Market

Let's talk about growth investments, one of the most crucial weapons in your Cash Flow War arsenal.

Stocks

Here we come to the crux of the matter, the stocks in the stock market. Here's where you can either lose your shirt or make a bundle. When you invest in a stock, or what some people call a growth asset, you're basically buying something that you hope to sell one day at a profit. You don't want stability of principal in this kind of investment. On the contrary, you want your principal to grow. Growth investments offer the highest potential return of the three asset classes we're discussing in this chapter (cash equivalent, fixed-income, and growth investments) and are your best chance to outperform inflation.

Here's how stocks work: When you buy shares of stock in a company, you're buying a share in a business, in its earnings and in its assets. You get a share of profits that the corporation pays out in dividends, and you benefit from increases in the company's value, which are reflected in its share price. Your total return from a stock investment is the dividends it pays plus or minus changes in its share price.

Here's something you probably would have never guessed: Over long periods of time, the stock market is the *only* non–real estate investment that has consistently outpaced inflation. Between 1926 and 2000, inflation has risen at an annual compound rate of 3.1 percent. Stocks have earned a 10.2 percent compound annual return, as measured by the Standard & Poor's 500 Index, which tracks the average performance of 500 widely held common stocks. So if you had invested in a stock fund that bought the S&P 500, you would have beaten inflation by 7.1 percent, despite all of the depressions and recessions in between. That's pretty good!

Understanding the Different Kinds of Stocks

There are two basic types of stock:

1. **Growth stocks.** These are stellar performers, fast-track companies whose earnings are expected to grow very rapidly.

2. **Value stocks.** These are ugly ducklings, out-of-favor companies that nevertheless promise a good long-term return. Value stocks are usually offered at a bargain; their selling price is cheap relative to the company's assets and future earnings potential.

Historically, growth stocks and value stocks have performed well in alternating cycles. While growth stocks are up, value stocks are down, and vice versa. That's why it makes sense to own some of both as many stock mutual funds do. So if you're picking stocks individually, try and buy several of each kind. If you want someone else to pick out your stock mix, there are also mutual funds that specialize in either growth or value stocks. The latter are called growth and income funds.

> The best investors I have met in the stock market are those that are able to make investment decisions that are not based on emotion. Smart traders will tell you to always sell a stock if it loses between 8 and 10 percent. Emotions, and speculating that the stock will come back, have lost investors more money than anything else. Find some good rules and live by them.

Allies

Large-, Mid-, and Small-Cap Stocks

A company's capitalization (market value) is determined by multiplying its total number of shares outstanding by their current market price. If a company has 500,000 shares available at two bucks a pop, then its market cap is $1 million.

- **Large-cap stocks.** Companies with market values of more than $10 billion. These companies are usually mature corporations with a long track record of steady growth and good dividends.
- **Mid-cap stocks.** Companies with market values of between $500 million and $10 billion. These companies tend to grow faster than large-cap companies, and tend to have less of a risk of going into the tank than small-cap companies.

- **Small-cap stocks.** Companies with market values of less than $500 million. Small-cap companies are the potential large-caps of tomorrow. Microsoft started as a small cap, for example. But while small-cap companies can grow much faster than bigger companies, they're also more volatile and they fail far more frequently.

> It's obvious you can make the most money with small-cap stocks, but you need to do your due diligence before you drop your cash into these companies. Do some market research and read up on the industry itself before you commit your Cash Flow reserves to this battlefield.

Stock Dividends

Profitable companies don't *always* choose to pay dividends. Rapidly growing companies, for example, often prefer to reinvest profits to expand their business which also benefits their shareholders. A mature company is a likelier source of dividends. So if you're looking for dividends, go with an older blue chip company. It won't offer the dramatic growth that a younger company will, but they will send you dividend checks.

> Stock dividends aren't a predictable source of income because companies pay dividends only after paying all their other bills like payroll, rent, taxes, and interest to their bondholders. But historically companies cut paying their dividends only as a last resort.

Dividend Reinvestment Programs

The stock market's total return over time includes both price changes and reinvested dividends, and the reinvested dividends have accounted for a very big chunk of that return. This is where a dividend reinvestment plan can make you some significant cash. More than 1,000 companies currently offer dividend re-investment plans, including several Dow industrial stocks, such as AT&T, Phillip Morris, and General Motors.

Dividend reinvestment plans (DRIPs) have several advantages over other investment vehicles in your Cash Flow War arsenal. Here's how they work:

- First, once you have one or more shares, the dividends you earn are then applied by the company toward the purchase of more shares.

- Second, often investors can send money directly into the company to buy more shares in amounts as little as $10 to $25.

When you use a DRIP, you avoid paying brokerage commissions. Here's how well a DRIP can work for you: According to Ibbotson Associates of Chicago, if you had put $100 into the S&P 500 stock average on the last day of 1925 and kept it there until June 30, 1990 but spent all the dividends, you'd have earned $2,806 on your investment. But if you had reinvested all the dividends instead of spending them, you'd have $55,091. Not too shabby for a hundred bucks!

> **Another way to avoid paying brokerage commissions, or at least lower the cost of transactions, is to go with an online brokerage like E-Trade (for example). Most of these online brokerages have some pretty powerful research tools and data that you can access.**

Allies

Thinking about Investment Risk

Most people think of stock investments as very risky mainly because stock prices fluctuate daily, often for no apparent reason. And guess what? They're right.

Any growth investment is subject to price swings based on changes in its perceived value in the marketplace. The price of a company's stock may rise or fall for any number of reasons: a rumor about an increase or decrease in the company's quarterly earnings; the apparent success or failure of a new product line; competition in the marketplace; or expected changes in the economy or in interest rates, or in government regulations that might have a positive or negative impact on the overall industry.

Allies

> **Remember to protect your return by using a Stop-Loss. A Stop-Loss is an order placed with a broker to sell when a certain price is reached. It's designed to limit a Cash Flow Warrior's stock market losses. It is also sometimes called a stop market order. If you set a stop-loss order for 10 percent below what you bought the stock for, you would limit your loss to 10 percent (or protect your gain), because when the stock dipped that far down, your broker would sell it. It's also a great idea to use a stop order before you leave for vacation or enter a situation where you will be unable to watch your stocks for an extended period of time.**

Cash Equivalents

Cash equivalents include money market mutual funds, bank CDs, and Treasury bills (T-bills)—both backed by the U.S. government—as well as commercial paper, and the IOUs of corporations with the highest credit ratings. When you invest in a cash equivalent you're basically making a short-term loan to a very high-quality borrower. (In some cases it's a really short-term loan—commercial paper maturity ranges from overnight to 90 days.) Money market mutual funds use your money to buy bank CDs, commercial paper, and T-bills. Cash equivalents are an excellent short-term investment.

The advantage of cash equivalents in the Cash Flow War are stability of principal and liquidity. You can tap your investment anytime without worrying about a temporary dip in its value.

In a money market fund, for example, your investment is converted into shares with a fixed value of $1, each of which you can always redeem for the same $1 value. Cash equivalents also offer great liquidity, which means that you can turn your investment into cash quickly and easily. A house, by contrast, is a very illiquid investment; it might take months or even years to sell. A money market fund pays fluctuating interest because the fund is constantly making new loans. As rates rise and fall so will your yield from the fund.

These characteristics make cash equivalents a good investment for any money you plan to use in less than five years and don't want to take any risks with. As a medium-term investment, cash equivalents are less attractive. If you know you won't use this money for eight years, for example, you'll probably want to get more money back on your investment. And you're in for a world of hurt if you use cash equivalents as your main long-term investment. Cash equivalents normally don't return enough money on your initial investment to keep up with inflation over a long period of time.

Bonds

You have probably heard people talk about bonds on every investor show or in the paper—yet very few people know anything about them. These are also called fixed-income investments, but the value of your principal in a fixed-income investment isn't fixed at all. Actually, the dollar value of your principal fluctuates with each change in interest rates. We'll talk more about this in a little bit.

When you're choosing a bond or a bond mutual fund to invest in there are two very important things to consider: the maturity of the bond (or the average maturity in a funds portfolio) and the credit rating of the issuers.

- Short-term bonds have an average maturity of less than three years.

- Intermediate-term bonds have an average maturity of three to ten years.

- Long-term bonds have a maturity of ten years or longer.

The obvious question here is: "How soon do you want the money back from your investment?" The longer a bond's maturity, regardless of the issuer's credit, the higher the yield. The reason is that the longer the term of the loan, the longer your principal will be exposed to the risk that the bond will lose value because the prevailing interest rate will change. The company that is borrowing your money when you buy their bond has to pay a higher yield to attract long-term investors for that reason. Make sure you check on the timeline before you plunge into the bond market!

As far as bond credit ratings, it's fairly simple. A bond credit rating is a rating agency's considered *opinion* of the borrower's ability to repay a loan. Standard & Poor's, for example, rates bonds with AAA (excellent), AA (very good), and A (good). The next tier of S&P bond ratings is BBB (adequate), BB (speculative), B (very risky) and B minus (very, very risky). The bottom feeders are CCC, CC, C, and D—these are bonds that S&P believes are in the tank, or just about to go into the tank.

An investment-grade bond is one whose issuer has a credit rating of BBB or higher. A junk bond, or a high-yield bond, is one whose issuer has a credit rating of less than BBB. The lower the borrower's credit quality, the higher the interest you'll receive on the bond.

How Your Principal Can Fluctuate When Buying Bonds

Let's say you bought a $10,000 bond paying 10 percent. This means that for the term of the bond, you receive fixed 10 percent interest payments; and if you hold that bond to its maturity date (and the issuer doesn't default), you get your $10,000 back plus all those interest payments you will get over the years. But between the time you buy it and the time it matures, your bond won't always be worth $10,000. Its value can change almost daily, every time the prevailing interest rate changes. So if you need to pull your money out of a bond investment, you could end up taking a bath.

Land Mines

> If interest rates rise to 11 percent, your $10,000 bond immediately becomes less valuable. Why? Because if the prevailing interest rate is 11 percent, *nobody* is going to pay you full price for a bond that only yields 10 percent. If you need to sell a $10,000 bond that pays 10 percent at a time when people can buy newly issued bonds that pay 11 percent, you'll get less than $10,000 for it.

Allies

> If interest rates fall, your bond's value shoots up. If the prevailing rate drops to 9 percent, buyers will pay a premium for an older bond that yields 10 percent. You could now sell it for *more* than $10,000.

If you come to the conclusion that the most profitable time to invest in bonds is at the beginning of a period of declining interest rates, you're up for a battlefield commission in the Cash Flow War. When interest rates are just beginning to go down is definitely the best time to jump into the bond market.

> **The bottom line on bonds is that the value of your principal has the potential to grow or to shrink, depending on which way interest rates move. That's why it's a big mistake to judge a bond or a bond fund only by its yield, the way you would judge a money market fund. What counts in a bond is your *total return:* the yield, plus or minus any change in the bond's price.**

One more thing to be wary of: Buying shares in a bond mutual fund is *not the same* as buying individual bonds because mutual funds don't hold bonds until they mature. When you invest in a bond fund, you're buying a share in thousands of different bonds in an ever-changing portfolio. This means the income you receive from a fixed-income fund isn't fixed but will fluctuate as the mutual fund buys and sells bonds. The market value of your principal in the fund also fluctuates, depending on whether the fund is selling bonds at a loss or a gain. The longer the maturity of the bonds owned by the mutual fund, the more dramatically your principal can gain or lose value as interest rates change.

When considering bonds as an investment for the long term, don't consider investing only in bonds. While bonds are a good investment for anyone who needs a dependable stream of relatively high income, they have *not* been a good long-term investment because they don't provide enough growth to beat inflation. Fixed-income investments historically have not held up very well to inflation over long periods of time. However, you should have some fixed-income investments as a form of insurance in a long-term investment plan because there have been some economic periods when fixed-income investments have performed well and growth investments have performed badly.

This kind of irrational volatility seems like an excellent reason not to own shares of any stock. And you're right: Stocks are a very risky short-term investment. In fact, industry analysts say that over a 12-month period, you stand a 29 percent chance of losing money in the stock market. Clearly, you wouldn't want to invest your emergency account in the stock market. Stocks are very liquid—they can easily be converted to cash—but they don't give you stability of principal. If you're forced to sell stock investments in a hurry, you'll probably take it square in the face.

But in the long run, stock prices reflect the steady growth of the U.S. economy and of American business corporations. In a ten-year period your risk of loss in stocks drops to just three percent. In a twenty-year period, your risk of loss falls to zero. Check this out: *The S&P 500 Index has never had a negative 20-year return.*

Options: Here's Where It Gets Really Involved

Buying options is not something I recommend for beginning investors, and not really something I recommend for people who don't consider themselves expert investors. But it is something you should be aware of, and something you may want to consider at a later date, after you've got some investing experience.

When you buy an option you're buying the *right (but not necessarily the obligation)* to purchase a security like a stock at some later date, at a preset price. For the purposes of our preliminary discussion here, let's assume that every transaction we're talking about involves 100 shares of stock (1 option contract).

Let's say that you think that XYX Corporation's stock is going up and it is currently trading for $48 per share. You could buy the right (but not the obligation) to purchase that stock at, say, $50. If at anytime XYZ's stock price goes to $50 or above, you can purchase those shares for $50. Even if the stock goes up to $55, $75, $100, or a million dollars, you still get to buy it for $50 (because that is the amount you contracted for). If the stock never reaches $50, then your option simply "expires" and you get *nothing*. That is called a "call option." A "put option" works the other way around.

Let's say you think that XYZ's stock is going to go down and is currently priced at $48. You can purchase a put at, say, a strike price of $45. If the stock, anytime during the period of your contract goes below $45, the person must buy it from you for $45. Even if the stock is only trading for $25 per share, he or she must pay you $45 for the same stock. Again, if the stock never goes below the $45 strike price then you get *nothing*.

The option's expiration dates are the Saturday following the third Friday of the month. This makes the third Friday of the month the last trading day for all expiring equity options. This day is called "Expiration Friday." If the third Friday of the month is an exchange holiday, the last trading day is the Thursday immediately proceeding this exchange holiday. After the option's expiration date, the contract will cease to exist. At that point the owner of the option who does not exercise the contract has no "right" and the seller has no "obligation" as previously conveyed by the contract.

There's obviously a lot more involved here than what is given in this simplistic example. If you're really paying attention, and if you're really up on the stock market, you can make a bundle of money buying and even better, selling options. But—and it's a big but—I think it's best to back off from buying and selling options until you're a little deeper into the whole investment world.

Personally, I like options. And as you get more sophisticated in your trading you will find that there are some great ways to be a conservative investor and *sell* options—but that is simply too much to cover in this book.

> If you are intrigued by options, I suggest you either check out the Options information on the American Stock Exchange home page at *http://www.amex.com*, or pick up a copy of *Options as a Strategic Investment* by Lawrence G. McMillan. This is really an area that you need to do some much deeper research into before you plunk down any of your hard-earned Cash Flow War Assets.

Mail Call

How to Avoid Investment Risk

The message seems clear: Spread your money out through different stocks, reinvest their dividends, and hold on to them for twenty years or so and you'll do fine. Okay, it's not that simple . . . or maybe it is. Maybe all you really need to do is to diversify, and spread your risk out over a few kinds of investments.

If the bad news is that there are no risk-free investments, the good news is that by choosing and combining your investments with a little care and common sense, it's possible to reduce unavoidable risks to a level you can live with comfortably. Even better, you can do it while giving yourself a very good chance of achieving the return you need. This great strategy is called diversification. It's what professional fund managers do and there's no reason you can't do it too. After all, this book is all about telling you what the rich people already know—and you can bet they're already diversified. The reason for diversification, of course, is to protect against a single, devastating loss. If you own several investments, there's less risk that they'll all be clobbered at the same time.

You can design a very solid portfolio with just three to five different basic investments. If you own a few different types of investments, you reduce your risk even more because you increase the chance that some of your investments will skyrocket even while others bomb. An example: You own stocks, bonds, and a money market fund. Interest rates soar, which hammers your bonds and sharply reduces or eliminates your stock market earnings. But the interest you earn in your money market fund just cranks along with the prevailing rate.

In this example, your money market fund cushioned the short-term impact of higher interest rates on your total portfolio. But your stock and bond holdings are the combination that assures your portfolio's long-term return. We already talked about how stocks always work out in the long run, as long as you hold on to them.

To further reduce your overall risk, you should also diversify within each asset class. On the simplest level, this means that you don't buy bonds from just one or two issuers, or the stock of only one or two companies. *Any* mutual fund investment automatically gives you this diversification.

On a slightly more sophisticated level, you also diversify when you invest in more than one kind of bond or stock. You can diversify by investing in both growth stocks and value stocks, for example. You can diversify by investing in both U.S. stocks and foreign stocks. You can diversify by investing in bonds from different issuers that carry different maturities.

Diversification will reduce your risk—but no diversification plan can eliminate risk altogether. The U.S. stock and bond markets don't move in lock-step, but it is possible for both of them to bottom out at the same time. High interest rates and inflation, for example, have a very bad effect on both stock and bond markets. That's when you remind yourself that high interest rates and inflation are increasing your money market fund yield and the value of your house.

Whatever money you decide to invest (after what you're already investing in college plans, retirement account, and emergency savings) will always carry a certain amount of risk. You just need to decide what level of risk you're comfortable with and then go for it.

Marching Orders for Playing the Stock Market

✔ Learn the differences between the three asset classes.

✔ Decide where you fit in when considering the level of risk involved in an investment.

✔ Make sure you diversify.

Bankruptcy and How to Avoid It

> *People who are always making allowances for themselves soon go bankrupt.*
> —Mary Pettibone Poole, author, *A Glass Eye at a Keyhole*

Obviously, the whole point of reading this book is so you never even have to consider bankruptcy. But, just as obviously, I know that some people sometimes hover on the edge of bankruptcy, and may read this book in hope of finding a way to avoid bankruptcy. Let me say right now that you probably can get through whatever problems you find yourself in right now if you start working on it immediately.

As they say, "I've been there and done that." I declared bankruptcy, and worked my way back to top. So, if you really need to take this drastic step, don't lose all hope of ever winning the Cash Flow War. It can still be done! I'd rather not see you declare bankruptcy (it set me back years in winning the Cash Flow War) and in this chapter I'll offer you some advice on how to avoid that drastic step.

First, let's take a look at just what bankruptcy actually is, and examine the differences between different sorts of bankruptcy.

What Is Bankruptcy?

Most often, normal people who declare bankruptcy are just looking for a fresh start. These people have maxed out their credit limits and have no savings, and when a crisis hits such as losing their job, accident, or illness they simply cannot pay their bills. Bankruptcy provides relief from creditor pressures and an opportunity at a new beginning.

There are typically two ways an average person can go when declaring bankruptcy:

1. **Chapter 7 bankruptcy.** Liquidation or straight bankruptcy. This allows you to discharge your debts, with certain exceptions, through a liquidation of your assets. After you file a Chapter 7, most creditors will be prohibited from taking your wages to pay your debts.

2. **Chapter 13 bankruptcy.** Reorganization. This allows you to pay your debts *to the best of your ability* without creditor pressure. To be considered for a Chapter 13, you need to have some sort of income, such as a steady paycheck, alimony, disability, or monthly Social Security benefits.

What's the Difference between the Two Types of Bankruptcy?

Before we get started here, remember that any numbers I use as an example will vary from state to state. What I'm doing is using the current federal numbers as a guideline, and they may not even be current when you read this. You need to check with a bankruptcy attorney in your own state. But these figures should give you a good ballpark idea.

Chapter 7

Under a liquidation bankruptcy (Chapter 7), you ask the bankruptcy court to wipe out (discharge) the debts owed. When you declare Chapter 7, just about everything you own will be sold by a court-appointed Chapter 7 trustee and the money will be given to your creditors. You can keep *some* of your property if it is considered to be exempt property under the laws of your home state. This varies from state to state, but basically it will leave you with clothes and basic living essentials.

If you own the house in which you live, it might be sold in bankruptcy; the same thing goes for cars and boats and the like. However, (and this varies from state to state also) you will be able to keep a small sum, like $5,000 to $10,000 that will be considered exempt from your creditors. They won't sell everything you own and leave you with absolutely *nothing*. There are other exemptions a local bankruptcy attorney can discuss with you, but that's really the big one.

> **You have probably seen numerous advertisements offering to "erase your poor credit" or "start fresh, all bad accounts removed from your credit report." Well, you can't—not legally anyway. You will find that this is a big waste of money. There are provisions for when you have inaccurate information on your account. You can report the misinformation to the credit reporting agency and if they confirm the error, it will be removed. But you don't need to pay anyone for these services.**

Enemies

Also, in a Chapter 7, if you owe money on your mortgage or a car loan, you'll probably have to give the house and car up to the lender. Unless, and this is a big one, you and your attorney can work out new loans with your creditors, which is called reaffirmation of debt. In all honesty, I wouldn't count on this happening because if you had an income that would allow you to reaffirm debt, you would most likely file Chapter 13.

Chapters 11, 12 and 13

Under a reorganization bankruptcy (Chapters 11, 12, and 13), you file a plan with the bankruptcy court proposing how you will repay your creditors. Some debts must be repaid in full; for others you pay only a percentage of the balance due. Others aren't paid at all. In a Chapter 13, you get put on a court-ordered payment schedule until you make good on all your debts. You usually get to keep all of your exempt and nonexempt property *so long as you make monthly payments*, as approved by the court, to the Chapter 13 trustee. The Chapter 13 trustee then pays off your creditors.

By the Numbers

Under federal bankruptcy laws, people with secured debts under $871,550 (mortgage, car loans, etc.) and unsecured debts (credit cards, personal loans, student loans) under $269,250 can file for Chapter 13. If you have debts in excess of the Chapter 13 debt limits you can file for Chapter 11, but it is usually used only by businesses because it allows them to stay in business rather than close their doors. Only family farmers can file for Chapter 12 reorganization, regardless of debt level. For the purposes of this book, we'll just be talking about Chapter 13.

Allies

If you can swing it, a Chapter 13 is the best way to go because it leaves you with more of your own personal possessions, and the climb back to solvency—and beyond—is not quite so rough.

Just Why You Would Choose Chapter 13 over Chapter 7

Although most people who have to file for bankruptcy choose Chapter 7, there are good several reasons why people select Chapter 13:

- You can't file Chapter 7 if you have received a Chapter 7 or Chapter 13 discharge within six years (*unless* you paid off at least 70 percent of your debts in a Chapter 13 bankruptcy). With Chapter 13 you can file bankruptcy at any time.

- You have valuable nonexempt property. More on this later in the chapter.

- You're in trouble with your mortgage or car loan. In Chapter 7, you will have to give up the property, or pay for it in full during your bankruptcy case which is not likely to happen. In Chapter 13, you can repay the back debt according to your plan, and *keep* the property by making the payments required under the contract.

- You have debts that cannot be discharged in Chapter 7.

- You have cosigners on your personal loans. In Chapter 7, the creditors will go after your cosigners for payment. With Chapter 13, you can protect the people who were trying to help you out by cosigning; your creditors can't seek payment from your cosigners for the duration of your case.

- New creditors will be more inclined to grant you credit after a Chapter 13 than they would after a Chapter 7.

- The best reason to choose Chapter 13 (if it is an option): You feel like you should repay your debts and you want to learn money management.

What You Will Lose When You Declare Chapter 7 Bankruptcy

When you toss in the towel and declare Chapter 7, you might as well throw in the keys, too—because whatever you had to lock up you'll probably have to give up. Certain kinds of property are exempt in almost every state while other types are almost never exempt.

This is what you can typically keep (exempt property):

- Motor vehicles, as long as they're not luxury cars
- Reasonably necessary clothing (you'll have to sell your chinchilla coat)
- Necessary household furnishings and goods (the second TV is gone, and so is the good stereo)
- Household appliances
- Jewelry (to a certain value determined by the state by in which you live)
- Personal effects
- Life insurance (to a certain value determined by the state)
- Pensions
- Part of the equity in your home (to a certain value determined by the state)
- Work tools
- Public benefits (welfare, Social Security, unemployment compensation)

The following items that you must typically give up (nonexempt property) are:

- Stamp, coin and other collections
- Family heirlooms of value
- Cash, bank accounts, stocks, bonds, and other investments
- Second car or truck
- Motorcycle (unless it's your only vehicle)
- RV
- Snowmobile, ATV
- Boat(s)
- Second or vacation home

Exempt items are the things you need to live, and nonexempt items are the things that you'd love to have, but don't necessarily need to have.

What Normally Happens When You Go to Bankruptcy Court?

In a Chapter 7 case, you have to file forms with the bankruptcy court that list your income and expenses, assets, debts, and property transactions for the past two years. It costs a few hundred dollars to file, but that may be waived for people who receive public assistance or live below the poverty level. A trustee is assigned to oversee your case. About a month after filing, you have to attend a meeting of creditors where the trustee reviews your forms and asks questions. The creditors rarely ever show up. If you have any nonexempt property, you hand it over to the trustee. The meeting lasts about five minutes. Three to six months later, you receive a notice from the court that "all debts that qualified for discharge were discharged." Then your case is over, and you're ready to begin your climb back out of the hole.

Filing for bankruptcy puts you into a little loophole called the "automatic stay." This immediately stops your creditors from trying to collect what you owe them. So, at least while your case is being considered, creditors can't garnish your wages, empty your bank account, repossess your car or property, foreclose on your house, or cut off your utility service or welfare benefits.

Until your bankruptcy case actually ends, your financial problems are now in the hands of the bankruptcy court. It assumes legal control of the property you own (except your exempt property, which is yours to keep) and the debts you owe *as of the date you file*. You basically can't sell or pay anything without the court's consent. You do have control of the property and income you acquire after you file for bankruptcy.

Chapter 13 is a little different. You file the same forms, but you also need to file a proposed repayment plan wherein you tell how you intend to repay your debts over the next three, or in some cases five, years. The cost to file cannot be waived, and a trustee is assigned to oversee the case. There's also a meeting of creditors, but they sometimes show up for Chapter 13 cases especially if they don't like something in your plan. The next step is to go to a hearing before a bankruptcy judge who either confirms or denies your plan. If your plan is confirmed and you make all the payments called for under your plan, you can continue with your Cash Flow War Battles. You'll be the one in control of making all the payments you agreed to in your plan.

Some Debts Are Simply Not Dischargeable

Bankruptcy won't solve all of your money problems, nor is it meant to. In fact, there are some debts that you have to pay no matter what sort of bankruptcy you choose to file. The following debts are nondischargeable in any bankruptcy proceeding. If you file for Chapter 7, you will still have to pay these debts when your case is over. If you file for Chapter 13, they will have to be paid in full during your plan, or they will still be hanging over your head when you're done with your repayment plan.

- Any debts you neglect to list when you file for bankruptcy
- Every single penny of child support and alimony
- Any debts for personal injury or death caused by drunk driving
- Student loans

- Fines and penalties imposed for breaking the law
- All tax debts (Uncle Sam *always* gets paid!)

Also, the judge always has the option to declare some debts nondischargeable in Chapter 7 if a creditor challenges them. However, you can pay these debts off in Chapter 13, if you include them in your plan.

- Debt you incurred fraudulently, such as lying on a credit application
- Credit card purchases in excess of $1,150 if made within 60 days of filing
- Loans or cash advances in excess of $1,150 if taken within 60 days of filing
- Debts from willful or malicious injury to another person or another person's property
- Debts from embezzlement, larceny, or breach of trust

What most of these nondischargeable debts boil down to is that you can't get away with being a bad guy by declaring bankruptcy.

> If you're the type of person who incurred debts by basically being a ne'er-do-well, don't expect to slide out of the consequences by declaring bankruptcy—because it won't work. All *you* really need to know is that student loans and taxes are nondischargeable.

How to Avoid Declaring Bankruptcy

The easiest answer here is to go back and reread Part One of this book. If you follow all the advice I offered in the sections of this book on budgeting, credit cards, and saving your money, then you'll never find yourself in this pickle except perhaps in the case of life-threatening medical hardships outside insurance coverage. However, if you're already in deep trouble financially and bankruptcy is looming, and you just started reading this book to learn about money management, then there are a few things you can do to stave off bankruptcy.

Don't Do Anything

If you're already living simply, with just a little income and property, and you plan to do so in the future, you're judgment-proof. Anyone who sues you won't be able to collect because you don't have anything they can legally take. Except for being a tax protester or willfully failing to pay child support you can't be thrown in jail for not paying your debts. And nobody can take away your basic clothing, ordinary household furnishings, personal effects, food, Social Security, unemployment, or public assistance. If you don't anticipate having a steady income or owning anything for a while, bankruptcy is probably not necessary. Your creditors will simply write off your debt as a deductible business loss for income tax purposes. In several years, it will become legally uncollectible under state law, and in seven years, it will come off your credit record. If you have seven years to kill, and you don't incur any new debt during that time, you can just forget about the whole thing. Of course, I would seriously question what you're doing reading this book if this sort of life is a viable option for you!

Get the Collection Agencies off Your Back

If your main concern is that creditors are harassing you, you don't need to declare bankruptcy. You can still get creditors off your back by taking advantage of federal and state debt collection laws that protect you from abusive and harassing debt collectors. Just keep making small payments until you can afford larger payments, and tell them that it's illegal for a collection agency to call you at an unreasonable time. The federal Fair Debt Collection Practices Act (FDCPA) also bars collectors from calling you at work, harassing you, using abusive language, making false or misleading statements, adding unauthorized charges, and engaging in many other practices. Under the FDCPA, you can demand in writing that the collection agency stop calling you. But you also must pay them a little money every month until you clear your debt.

Negotiate Your Debts

If you're not completely broke, or if you have assets you're willing to sell, you'll be a lot better off by negotiating with your creditors rather than filing for bankruptcy. Negotiation may simply buy you some time to get back on your feet, or your creditors may actually agree on a settlement of your debts for less than you owe. Sometimes it's worth it to them to get some of the money you owe them if they don't have to go through a big hassle to get it. This actually works; some creditors can be surprisingly reasonable when you tell them they can either take a settlement or see what they get in bankruptcy court.

Ask for Help to Design a Repayment Plan

If you feel you can't negotiate with your creditors, get someone who can. The ability to negotiate is an art, and involves a number of skills. Sometimes people can't do this sort of negotiation because deep down they feel that the creditors are right to insist on full payment, or the creditors are so hard-nosed or just plain irrational that the process is too unpleasant to stomach. Whatever the case, if you don't want to negotiate with your creditors, you can turn to a lawyer, a bankruptcy service, or a nonprofit credit counselor. Let them negotiate for you, and make sure that you make the payments you agree to make.

Marching Orders for Bankruptcy and How to Avoid It

✔ **Follow the advice in Part One of this book and bankruptcy will never be a problem.**

✔ **Know the differences between Chapter 7 and Chapter 13.**

✔ **Exhaust all of your options before declaring bankruptcy.**

Part Four

Building on Your Victory

There are always opportunities through which businessmen can profit handsomely if they will only recognize and seize them.

J. Paul Getty, author, *How to Be Rich*

Building on Your Victory

> *A mind troubled by doubt cannot focus on the course to victory.*
> —Arthur Golden, author, *Memoirs of a Geisha*

Congratulations! Now that you've finished reading the previous chapters and begun implementing the knowledge you gained in the first three parts of this book, you're well on your way to enjoying a successful and prosperous lifestyle. If you put this book down right now, and only use the knowledge you've gained in the first three parts, you'd be justified in proclaiming victory in the Cash Flow War.

By taking complete control of your personal finances, and taking complete control over all of your investment vehicles, you have *forever* separated yourself from the vast majority of the population. Most of us are content to keep our noses to the grindstone, working hard every day to make a better life—but surprisingly few of us have the knowledge to really make the fruits of our labor *go to work for us*. By acting on the knowledge you gained in those pages, you're putting yourself in very elite company. With what you've learned, you can virtually assure yourself a good financial life. All you need to do is to implement what you've learned and stay the course.

Enjoy your success. You've earned it.

And now that you've got the tools to enter the winner's circle, you've also earned the right of entry into the *inner circle*. You can take this whole thing one step further—and go from having a successful and prosperous lifestyle to enjoying *complete financial freedom*.

You'll find the final necessary pieces of your Cash Flow War arsenal in Part Four. The whole world is spreading out in front of you, and all you have to do now is learn these advanced Cash Flow War tactics and commence your final campaign.

Here's what we'll be looking at in Part Four:

Chapter 17: Exploring Self-Employment

Not very many of the truly rich people I know work for anyone but themselves. In this chapter, we'll explore the steps you need to take so that you can look in the mirror every morning and see the boss!

Chapter 18: The Shortest Chapter in This Book

No kidding, it really is! I put this chapter in because I wanted to make sure that every Cash Flow Warrior out there fully understands that yield is the one true way to judge the success or failure of a financial investment.

Chapter 19: Marketing Your Business

This is a basic training course in the rudiments of marketing; these are the sorts of things you'll need to be thinking about as you venture into self-employment. The one surest way to fail in your initial attempts at entrepreneurial activities is to walk into the situation without a clear understanding of marketing. This chapter will give you the basics you need to know about marketing.

Chapter 20: Understanding Franchises

Franchises are a very good opportunity for those Cash Flow Warriors who have amassed a solid chunk of change to invest. In this chapter, we take a hard look at franchises, the pros and cons of being a franchise owner, and how to determine the worth of a franchise program.

Chapter 21: Bad Business: Opportunities to Avoid

In this chapter, I'll give you a gentle reminder that not everyone is as honest as you are. We'll take an in-depth look at how and *why* to avoid things like multi-level marketing schemes.

Chapter 22: Cashing In on Cash Flow

The Cash Flow industry is where I've achieved my greatest success, and I'd like to show to just how lucrative it could be for you as well.

Chapter 23: The Real Estate Industry

Real estate is where Cash Flow Warriors can really make their mark, if they've got the right tools in place and know what to look for in investment properties. What I'll do in this chapter is give you an idea of the different types of real estate investing that you can do, and then if you're still interested you should really take some real estate courses.

Chapter 24: Death, Taxes and Your Business

Once you have a company set up—be it real estate, cash flow, or some other opportunity—you can begin to realize the benefits of additional tax deductions. This chapter will delve into the tax advantages of owning a small business.

Chapter 25: Declaring Victory in the Cash Flow War

Although you can have a very good life if you just apply what you learned in the first three parts of this book, if you really want to proclaim total victory in the Cash Flow War and issue a statement of financial freedom, then you need to go beyond what we learned in Parts One, Two, and Three and act on the advanced intelligence reports you'll receive in Part Four!

You're on Your Way

You're way ahead of all your friends and neighbors now, as they still haven't learned the rules of the Cash Flow War. As I stated in the introduction to this book, the two things they don't teach us in school are relationships and money. I think you know by now this book is not about relationships, but it is about money and taking control of your financial destiny. It is all about winning the Cash Flow War. Most people end up as casualties in this conflict, and it's simply because they were never taught the rules of engagement. This book has changed all of that for you.

You've gained a complete mastery of the rules of the Cash Flow War in Parts One, Two, and Three. But now is not the time to become paralyzed through analysis. Please be aware that you don't want to get stuck in a cycle of continually searching for knowledge. You've got the weapons in your arsenal that you need for a preliminary assault!

There is an old saying that goes "The more you know, the more you find you don't know." It would be impossible to know everything there is to know on any subject. It goes without saying that the more you know, the better off you will be. But it is far better to know a lot about a specific subject than it is to know a little bit about a lot of subjects.

So what do you do with the knowledge you've already gained? That's simple. You apply it. Begin using the tools and Cash Flow War weapons you've acquired. Apply them to your life, and you will quickly see the dramatic changes that occur. After all, wisdom is the application of knowledge.

With practice, you'll remember to keep your eyes and mind open while continuing to move forward, and all the while taking the appropriate actions. That is the first, crucial key to success: putting your knowledge to work for you.

Let's get started with one final important push!

Exploring Self-Employment

> *Never fear for want of business. A man who qualifies himself well for his calling, never fails of employment.*
> —Thomas Jefferson, third president of the United States

Let's start this section out with a deceptively easy topic. This is probably one of the most important lessons you can learn about the weapons in your Cash Flow War, and it's a very simple one: *Most millionaires do not work for someone else.*

I'm sure you think that you'd have to quit whatever it is you're doing now and devote your whole life to a new endeavor but I'm here to tell you that owning a company does not need to be a full-time endeavor. Many Cash Flow War winners run a company in their spare time, and still reap the same key benefits as people who are dedicated full-time to their own companies.

Here's a quick look at the three main benefits of owning your own company:

1. Improved retirement savings

2. Tax advantages (covered in Chapter 24)

3. Ability to expand or sell your company

Allies

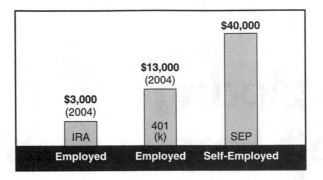

Retirement savings. Take a look at the figure above, and you will see what I mean by the improved retirement savings advantages of being self-employed. When you own your business, many more doors are open to you in planning for your retirement while realizing tax benefits today.

You can easily see in that the amount of money a self-employed individual can put away for retirement far exceeds that of a traditional employee. Just refer to Chapter 13 on taking control of your retirement plans and you can see we're talking about significant sums here.

Ability to expand or sell your business. One of your goals when starting a business, in addition to the two items we have already covered, should be to realize passive income at some point. That may be handled in one of two ways:

1. *Sell your company.* If you are able to build something that someone else would like to buy you can sell the company. Most likely, you will need to create some sort of note and the buyer will make payments to you for the business. Typically the note should be paid in full within 7 to 10 years (unlike your 30-year mortgage). You could also potentially "franchise" your company, thereby allowing others to do the same thing as you and pay you a continual fee. You could then move on to another project and/or company. *Remember:* If you sell your company, it is highly unlikely that you will be able to continue to take advantage of some of the tax benefits we have mentioned. You will need to start another company (which is sometimes the most fun of all).

2. *Let someone else run your company.* Owning your own company can quickly turn into your company running you. If you are dealing with something that involves money (particularly *your* money), then you are going to want to stay involved. However, you always want to pay attention to your time. What is the best use of your time? If you are spending four hours a day licking stamps then you could certainly hire someone else to do that—for not a lot of money—thereby freeing up your time to go after things that will make you more money.

Recognizing an Opportunity

So, how do you choose a business to open? It seems that these days you can't open a magazine, read the newspaper, or turn on the television without a new money-making opportunity being pitched to you. Some of these are legitimate opportunities, but most of them are just get-rich-quick schemes that only work for the entrepreneurs that are pitching them.

However, there are certainly legitimate opportunities all around us—it's just a matter of sifting through the junk and finding the real money-making ones. In Chapter 22, I discuss in depth the Cash Flow Industry that I am involved in. It's certainly not the only way to make money—far from it! In Chapter 20 we'll take a deep look into franchising opportunities, and there's lots of room there for an enterprising Cash Flow Warrior. Of course money can be made in anything from the stock market to eBay to real estate.

Whatever opportunity you choose to follow you should adhere to a few simple rules. These rules will help you weed out choices that will simply result in you losing a boatload of money. As you contemplate opening your own business, look at it closely and see if the opportunity and the industry fit within these following rules:

Rule One—There must be an *existing* industry or need. Everyone knows a story about people who come up with a great new idea, start a business from their garage, and then obtain financing and take it to the general public and make more money than they know what to do with. Here's the plain truth: This is rare—and I mean *really* rare. The problem with this approach is that most of these businesses rely on the entrepreneur to create a market! Developing a product or

Allies

service and then trying to create a market of people that will buy it, or creating a need, simply does not work in most cases. This is a long shot, to say the least. What a seasoned Cash Flow Warrior looks for is a product or service that people *already* want or need. You want to fill a need that people have, not convince them they need something they never even heard of before. Starting with a new product or service is extremely risky.

Allies

Rule Two—You must get accurate and up-to-date information. A lot of the opportunities that will present themselves to you are things that were actually a good idea at one point. The problem is that their time has passed. Some of these tired opportunities are like getting a "stock tip" from a friend—too many people have already taken advantage of it and *if* there was once money to be made, it probably already has been. Since you'll be doing your due diligence and thoroughly investigating any business venture you may choose to launch, make sure that whatever materials you obtain (such as books, CDs, DVDs, training manuals, videos, etc.) are current and up to date. Market conditions in almost every business change often; if you're operating under the assumption that the statistics that somebody gathered regarding a certain marketplace two years ago are still valid, then you might be operating under a false assumption. If there is not accurate and up-to-date information available to you about a marketplace or an opportunity, then you should pass on that opportunity.

Allies

Rule Three—Live trainings, conventions, or seminars. There are lots of opportunities that are based on programs that allow you to "study at home" and "at your own pace." In some cases, you might find out what you need to know about a marketplace or an opportunity through this method, but I'm inclined to think that the rate of failure is high among would-be entrepreneurs who follow this approach. Most people will read the first couple of chapters of their manual, or listen to a couple of the tapes and simply lose focus.

The problem is that you can't ask a book questions, and you can't interact with a tape. When you're exploring a business or a market, you need to find an instructor or a mentor. And here's the most important part: You must learn from someone *who actually makes money in the field that he or she are teaching you about.* There's a glut of people out there who are simply paid teachers, and they're willing to teach you the latest money-making techniques. However, when they're cornered they have to admit that they don't actually do any of it themselves—because they make their money teaching others!

Since we've already talked about the need to set up shop in an existing industry, it should follow that the marketplace you've chosen will have some sort of association that presents seminars, conventions, and tradeshows. This is a fact: Every legitimate industry is supported by an infrastructure of seminars, networking opportunities, and/or conventions. All you need to do is a simple Internet search to find them.

Rule Four: There must be some sort of support. This is really an extension of the preceding two rules: No matter how good the training, materials, and mentors, you *must* have someone you can call on later. You must have, at the very least, a place to get more information as you develop your new business.

Allies

As you'll see in the coming chapters, both the Cash Flow Industry and franchising opportunities fall within the guidelines set out in these four basic rules as do many other businesses; if the business opportunity you're contemplating does not, then I would suggest that you look into other opportunities.

What Sort of Business Are We Talking About?

There are basically two ways to go when you set up your own business. Since we're talking about setting up your own business, we don't need to look into partnerships or corporations. We just need to look at sole proprietorships and Limited Liability Corporations (LLCs), and as you'll see, even though it involves a little bit more set-up time in the beginning, an LLC may just be the way to go.

There are numerous other choices like S-Corps and C-Corps. Ask your tax advisor what meets your needs!

Allies

Sole Proprietorship

Most of us, when we embark upon starting our own business, will open up a sole proprietorship. This is the simplest form of business organization. For all intents and purposes, the business entity and your other affairs (personal and business) are merged together. As the proprietor, you own and control the business. From the standpoint of nearly all legal rights and responsibilities, your sole proprietorship business and you are considered to be one and the same.

Although as a sole proprietor you are merged with your business, it's best for financial management purposes to maintain separate records for your business unit and your family or household. To make sure that you have the documentation you need for tax reporting purposes, you should maintain separate bank accounts and separate credit cards for your business and your family affairs.

If you're using credit in your business operations, it's even more important to maintain the separation of finances and records for your business unit and household. Interest payments on personal debt are not a deductible expense for federal and state income tax purposes, while *interest payments on business borrowing are fully deductible.*

Some business and household costs will be incurred jointly if you have a home-based business, like utilities and phone bills. You'll need to allocate the respective portions to the business unit and the household and then pay the business and personal amounts from the respective bank accounts. A relatively small investment of effort in bill paying and record keeping can ensure you have the data needed for filing and substantiating your income tax returns.

Allies

Advantages of sole proprietorship
It's simple: You can just open up a home office one day and decide you're working for yourself. You don't need to do any formal business planning or organizational arrangements (bylaws, organizational charter, etc.) when a sole proprietorship is established. Depending on what sort of business you're engaged in, other than routine permits and licenses required for your business activities, no public notification or legal assistance is *required* to start, terminate, or modify the business.

Land Mines

Disadvantages of sole proprietorships
You can lose it all: Because you're not a separate business entity, mingling of business and household finances can occur, and you end up operating with your whole net worth. This means that everything the proprietor and family owns is at risk in both personal and business activities. Legally, a sole proprietorship is inseparable from its owner: The business and the owner are one and the same. As a result, the owner of a sole proprietorship is personally liable for the entire amount of any business debts or court judgments. This means that if you form a sole proprietorship, creditors of the business can come after your personal assets—your house or your car, for example—to collect what the business owes them.

Limited Liability Corporation

If you set up a Limited Liability Corporation, or LLC, you'll need to do a little more work before you actually begin. You'll need a lawyer and an accountant, but by laying the groundwork out a little bit before you jump in, you'll be protecting your personal assets much more than you can in a sole proprietorship. Basically, the name says it all: limited liability. You're only liable for the amount of money you put into the business, so if you invest $25,000, you can only lose $25,000.

LLCs are a relatively new breed, but you can now form an LLC with just one person in every state except Massachusetts, which requires, at the time of writing, an LLC to have two owners.

The LLC provides its owner with a very flexible and adaptable form of business organization that gives you liability protection comparable to the protection provided by forming a corporation with incorporation of a business unit. Unless you give your personal guarantee on a business loan, your liability is limited solely to the amount invested in the LLC—except, of course, for unpaid taxes. Your Uncle Sam always gets paid!

An LLC can be established at a relatively low cost in a short time frame. You'll need to come up with a business plan and articles of organization. (The articles of organization simply state who is managing the LLC, and who makes what decisions.) Filing fees are typically $100 or less. Many states supply a blank one-page form for the articles of organization on which you need only specify a few basic details about your LLC such as its name and address and contact information for a person involved with the LLC who will receive legal papers and tax forms and such.

In addition to filing articles of organization, you must create a written LLC operating agreement. While you don't have to file your operating agreement with the state, it's a crucial document because it sets out the LLC members' rights and responsibilities, their percentage interests in the business, and their share of the profits. This is what you may need a lawyer for, and this is crucial, because this is the document that limits your liability.

Mail Call

The main reason to make an operating agreement is as simple as it is important: It helps to ensure that courts will respect your limited personal liability. This is particularly key in a one-person LLC where, without the formality of an agreement, the LLC will look and feel a lot like a sole proprietorship. Just the fact that you *have* a formal written operating agreement will lend credibility to your LLC's separate existence.

While many states do not legally require your LLC to have an operating agreement, it's foolish to run an LLC without one. An operating agreement helps your LLC by guarding your limited liability status, heading off financial and management misunderstandings, and making sure your business is governed by your own rules—not the default rules of your state.

Since you'll essentially be a corporation, you'll need an accountant to file your taxes for you. This is not a bad thing, as I have never hired an accountant that didn't end up saving me money in the long run by discovering deductions and tax advantages I had never considered before.

The Differences Between the Sole Proprietorship and the LLC

There are a few basic differences between the two forms of business organization. While the taxes are essentially paid the same way, you'll have more latitude when making deductions as an LLC. And, as an LLC, you'll have the paid preparer's name at the bottom of you tax form so if there is any trouble with the IRS you can have your accountant sort it out!

I've already talked about how an LLC protects your assets, unlike in a sole proprietorship where everything you own is at risk. The only clear advantage I can see in a sole proprietorship form of business organization is that you could start your own business *tonight.* But I'm not so sure that's a good thing—it should take you significantly longer than that if you're checking your opportunity against the four rules I laid out earlier in the chapter.

When it comes right down to it, after you identify and qualify an opportunity, there are really only five basic steps to starting an LLC:

1. Choose an available business name that complies with your particular state's LLC rules.

2. File formal paperwork with the secretary of state's office in your state, usually called articles of organization, and pay the filing fee.

3. Create an LLC operating agreement, which sets out the rights and responsibilities of the LLC owner(s).

4. Publish a notice of your intent to form an LLC (required in some states).

5. Obtain whatever licenses and permits may be required for your business

In the end, start up whatever works for you now! You can always change later to meet your needs.

Marching Orders for Exploring Self-Employment

✔ Identify an opportunity.

✔ Qualify an opportunity by applying the four rules.

✔ Set up an LLC or sole proprietorship.

✔ Remember, there are many other choices such as "S" or "C" corps. Be sure to check them all out before making a decision.

✔ Once you have identified your business, contact a professional to see what kind of company structure best fits your needs.

18

The Shortest Chapter in This Book

It Is All About Yield

> *Everything should be made a simple as possible, but not one bit simpler.*
>
> —Albert Einstein, inventor

My point in writing this chapter is a very simple one: You need to understand that the concept of yield is the single most important factor when choosing an investment. Most people only look at how much *money* they will make on a particular deal. This is often a mistake. A sophisticated investor will only look at *yield*.

Simply stated, yield expresses the percentage return on your investment. If you invest $100 and end up with $120, then you have an investment that yields 20 percent. If you invest $100,000 and end up with $120,000 then you still have an investment that yields 20 percent. And that, my fellow Cash Flow Warriors, is a darned good investment.

Let me put it another way. Some people would not invest $100 to only end up with $120, thinking that the $20 is not worth the investment time or effort. Well, forgetting risk or cost for a moment, we already know that it is a 20 percent return.

The fact it is only $20 is because you only started with $100. The return is still 20 percent.

A one-time investment of $100 (at 20 percent) for 20 years becomes almost $4,000. Not bad—just imagine if that was a $1,000, $10,000, or $100,000 investment!

Here endeth the lesson.
— Sean Connery, actor, in *The Untouchables*

Marketing Your Business

> *The aim of* marketing *is to know and understand the customer so well the product or service fits him and sells itself.*
> —Peter F. Drucker, author,
> *Management Challenges for the 21st Century*

Marketing is a buzzword you hear all the time. More than likely, you have a vague idea of what it is, but more than that you are unsure of. Is it advertising? Is it sales? Is it spending a lot of money? Is it something that can be done for free? In truth, it is all of these things and more. In fact, the topic of marketing is a subject big enough to have dozens and dozens of books written on it. There is no way I could hope to completely teach you everything you will need to know in one chapter. However, I can give you some tips and pointers so you will better understand why you need marketing, what marketing is, and how to get started.

We discussed various ways to go about opening up your own business in Chapter 17. If you've decided that this is part of your Cash Flow War strategy, your very next thought should be: "Where do I find my clients or customers?" Obviously, without clients or customers, you haven't got a business. So many good ideas have died a lonely death because the entrepreneur that brought them to the table had no idea how to go about marketing to them. Because that's the heart of what marketing is—it is letting people (your market) know about your goods or services.

We knew one guy who had a great idea. He dumped twenty grand or so into product development—making up prototypes, coming up with a great name, and now he's got about 1,000 cases of this product sitting in a shed at Storage USA. It was a real Ben Franklin–type idea: simple, inexpensive, and everyone could use the product.

You can have the best business idea in the world, but if you're not marketing it properly, nobody will ever hear about it.

Here's his idea: You know those little hinge-tabs that open and close your CD cases? Well, we all know that those tabs inevitably break off, and make using the cases a real pain in the neck? This guy had a nice, thick, clear tape, precut to CD size, that you could put right on the hinges of the CD and then the case would work perfectly. He designed a dispenser that worked beautifully—he even figured out how to sell enough tape to fix 50 CD cases for less than a buck, and still make a very hefty profit on every unit.

If something like that was sitting next to the register the next time you picked up some CDs, would you buy it? I know I would! It's a great impulse item, a perfect stocking stuffer. But they never made it next to the register *anywhere* because this guy never figured out how to go about marketing his idea. So he pays the storage every month, and he's still driving his UPS delivery truck every day. He doesn't even like to talk about it anymore because the whole experience disheartened him so much—he's a Cash Flow War casualty.

Before you go into business, you need to understand marketing and you need to develop a marketing plan. Marketing is the most important aspect of your business, and most of your time should be spent in this area. Even if you have the best product on the market at the best price, it doesn't do you any good if no one knows that you exist.

Marketing 101: The Big Three

We can all agree that marketing is one of the most basic and fundamental components of any successful business. What we will probably have a harder time agreeing on is just what marketing is.

Here's my take on it: Put very simply, marketing is the process of identifying and communicating with prospective clients efficiently. It's a three-step process:

1. Identifying qualified prospects.
2. Communicating with qualified prospects.
3. Evaluating communication.

Identification centers on defining your product, defining your competition, and defining just who should hear your message. This includes performing research and planning whenever any new venture is being attempted. This stage is crucial.

Communication focuses on the medium of conveying your message effectively. This is accomplished through a variety of methods. *These include branding, advertising, public relations, publicity, and passive marketing.* Some people confuse marketing with advertising; however, marketing and advertising are not the same thing. Advertising is just one portion of the marketing communications activity.

Evaluation is an ongoing process to determine effectiveness before, during, and after you've delivered a communication. Proper analysis can help you to deliver the proper message to the right prospect at the right time through the right medium. Plus, by evaluating what you've done before, you can help ensure future success by making adjustments where necessary and forecasting your results.

Creating a Marketing Plan

It's *critical* that you develop a marketing plan, budget marketing into your financial plan, and constantly get the word out about your product. If you don't, your great idea could end up gathering dust in a storage shed somewhere.

I've put together an *Eight-Step Action Item* program, based on the Big Three that should get your marketing blood flowing.

Identification Action Items

Step One—Identify Your Product or Service

List in detail your product or service's features and benefits. A feature describes your product or service; the benefits describe what your customer will get from this product.

For example, if you're selling an attachment for a hose for washing cars, the features may be that it has a non-slip grip, it can use any common liquid dish-washing soap, all the metal parts are guaranteed rust-free, it's ultra-light, manageable, so simple your 10-year-old kid can use it, and it only costs $8.95. The benefit of this product can be that you can wash and rinse your car completely clean in less than five minutes, it has no brushes that can damage your car's finish, and you make your money on it after you skip two visits to the car wash.

It is important that you are clear about what is unique or different about your product or service. Why should people come to you instead of your competition? Let your customers know *why* you are different. If you offer lower prices than your competition, let your customers know how you can do that. Do you have lower overhead? Can you purchase in volume and pass the savings on to the customer? Do you provide extra service or guarantees? Whatever your advantage, make sure you communicate it to your customers.

Think about the product or services you're considering offering and on a separate piece of paper jot some of your ideas down. First, list your product or service's features. Then list the benefits of your product(s) or service(s).

Step Two—Identify Your Market

Just who is the type of person who would buy your product or service? Or, is it even a person? Are you planning on selling a service to other businesses? You need to identify who your target customer is. Taking our example of the car-washing device, you might decide that your target is men aged 18 to 34. If you're targeting businesses, what sort of business? Do you want to sell to IBM or the local pizza joint? If you're targeting people, you need to describe your target customer in terms of demographics:

- Age
- Sex
- Family composition
- Geographic location
- Income

> **Many first-time entrepreneurs on a limited budget try to market to a wide range of prospects. If you try to market to everyone you will soon run out of money and will experience little success. If you narrow your marketing efforts to focus on your target customer, your success rate will greatly improve. Make sure you create a profile of your best prospects, and make them the focus of all of your marketing efforts.**

If you're targeting businesses, then you'll need to figure out the sort of business you're shooting for; after that, you can identify specific targets with these resources:

- **Chambers of Commerce directories.** Chambers of Commerce typically maintain directories of member companies along with descriptions of the businesses.
- **CD-ROM directories.** Computer CD-ROM directories contain thousands of names and addresses of businesses. They are typically classified by industry or geographic area
- **Local book of lists.** These inexpensive guides are published annually by city business journals. They typically rank local businesses by industry, annual sales, number of employees, or size.
- **Public library or university library.** At the library, you can find directories of thousands of domestic companies classified by industry, location, size of assets, or SIC code. Examples include *Dunn's Regional Business Directory* and *The Manufacturer's Register.*

- **Member lists.** Some professional associations or organizations will provide you a copy of their member list or they may be available in your local library. This could be especially helpful if you are marketing to attorneys, financial planners, doctors, or other professionals.

- **List brokers.** List brokers compile a list based on the parameters of your selection. For example, you could request a list of all people who have sold a home in your county or all newcomers to your zip code. They charge a fee per name for this service. Lists are only effective if they are current and accurate, so use caution if you decide to buy one.

- **Government vendor lists.** Vendor lists from any type of government agency are available to the public. To obtain them simply call the Accounts Payable department of the government agency and ask them how to get a vendor's list.

- **Yellow pages.** As simple as it sounds, most people don't realize that the Yellow Pages can be a useful tool for identifying prospects. Just look up the page for the sort of business you're targeting.

- **Local newspaper and business journals.** Scanning the business section of the local newspaper or a local business journal can lead you directly to highly qualified prospects.

- **Internet.** The Internet is another useful tool for identifying prospects, particularly businesses. If you market to businesses in a particular industry, for example, you can use the Internet to search for companies that fit your prospect profile.

Trade associations and publications are also a great place to get information about your potential market, especially if you are targeting businesses.

Step Three—Identify Your Competition

If you're marketing to businesses you can combine Steps Two and Three simply by looking for companies that are advertising a similar product or service to your own as you search for customers. If you're marketing directly to the consumer, then you can use the resources in Step Two to identify your competition.

You need to answer these questions:

- Who is your competition?

- What are their strengths?

- What are their weaknesses?

- How are you different or better than your competition? How are you unique?

- Why should people come to you instead of them?

- How does your product or service's features and benefits compare to the competition?

Communication

Step Four—Determine Your Position

Now that you have determined how you plan to be different, you need to develop a position for your business, make a slogan with this position, and put this slogan on everything—your business cards, letterhead, advertisements, and so on.

This is your first step towards developing a brand, and this is a key element to your Cash Flow War success. As with many things in marketing, a lot of confusion surrounds the term *branding*. Many people think of branding as simply creating a slogan or a logo.

Branding is creating an easily recognizable image and message for a person and/or product. The process of creating this identifiable *brand image* should be the primary driving factor behind any message you project to your prospects.

You must ask yourself the following question when determining exactly what brand image is: "What do I want people to think about me and my services?"

Here are some sample branding statements, or slogans, to get you thinking:

- *We do chicken right.*—Kentucky Fried Chicken

- *Progress is the most important product.*—General Electric

- *I love what you do for me.*—Toyota

- *Did somebody say McDonald's?*—McDonald's

- *Where do you want to go today?*—Microsoft

- *A different kind of company. A different kind of car.*—Saturn

- *For the life of your business.*—AT&T

- *Solutions for a small planet.*—IBM

- *You'll love the way we fly.*—Delta Airlines

- *Just for the taste of it.*—Coca-Cola

Action Items

- *Our most important package is yours.*—Federal Express
- *Good to the last drop.*—Maxwell House
- *You'll love the stuff we're made of.*—Pizza Hut

Think up as many branding and positioning slogans as you can, then narrow them down to five and get other people's feedback, then narrow them down to one.

Step Five—Advertise

You could read volumes of material describing in great length exactly what advertising really is and end up knowing less than you did when you began. For our Cash Flow War purposes, let's just define advertising as any means of communicating with a prospect that costs you money.

There are two main types of advertising: direct and indirect. In *direct advertising,* you promote your product or service directly by placing ads various media outlets. *Indirect advertising* uses the logo and slogan that you have plastered all over your letterhead, envelopes, invoices, and signs.

Now that you have determined what your market is, who your target customer is, who your competition is, and how you are going to be different, *what are the best vehicles to get your message out?*

Here's the only rule you need to know when you're selecting a media outlet: Put your ads in front of prospective customers. What would your prospects be most likely to read? The Yellow Pages? The local newspaper? The local business journal? A medical or law journal? What is likely to get their attention?

Your personality type might lend itself to a particular type of marketing. If you are outgoing, you might rely solely on personal contact; on the other hand, if you are shy, you might avoid personal contact and stick with direct mail. It is important to vary your methods in order to reach more prospects and to offer your business better exposure.

You need to focus your efforts on *direct response* advertising. Direct response advertising contains a very definite call to action. It presents your marketing message, and then tells the prospect how to participate. The call to action may be instructions to call, come in, return a reply card or use a coupon. The point is that direct response advertising elicits a direct response from the prospect.

Study the demographics of the advertising media you are considering. The sales representative should be able to tell you who a publication's audience is—he or she has that sort of information right at hand. Remember: Never buy an ad just because the rates are low. If nobody responds to your ad, it's not a bargain! Always ask for an agreement in writing before committing yourself to any advertising medium.

Step Six—How to Secure Word-of-Mouth Advertising through Customer Service

It should go without saying that word-of-mouth advertising from happy customers is the best advertising that money *can't* buy! You can increase your chances at this by having a reputation for excellent customer service. You already know that when you're happy with a business transaction you've made that you tell their friends and colleagues. Word-of-mouth referrals are what you are looking for. These referrals are already just about sold on your product or service because their friends or colleagues referred them.

Build a reputation for:

- **Speed.** Take care of your customers or clients as quickly as possible; return phone calls

- **Promptness.** Get your product to them quickly; handle complaints quickly.

- **Quality.** Offer a guarantee in writing with reasonable conditions.

- **Personal service.** Go the extra mile. Give clients more than they expect. You can send a thank you note after the sale, offer a discount on their next purchase, and so on.

- **Accessibility.** Make sure that your customer or client can reach you easily. Include phone numbers on your business card, along with e-mail, fax number, and cell.

- **Keep your promises.** Make sure that your client or customer can rely on you. If you say you will be there Thursday at noon, be there. If something unavoidable comes up, call your appointment and let him or her know the situation. If you guarantee your product or service, be prepared to back up that guarantee.

Evaluation Action Items

Step Seven—Marketing Analysis

Marketing analysis is when you sit down and figure out if what you're doing is effective. Whenever you start any marketing effort you must be certain to test and track every campaign.

> **When the orders are rolling in, it's easy to get caught up in this wave and think that you no longer need a targeted marketing plan. Many new entrepreneurs spend all their time on their existing clients. While it is important to have good customer service and you want to maintain your clients, client (or customer) attrition is inevitable in any business. If you don't maintain a targeted marketing program, you will soon find yourself without clients.**

For instance, if you're advertising, start with a small ad and see what kind of results the ad generates before you spend a lot on a widespread ad campaign. If you see that it is successful, you can go larger. If there were some minor changes needed, you can fine-tune from there before spending the big bucks.

You can measure your advertising effectiveness very easily if you track inquiries and sales. To determine your cost per sale, track the number of people who purchase or buy, and divide the cost of the ad by that number. If you're not making at least twice the cost of your ad with sales, then you should try a different approach next time.

Step Eight—Forecasting

The ultimate goal of analysis is forecasting. Once you've figured out what works and what doesn't, you will be better armed to project what the results of future marketing campaigns will be. By focusing on marketing efforts with which you have a proven positive track record you can almost nail down just how successful any marketing campaign you embark on will be.

Forecasting is, of course, not an exact science. As with anything, there are a series of variables that can be changed and fine-tuned to make efforts successful. But forecasting can give you a good idea of what to expect, and better yet, the knowledge to avoid what you know doesn't work.

Develop a Marketing Budget

Now that you've got the *Action Items* needed to set up a marketing plan, you've got to figure out how to pay for it. This is a critical step, especially in the beginning. Marketing expenses should be given priority. Eventually, your marketing expenses will pay for themselves in increased volume of business. But how are you ever going to attract business if you don't let people know about your business?

You need to sit down and take a hard look at how much money you have in your budget for marketing. And then you need to determine how and where to spend that money.

> **What did you determine were the best vehicles to get the word out about your business? For each form of advertising, you need to contact a sales rep and determine the estimated cost of each advertisement. Once you know that, you can then determine what form of advertising fits into your budget.**

Regardless of the medium you choose, your advertising should be:

- **Relevant.** Advertisements should be tailored to meet the needs of the prospects with whom you are communicating. Advertising should show how your service will directly benefit the prospect.

- **Repetitive.** Once is not enough when it comes to marketing. You may have to make repeated phone calls, send out multiple mailings, or run print advertisements for weeks before you receive a positive response.

- **Intrusive.** Advertisements must "get close to the prospect" and encourage a response. Communications delivered in person are the most intrusive; communications in writing are the least intrusive because they can be thrown away and forgotten. The more intrusive the communication, the better.

Marketing on a Budget

Marketing is critical for the success of your business, and the overall success of your Cash Flow War campaign. But, and this is good news for those of you who are pursuing a more aggressive strategy, it doesn't have to be expensive. Here are some suggestions of things you can do with little or no money.

Write Articles

Allies

Getting articles published in magazines, journals, newsletters, or newspapers your customers read is an excellent way to establish yourself as an expert. Some trade publications will pay you for articles they publish; others may not pay in dollars but will close each article with a byline identifying you, your company, and your location. Don't worry about getting paid for your piece—the publication that *doesn't* pay you will probably be more lenient about letting you do a little blatant self-promotion.

Don't overlook the op-ed (opinion/editorial) page in your local newspaper. Most papers publish guest editorials and identify the writer. Contact the publications serving your community and ask for their submission guidelines (or check their Web sites).

Allies

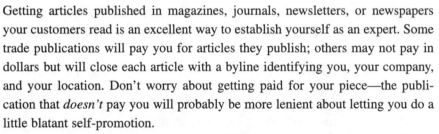

If you can't write well enough for publication, hire a freelance writer to do it for you. Your business is judged by the type of marketing material you produce. Make sure that everything you produce is of the highest quality you can afford. If you hand out shoddy, unprofessional marketing materials to your prospects you will likely lose prospects to your competitors. Nothing makes a person look less competent than a poorly written piece, especially when it sits next to better articles.

> If you can't afford a freelance writer, contact the school newspaper at the university closest to your house. Get the editor on the phone, as he or she is typically the best writer on the staff. You can hire a college kid for a fraction of what it costs for a professional writer!

Allies

Distribute Press Releases

The purpose of a press release is to get the media interested in covering your story, either in a printed news story, on the radio, or on television. Ultimately, you want to generate calls from people who see the story. Again, if you can't write well, farm this task out.

> What exactly is a press release? A press release is a standard document that informs the media about your service. Rather than selling your services, it will simply inform your audience about some aspect of what you do.

By the Numbers

Public Presentations

Public presentations and free seminars are another publicity-generating method to communicate your marketing message and are especially useful if you are not comfortable conveying it in writing.

Internet Marketing

There is possibly no more cost-effective method of marketing to your prospects than the Internet. Practically every business has its own Web page, and thousands of individuals have personal pages. In today's Internet-based culture, the only mistake you can make is not to have a Web page—even if it just lists basic contact information for your business, with a logo and slogan slapped on top of it.

As the Internet continues to expand and grow there will be a variety of marketing methods. Currently these options include:

- Banner advertising
- Link exchanges
- Newsgroups
- Bulletin and message boards
- E-mail campaigns
- Informational databases
- Directory listings

Another way to use the Internet is to identify prospects. If you market to businesses in a particular market, for example, use the Internet to search for companies that fit your prospect profile. Then, write down the companies' addresses and phone numbers so you can contact them directly.

We could devote an entire book to Internet marketing of your business; however, I'm devoting this book to Winning the Cash Flow War! Check out what your competitors are doing on the Web—do a Google search on their name, your industry, your hometown. You might be surprised at the depth of important information you come up with.

If using the internet as a form of marketing, *never*, under any circumstance, use spam e-mail. Period!

Marching Orders for Marketing 101

✔ **You must have at least a basic understanding of marketing to launch a business.**

✔ **You need to develop a marketing plan and a marketing budget.**

✔ **Stick to the plan, and don't stop advertising just because you have all the business you can handle.**

Understanding Franchises

> *Spare no expense to save money on this one.*
> —Samuel Goldwyn, movie mogul

Franchising is a business opportunity that may fit the bill perfectly for Cash Flow Warriors looking to start up their own businesses but who don't necessarily have an idea of their own to kick off. This chapter illustrates just the sort of thing you should be looking for—the good franchise opportunities offer training, marketing and advertising support, and the opportunity to grow a business with an eye towards expansion or future sales. Of course, some franchise opportunities are better than others, and we'll talk about the steps you can take to identify a good opportunity in this chapter.

So just what is a franchise? Your local Dunkin' Donuts™ or Subway™ sandwich shops are perfect examples (and good franchises to own!). Even though these are national chains, the stores are owned locally. Here's a very basic definition of how it works: You (the franchisee) pay an initial fee and ongoing royalties to a franchisor (the parent company). In return, the franchisee gains the use of a trademark, ongoing support from the franchisor, and the right to use the franchisor's system of doing business and sell its products or services.

Allies

> **Beyond the bang of a well-known brand name, buying a franchise offers many advantages that are not available to Cash Flow Warriors starting a business from scratch. The most significant is that you get a proven system of operation and training in how to use it. New franchisees can avoid a lot of the mistakes start-up entrepreneurs typically make because the franchisor has *already* perfected daily operations through trial and error. Remember, if you go under, it makes the franchisor look bad, too; a good franchisor will make sure you learn everything you need to know before you open up.**

Another large advantage for Cash Flow Warriors when considering their own business is the fact that franchisees enjoy the benefit of strength in numbers. You'll gain from economies of scale in buying materials, supplies and services, such as advertising, as well as in negotiating for locations and lease terms. By comparison, independent operators have to negotiate on their own, which usually means getting less favorable terms. Depending on the sort of business opportunity you embark on, some suppliers won't even deal with new businesses or will reject your business outright because your account just isn't big enough.

On the surface of it, owning a franchise seems like a pretty good deal, doesn't it? Let's take a look at the major *advantages* and *disadvantages* of purchasing a franchise. There are good and bad points on each side, and you need to think about all these points before you decide which way to go.

The following are major advantages of buying a franchise:

- Business failure risk is vastly reduced when the business plan has already proved to be successful in the marketplace.

- Turnkey operation with standardized products and systems, and standardized financial and accounting systems.

- As well as sales and marketing assistance, financial assistance may be available from the parent company.

- Using an established trademark saves the business owner the cost of creating and advertising a name that customers will recognize.

- Group advertising and purchasing reduces your cost of operations, making the day-to-day expenses less costly.

- Ongoing training provided by the parent company gives you operational expertise that you would otherwise have to learn through trial and error.

- Expansion is a natural part of franchising; operating a successful franchise, in most cases, leads to purchasing second and third franchises in the same organization.

The following are major disadvantages of buying a franchise:

- People with a strong independent streak, and Cash Flow Warriors who see themselves as innovative entrepreneurial types, will not enjoy the strict operational requirements and specifications of a franchised business. When you purchase a franchise, you must play by the franchisor's rules.

- You are not in control. You have signed a binding contract that states that you must follow all corporate level directives. You cannot differentiate in the slightest way from the franchisor's product line or business methods. The fact that you can walk into a Subway in Yuma, Arizona or in the Yukon and get the same sandwich the same way is one of the things that makes it a great franchise—but it just may be an aspect of the business that bores you to tears.

- Some franchise systems are better than others. Some franchisors offer inadequate training, do not have a good job support systems for their owners, and will not make the best use of your advertising dollars.

- You're never done paying for a franchise. In addition to the one-time charge that a franchisor charges you for the privilege of using the business concept, attending their training program, and learning the entire business, there will also be an ongoing royalty fee.

- Don't forget the advertising costs. As a rule of thumb, the cost for franchise royalties and advertising contributions is between 6 percent and 12 percent of the gross sales of the business, payable weekly or monthly. Forever.

With that all said, you can still make a lot of money once you're up and running with a few franchises. If you're the kind of person who doesn't mind playing by somebody else's rules as long you know there may be a big payoff one day, then franchising is for you. But, and you need to be honest with yourself, if following directions from corporate headquarters would eventually begin to irritate you, then franchises are not the way for you to go. If you're the kind of Warrior who absolutely needs to go into battle solo, I've got some other battle gear that you can try on for size. But, if you can follow orders well enough, the payoffs in franchises can be spectacular.

Choosing the Right Franchise

Just like anything else, there are good and bad franchise opportunities. And just like with any other business opportunity, if you do the proper preparation before you embark on a course of action, you'll be able to sift out the bad franchises and choose a good company to sign up with.

First, just so you can get an idea of how varied the opportunities in franchising are, let me show you a list of the Top 30 Franchise Opportunities as listed by Entrepenuer.com. I'll also include some ballpark figures for what it costs to open up one of these franchises. Just look at the diversity of industries covered in the top 30 alone (there are over 500 franchise opportunities listed on that site)—and the start-up costs range from just a few thousand dollars to over a million.

- **Subway:** sandwiches and salads. Cost: $86,000 to $213,000.
- **Curves:** women's fitness and weight-loss centers. Cost: $35,600 to $41,000.
- **Quiznos:** sandwiches, soups, salads. Cost: $208,400 to $243,800.
- **7-Eleven:** Convenience store. Cost: Price varies.
- **Jackson Hewitt Tax Service:** tax preparation services. Cost: $47,400 to $75,200.
- **The UPS Store:** postal, business services. Cost: $141,000 to $239,000.
- **McDonald's:** hamburgers, chicken, salads. Cost: $506,000 to $1,600,000.
- **Jani-King:** commercial cleaning. Cost: $11,300 to $34,100.
- **Dunkin' Donuts:** donuts and baked goods. Cost: $255,700 to $ 1,100,000.
- **Baskin-Robbins:** ice cream. Cost: $145,700 to $527,800.

- **Jiffy Lube:** oil change. Cost: $174,000 to $194,000.

- **InterContinental Hotels Group:** Cost: Price varies.

- **Sonic Drive-In:** drive-in restaurant. Cost: $710,000 to $2,300,000.

- **Domino's Pizza:** pizza, buffalo wings. Cost: $141,400 to $415,100.

- **Super 8 Motels:** economy motels. Cost: $291,000 to $2,300,000.

- **Kumon Math & Reading Centers:** supplemental education. Cost: $8,000 to $30,000.

- **Chem-Dry:** carpet, drapery, and upholstery cleaning. Cost: $23,600 to $82,800.

- **ServiceMaster:** commercial/residential cleaning. Cost: $26,000 to $90,000.

- **REMAX:** Real estate. Cost: $20,000 to $200,000.

- **Snap On Tools:** professional tools and equipment. Cost: $17,600 to $254,700.

- **Burger King:** burgers, fries, breakfast. Cost: $294,000 to $2,800,000.

- **Jan Pro:** commercial cleaning. Cost: $1,000 to $14,000.

- **Merle Norman:** cosmetics studios. Cost: $33,100 to $162,000.

- **Papa John's:** pizza. Cost: $250,000.

- **Jazzercise:** dance/exercise classes. Cost $2,600 to $32,800.

- **Radio Shack:** consumer electronics. Cost: $60,000.

- **Days Inns:** hotels and inns. Cost: $400,000 to $5,400,000.

- **Liberty Tax Service:** income-tax preparation services. Cost: $38,100 to $49,100.

- **Midas Auto:** auto repair and maintenance services. Cost: $379,400 to $528,000.

- **Dairy Queen:** ice cream/sandwiches. Cost: $655,000 to $1,300,000.

You'll notice a wide price range in some franchise opportunities. That's because with some franchises you can go from just a kiosk in a mall to a free-standing building with your own parking lot. That's just one of the many decisions you'll be making after you narrow your choices. The best way to begin the selection process is to learn how to spot a good franchise opportunity.

Avoid a "franchise" that requires you to own a piece of the company or makes your income dependent on its actions. This often happens with scams like ATM machines and the like (where you invest in the machine and they put it somewhere for you). If you are in doubt, contact the Better Business Bureau and check them out first.

Here are six Action Items you can follow that will help you pick out the winners from the losers:

1. **Identify an industry.** Start by investigating various industries that interest *you* to find those with growth potential. For example, if you can't stand the thought of hanging out in a garage all day, then cross Jiffy Lube and Midas right off your list. Narrow the choices down to a few industries you are most interested in.

2. **Look at the area you want to work in.** Is there a market for the type of business you're thinking about? If you live in an urban area, chances are there are already well-established 7-Eleven, WaWa, or Circle K franchises in your neighborhood.

3. **Does the industry make sense?** A perfect example of a new franchising opportunity that doesn't make sense to me is the new low-carb food outlets that are opening up. The whole low-carb thing has moved from a fad to a trend so all the big supermarkets are carrying more and more low-carb items every day. You can't compete with the Wal-Marts of the world, so don't even try!

4. **After you find an industry, make some calls.** Let's say you decide that a commercial cleaning franchise would be just right for the geographic area you're looking to operate in. Your next step is to contact all the franchise companies in those fields and ask them for information. Any reputable company will be happy to send you information at no cost. If they want to charge you for information, cross them off your list. If they don't respond promptly, cross them off your list—it can only be indicative of future non-support down the road.

5. **Use these sites to find contact information.** The Internet is a great place to pick up contact points for information on franchises in your chosen industry. Try *entreprenuer.com*, *franchisegator.com*, *franchisesolutions.com*, and others. Or, simply type the name of the company you're interested in into a search engine like Google, and the contact information will be on the site.

6. **How much money are you willing to put up?** You can eliminate a lot of choices just by putting a limit on the sort of money you're willing to invest. While some franchisors offer financing, you may want to really, really investigate these franchises. It could be a sign that the companies can't attract blue chip franchisees, or it could simply be a bad business model of a company expanding too fast (like Boston Market did). Or, it could be a great opportunity. But make sure you check out a company that offers financing—get a copy of their latest annual report, or pay a few bucks and get a Dunn and Bradstreet report on the company. Do your due diligence!

> Don't pay anyone *anything* for the initial information on a franchise. You can do this all for free—just use the sites to get an idea about what franchising companies exist in your chosen industry.

Now That You've Got the Preliminary Information

Once you've gotten the information from the franchisors, you need to mount up and make some inspection tours, soldier! You should have, by this time, focused in on an industry and a price range, and that should narrow your choices down to a manageable number.

Here are the next steps in continuing your franchise opportunity investigation:

1. **Go to a franchise trade show.** You can find a good list of upcoming shows at www.franchiseworks.com. You can also do an Internet search on trade shows—just type "franchise trade show" in a search engine and

you'll be set. There will be one coming to a city near you in the near future—guaranteed. Going to these shows is an easy way to gather preliminary information and survey the field in a time-efficient fashion. Dress in business attire, but make sure you have comfortable shoes. A long day at a trade show can be tough if your feet are killing you halfway through.

WARNING
Land Mines

> **If a company has an awful booth at the trade show, pass them up. If they can't market themselves to people that are self-selected to seek information on their company, how can they possibly market your franchise to the general public? Pass on these losers and hit a booth that has a professional appearance and well-presented marketing materials.**

2. **At the show.** Maximize your time; study the floor plan before you hit the convention hall and map out a campaign that will enable you to gather information form your targeted companies. Allow time to visit companies you hadn't preselected—there's always the possibility you could get in on the ground floor of the next McDonald's—but be sure you are well-armed with skepticism. Make these companies prove themselves to you, that's why they paid to be there.

3. **Gather information.** You're at this show to pick up information. Gather all the documentation you can; ask if a company will let you have a copy of a standard contract. Some companies will, some won't. Ask to see the UFOC (Uniform Franchise Offering Circular): This is a document that contains information franchisors must provide you by law, to assist you in analyzing the merits of your potential franchisor. A franchisor must provide a prospective franchisee with a UFOC at their first face-to-face meeting or at least ten business days prior to the signing of the franchise agreement, whichever is earlier. Get business cards, in case you want to follow up.

4. **Select companies to interview.** After you've reviewed all the documentation and the marketing collateral, you need to sit down with a few of your top candidates and get down to brass tacks—ask some hard questions and get substantial answers.

Setting Up the Franchisor Interview

If you've been following the Action Items, you're continuing your selection process by whittling out the less desirable industries and franchises. Now that you've got the business cards from the show, it's time to get on the horn and set up a face-to-face interview.

These are the sorts of question you should ask—I have adapted some questions for you from the *www.enterpreneur.com* Web site (which is really a great site for you to check out when you're considering franchises). You can add your own questions, and customize the questions a bit to better fit the industry you're investigating. But you shouldn't pass on any of these questions; these are all things you need to know.

Interrogation Techniques

During your interview, you'll need to get some concrete answers to what you should consider key areas to help you determine the strength of the franchise. If the franchisor can't answer these questions on the spot, it's okay if he or she sends you the information later, via e-mail or regular mail. Franchisors can't be expected to have all information at their fingertips. If, however, the franchisor rep *refuses* to answer some of these questions, or promises to get back to you and never does, then you should consider this failure a red flag and cross the opportunity off your list:

- Ask what the pretax net profits of existing operations are and compare them against the earnings statement or pro forma that the franchisor should have already supplied you.

- Find out what is included in the training program, field assistance, store design, facility construction, site selection, and feasibility studies.

- Will there be any additional working capital required after the initial fee and investment, and if so, how much?

- How will the franchisor arrange for the supply of product to the business? Ask to see a current price sheet.

- Ask the franchisor to detail exactly what the territorial restrictions and protections are.

- Find out how many franchises have been sold to investors in the state you will be operating in during the last 12 months, and how many have opened a franchised business in that time.

- Ask if the company has any plans for further expansion in the state. Has it identified any locations it plans to develop?

- If purchasing a current franchise, ask to see the operating books and records of the business for the past two years.

- What type of support will the franchisor provide once your franchise has opened its doors?

- Find out if any franchisees have been terminated. If some have, ask the franchisor to detail the reasons. Have any franchisees failed or gone bankrupt?

- What kind of financing is available from the franchisor, if any?

- Find out if there are any current lawsuits pending against the franchisor. Have them elaborate on any past judgments.

- Find out how disputes between the franchisor and franchisees are settled.

- Will the franchisor assist in site selection? It will be of enormous help if it does. Whether it does or not, do your own demographic study so you are familiar with the profile of the audience within the market area.

- Don't be afraid to ask questions. And don't be afraid that you'll appear foolish because, frankly, very few people understand the franchise agreement or the UFOC in full. Primarily, you're trying to pinpoint any problems that may exist in a franchise. Don't just settle on any franchise.

- If you run across a franchisor that is reluctant to pass along a list of current franchisees, makes promises that you'll earn a fortune on a limited investment, insists on deposits for holding a franchise unit, tries to convince you to sign before someone else does, or is full of empty rhetoric when answering your questions, head for the door. These are franchisors that are probably trying to pull a fast one to get your money.

Things to Keep in Mind during Your Interview with Franchisors

While researching this chapter, we came across a group known as the Canadian Franchise Association. You can find them at *www.cfa.ca*. They have a list on their

Web site that is sort of a gold standard that they apply to franchisee-franchisor relationships, and if a company hits all these marks, then they can be awarded by the CFA. I thought that these standards summed up exactly the sort of things you should be looking out for when you get into a franchisee-franchisor relationship, and you might want to keep this list in mind while you're interviewing franchisors.

- **The selection process.** The franchise follows a system of presale steps to match qualified candidates with the franchise, so the needs of both parties are met. Franchisees are told what to expect financially, and are encouraged to get independent legal and accounting advice. A reasonable time is allowed to review the offering.

- **The disclosure policy.** Franchisees receive a disclosure document, which is updated immediately whenever the franchisor makes a significant change.

- **The franchise information package.** The franchisor provides sufficient documentation for the franchisee to make an informed decision. The franchisee also gets plenty of help in selecting a site, negotiating a lease, and financing the business.

- **The initial and on-going training.** Franchisees undergo a comprehensive training program and receive thorough and up-to-date operating manuals that prepare them for all aspects of business. Franchisees are prepared for day-to-day operations, marketing, business development, and administration. They can expect help with their grand opening, assistance immediately following the startup of the business, and periodic refresher courses to reinforce the franchisees' concepts and practices. Ongoing training is available to keep franchisees current with industry trends, and allow them to improve their skills and competitiveness for as long as they're part of the franchise system.

- **The level of support and communication.** Formalized support and communication indicate that the franchisor is prepared to address any problems as soon as they arise. The system has measures in place that:

  ○ Preserve the integrity of the system for the benefit of all its franchisees.

  ○ Allow franchisee input and resolutions of concerns.

  ○ Inspect and evaluate stores effectively.

- Create and analyze budgets and cash flow projections.
- Provide system-wide communication.
- Provide comprehensive launch of new products.
- Allow for franchisee input into programs and concept development—for example, on advisory councils, special committees, or associations.
- Provide administrative, financial, and planning support prior to store opening.
- Meet the franchisee's expectations in terms of financial disclosure, based on actual performance of existing locations and a realistic forecast for reaching the financial break-even point.

- **Effective marketing.** The franchisor provides effective marketing strategies and materials that help the franchise become profitable and increase market share. The franchisee has some input into marketing, with full disclosure of the use of advertising funds.

- **The ability to solve problems.** A number of common issues come up in the life of any franchise, and the franchisor should be prepared to help franchisees resolve them. The problem-solving mechanism pinpoints trouble early, helps underperforming locations or franchisees in crisis get back on their feet, deals with disagreements in good faith, deals with disability or death of a franchisee compassionately, and helps with financing and renegotiation of loans or leases.

- **The viability of the concept.** The franchisor makes sure the concept stays viable over the years through research and development, technical and marketing improvements, competitive analysis, and well-defined strategies for growth. At the store level, the franchisor conducts thorough market analysis to determine the viability of each location.

- **The corporate culture.** The franchisor cultivates a corporate culture that embodies a spirit of integrity, support, compassion, and fair dealing toward its franchisees.

- **Rewards and recognition.** Franchisees are recognized and rewarded for outstanding achievements in sales, quality of operations, and other essential areas of success.

Source: Canadian Franchise Association

The Final Information-Gathering Step

It's time to get back on your horse, soldier. You've interviewed the franchisors, held them up to the standards I've laid out, and now you're down to one or two choices. Now you need to go talk to fellow franchisees.

You should have gotten some contact names in the UFOC the franchisor supplied you. Get on the horn with a few of these folks and see if you can't set up a meeting with them. They should be willing to talk to you—after all, it's only in both of your best interests to check out a future co-franchisee. Remember: If the company you're looking at has a franchise already in the next town over, the performance of that franchise will reflect on your own (and vice versa). If people have a bad experience at one Burger King, they'll carry that opinion with them into the next Burger King they walk into!

At any rate, you'll want to ask the franchisee some pretty specific questions.

- Could you tell me how a normal day goes for you?

- Was the training from the franchisor adequate? Did you feel you were prepared when you opened your doors for the first time?

- Does the franchisor respond quickly when you ask for assistance and support?

- Does the franchisor follow through on its promises?

- Was the investment and cost information supplied to you by the company realistic? Or were there hidden expenses?

- Do you feel like you're getting bang for your buck when it comes to the advertising fees? Are you getting good marketing support from the company?

- Are you making the sales and profits that you were led to believe you would?

- Are there expansion opportunities for additional franchise ownership in this system?

- If you had to do this all over again, would you make this investment again?

- Have you had any problems or conflicts with the franchisor? How were they resolved?

Don't be afraid to ask tough questions, and get a little nosy. Don't be shy! You're thinking about sinking a significant amount of time and money into this thing. Some people will answer you truthfully, and some will tell you to hit the road, so you should probably schedule a few of these interviews if you can.

Does It Still Seem Like a Good Idea to You?

You've done all your soul-searching regarding whether you want to be involved in a business that has a parent company to which you are tightly bound. After all of your research into viability, location, the parent company, and so forth, does this still seem like something you want to do? If you've found a good franchise opportunity that offers training, marketing and advertising support, and the opportunity to grow a business with an eye towards expansion or future sales, maybe this is the final weapon you need in your Cash Flow War arsenal.

If a franchise seems to fit all the criteria I've laid out, then this might very well be your ticket to victory in the Cash Flow War.

Marching Orders for Understanding Franchises

- ✔ Identify an industry.
- ✔ Research all the main franchisors.
- ✔ Ask all the right questions before you commit and sign a binding contract.
- ✔ Patience and due diligence are the keys to choosing a good franchise.

Bad Business "Opportunities" to Avoid

> *Success in business requires training and discipline and hard work. But if you're not frightened by these things, the opportunities are just as great today as they ever were.*
>
> —David Rockefeller, US banker

I stated in the introduction to this book what I thought about get-rich-quick schemes: Either they don't work, or the only people who get rich are the ones who invent them and then get unsuspecting entrepreneurs to buy into them. In this chapter I'll show you how to spot some of the bad business opportunities out there with a special emphasis on a particular sort of business I think you should avoid like the plague: multilevel marketing opportunities (sometimes known as network marketing).

Since by now you're a valiant Cash Flow Warrior, we can assume that we're all honest people here. And since we're all adults, we know by now that not everybody is as honest as we are. As a matter of fact, there are some real rats out there.

Spotting the rats is no easy task. There are plenty of good, honest, hard-working individuals out there who are seeking to expand their businesses in a straightforward fashion by marketing them to new entrepreneurs. There are also plenty of companies, like my own, that have developed a secondary revenue stream by teaching a unique philosophy of wealth building. So while there are certain clues to look for when spotting a scam, remember that these clues I mention don't necessarily mean that an opportunity is a scam. What you need to do is to keep an eye out for the clues, and then submit the opportunity to the Action Items I lay out later in this chapter. If it can't pass the Action Items scrutiny, then stay away—but if the opportunity holds up, then it might just be a legitimate Cash Flow War strategy.

One clue may be the type of business opportunity being advertised. According to the Federal Trade Commission, fraud is most often associated with vending machine, display rack, pay phone, medical billing, ATMs, work-at-home, and some Internet-related business opportunities.

Another clue may be how the opportunity is presented. Promotions for fraudulent business opportunities often appear in the classified pages of daily and weekly newspapers and magazines, as well as online. They also may be marketed in television commercials and infomercials. Be careful: Don't just assume an infomercial is a scam. In fact, the people conducting scams often don't like the exposure of television media. I use infomercials sometimes, and they can be a very effective way to disseminate information. If an infomercial is backed up by seminars and all the appropriate documentation and credentials you'll learn to look for in the Action Items, then you'll probably come to the realization that it could be a good business opportunity.

Some scam artists use tried-and-true bait: Great money (say, $160,000 a year) in a short period (weeks or months) for no work at all or very little effort. Guess what? Nobody ever made six figures without putting in a little sweat equity! They trumpet an ideal work situation—the ability to set your own hours, be your own boss, and work from home.

What the ads don't say is that the scam artists behind these so-called business opportunities aren't interested in helping you run a successful business: They're interested only in getting your money. To get you to buy in, they may mislead you about the business opportunity's earnings potential and promote a nonexistent opportunity that has little chance of succeeding—for example, a business with little or no market. They may doom your chances of success by providing cheap, low-quality, or outdated merchandise; poor-quality equipment (such as defective pay phones and vending machines); and locations that get little foot traffic, like rural gas stations, out-of-the-way snack shops or stores in deserted strip malls.

What it all boils down to is that you need to thoroughly check out a business opportunity before you invest your time and money into it.

How to Spot a Scam

In Chapter 20 I explained the franchise industry to you, and I think you'll agree that there are some fine opportunities in franchising. We also laid out some pretty clear rules on how to spot good franchising opportunities. However, there are some real scam artists out there, too—just waiting to take first-time entrepreneurs to the cleaners. Before you get involved with a franchising opportunity or buy into a similar situation, run the whole deal through these Action Items and see how it stands up to the scrutiny.

- Run—don't walk—if you see the words "get-rich-quick" or "make money in your sleep" in the advertising.

- If the company can't supply written proof of the claims in their presentations, especially those about success rates, just say no.

- Be skeptical of the experts who endorse a product—especially if they are paid by the advertiser.

- Be very careful when listening to or reading testimonials. These may well be paid for and may not actually reflect the experience of most consumers.

- Don't even think about buying into a scheme if the company reps can't answer your questions clearly, give evasive answers, or just aren't willing to answer your questions at all.

- Before you buy anything, perform your due diligence and decide whether the price reflects a fair market value.

- If the promoter requires a deposit, tell him or her that you'll establish an escrow account where the deposit can be maintained by a third party until you actually make the deal. If the rep balks, you should walk.

- Anytime some slick representative starts spinning a yarn about promises of free funding or low-interest government loans, take off your rose-colored glasses. This sort of money is available only in very limited circumstances.

- Don't ever let yourself be pressured into purchasing anything immediately. If it's truly a good business opportunity, the company or rep won't need to give you a hard sell, because plenty of qualified prospects will be lined up. Good opportunities are never sold through high-pressure tactics.

- If the business opportunity involves selling products from well-known companies, get on the phone with the legal department of the company whose merchandise you would be selling. Ask some pertinent question, such as "Are the business opportunity and its promoter actually affiliated with the company?" Ask whether the company has ever threatened trademark action against the business opportunity promoter.

- Before you buy anything, ask what the company needs to know about you to fulfill their qualifying requirements. If they don't seem too interested in your background, abilities, and financial status, you can be pretty sure this is not a good opportunity.

- Here's one that will knock a lot of scam artists right out of the picture: Ask to see a written copy of their refund policy. Do they put their money where their mouth is? In my Cash Flow Trainings, people can come to a full one-third of the training. If they decide the business is not for them (for any reason), they can walk and get all their money back. Why would I do that? Because the opportunity is real and I want people to make an educated decision. Scam artists will apply pressure and go with "no refunds." If you don't have some sort of trial period, you may want to reconsider.

- And finally, if everything else checks out, make sure that you take the time to check out the company with your local consumer protection agency, Better Business Bureau, and state attorney general's office. This way you can find out if the company has any unresolved consumer complaints on file. One or two unresolved complaints are not necessarily a deal-killer—we all know how many spurious lawsuits are filed everyday. But if a company has half a dozen cases on the books against them, it's time for you to walk.

You Can Call on the Feds

The Federal Trade Commission is also on the case here—if you feel like you may be walking into a scam, you can call them up and have them run the whole deal through their database. It's nice to see your tax dollars at work for you! They also have a great Web site that you can access, and it is a powerful tool to help you identify scam tactics. You can find it at: *http://www.consumer.gov/sentinel.*

> **From the FTC Web site**
>
> **The FTC works for the consumer to prevent fraudulent, deceptive, and unfair business practices in the marketplace and to provide information to help consumers spot, stop, and avoid them. To file a complaint or to get free information on consumer issues, visit *www.ftc.gov* or call toll-free, 1-877-FTC-HELP (1-877-382-4357). The FTC enters Internet, telemarketing, identity theft, and other fraud-related complaints into Consumer Sentinel, a secure, online database available to hundreds of civil and criminal law enforcement agencies in the United States and abroad.**

Allies

You're now heavily armed, and you should feel confident when taking the field against a possible scam artist. Use the Action Items, access the government resources available to you, and do your due diligence and you will almost certainly avoid getting ripped off. However, and unfortunately in this case it's a pretty big "however," there are some scams out there that sometimes fly just under the radar when you're attempting to identify a scam. For the rest of the chapter I'm going to show you just how to identify the *Land mines* known as multilevel marketing or network marketing companies.

Exposing the Multilevel Marketing Myth

Here's one quick way to avoid multilevel marketing traps: Always remember that your friends and family are your friends and family, and they are not business opportunities!

Just what is a multilevel marketing plan? Also known as network or matrix marketing, these plans are a way of selling goods or services through distributors. What the come-on usually boils down to is if you sign up as a distributor, you will receive commissions on whatever sales you make of the plan's goods or services, in addition you get a commission on those of other people you *recruit* as distributors. The recruiting is key, and that's one of the big tip-offs to alert you to the fact that this is a multilevel marketing plan.

The hook to get you to recruit is that multilevel marketing plans usually promise to pay commissions through two or more levels of recruits, which are known as the distributor's "downline." As in all pyramid schemes, the incomes of those distributors at the top and the profits to the sponsoring corporations come from a continuous influx of new investors at the bottom. And the people at the bottom never get paid!

Land Mines

If a plan offers to pay commissions for recruiting new distributors, walk away! According to the FTC, most states outlaw this practice, which is known as "pyramiding." State laws against pyramiding say that a multilevel marketing plan should only pay commissions for retail sales of goods or services, not for recruiting new distributors.

Why would something that seems to pay everybody be prohibited? Because pyramid plans that pay commissions for recruiting new distributors will eventually collapse. This is a no-brainer because you will eventually reach a point where there are no new distributors to be recruited. And when a pyramid-type plan collapses, just about everybody (except, of course, the inventor and the first few in) will lose his or her money.

Allies

What follows is a quick checklist from the FTC that will help you to identify shady multilevel marketing plans. The Federal Trade Commission cannot tell you whether a particular multilevel marketing plan is legal. Nor can it give you advice about whether to join such a plan. You must make that decision yourself. However, the FTC suggests that you use common sense, and consider these seven tips when you make your decision:

1. Avoid any plan that includes commissions for recruiting additional distributors. It may be an illegal pyramid.

2. Beware of plans that ask new distributors to purchase expensive inventory. These plans can collapse quickly—and also may be thinly disguised pyramids.

3. Be cautious of plans that claim you will make money through continued growth of your "downline"—the commissions on sales made by new distributors you recruit—rather than through sales of products you make yourself.

4. Beware of plans that claim to sell miracle products or promise enormous earnings. Just because a promoter of a plan makes a claim doesn't mean it's true! Ask the promoter of the plan to substantiate claims with hard evidence.

5. Beware of shills. These are people paid by a plan's promoter to describe their fictional success in earning money through the plan.

6. Don't pay or sign any contracts in an "opportunity meeting" or any other high-pressure situation. Insist on taking your time to think over a decision to join. Talk it over with your spouse, a knowledgeable friend, an accountant, or lawyer.

7. Do your homework! Check with your local Better Business Bureau and state attorney general about any plan you're considering—especially when the claims about the product or your potential earnings seem too good to be true.

Why a Multilevel Marketing Plan Must Eventually Fail

All you have to do is take a hard look at the business plan that these people are perpetrating—it's flawed! Multilevel marketing plans have been around for almost thirty years now, so they can no longer claim to be a new and ground-breaking way of changing either the marketplace or the way goods and services are sold. These plans have been tried and, for the most part, have failed. In fact, some have been miserable failures despite the fact that they offered excellent products.

The problem is that while the product or service may well be good, the product is not the real incentive to join a multilevel marketing plan. If the product was so good, people would already be out pushing this particular product or service in the real world. The product is simply an excuse to make the real money-making engine look legitimate.

The whole multilevel marketing plan pitch boils down to this: A promoter convinces you that if you can convince ten people that everyone needs this product or service and they can convince ten people, and so on, you will make lots of money. And as long as you actually sell a few products along the way, it is not technically a pyramid scheme and it makes it all legal.

But the way to make money in all these plans is clearly not by only selling product, or else traditional markets would push the product. The hook here is selling others on the prospect of easy money. And that prospect is essentially flawed, because for anyone but the people who begin these schemes, the market eventually dries up. It's just simple math, and you don't even need the Calculator Clarity you learned back in Chapter 12 to figure it out.

Multilevel marketing plans work by geometric expansion where you get ten people to become distributors and they sponsor ten more to sponsor ten more, and on and on. The promoters usually show this as an expanding matrix or network of distributors (they never, *ever* say pyramid!), with corresponding royalties or commissions at various levels. Common sense alone will tell you that this cannot work. Once you get three levels deep, you're already talking about 1,000 distributors! At six levels deep, that would be 1,000,000 people who believe they can make money selling whatever the product is. But who can they sell this to? Can you think of a single product that needs one million distributors? It's a sucker bet!

By now you'll have figured out that the multilevel marketing plans' true target market constituency is not the consuming public at large; they're really aiming at people who are looking to make some extra money. Unfortunately, after a few years of economic downturn and jobs shipping overseas, the market for potential new distributors is growing.

Promises of quick and easy financial success without too much work play pretty well in a poor economy, so you can see why the marketing push or thrust of multilevel marketing plans is targeted at prospective distributors rather than at product promotions to purchasers. The plan's true products are not long-distance phone services, vitamins or whatever, but the investments that people get suckered into who lay out for distributorships.

They Can't All Be Bad, Can They?

I know what you're thinking: *Well, at least some of the multilevel marketing plans must be good; Amway has been around forever, hasn't it? And now they've moved onto the Web, with their Quixtar brand, so they must be okay.* Well, I don't want to get involved in a fight with a big corporation like Amway, so I'll let someone else carry the ball here. Here's a direct quote from an opinion filed with a Texas court in regards to a case in which Amway was being sued:

> It is my opinion that the Amway business is run in a manner that is parallel to that of major organized crimes groups, in particular the Mafia. The structure and function of major organized crime groups, generally consisting of associated enterprises engaging in patterns of legal and illegal activity, was the prototype forming the basis for federal and state racketeering legislation that I have been involved in drafting. The same structure and function, with associated enterprises engaging in patterns of legal and illegal activity, is found in the Amway business.

> —G. Robert Blakely, *professor of law, Notre Dame University*

Mail Call

What Can Happen to You if You Join a Multilevel Marketing Plan?

In the event that you actually lose your mind, forget everything you've learned about Cash Flow War strategies, and join a multilevel marketing plan in a fit of temporary insanity, what's the worst that can happen to you? Maybe you lose a few hundred bucks, or a few grand, and you get a little embarrassed about being scammed and you move on. Well, unfortunately, that's not the case.

The Federal Trade Commission has a few things to say about your responsibilities as a member of a multilevel marketing plan. If you decide to become a distributor, then you are legally responsible for the claims you make about the company, its product, and the business opportunities it offers. That applies even if you're simply repeating claims you read in a company brochure or advertising flyer. When you promote the qualities of a product or service, you're obligated to present those claims truthfully and to ensure there's enough solid evidence to back them up. The Federal Trade Commission advises you to verify the research behind any claims about a product's performance before repeating those claims to a potential customer.

Likewise, if you decide to solicit new distributors, be aware that you're responsible for any claims you make about a distributor's earnings potential. Be sure to represent the opportunity honestly and to avoid making unrealistic promises. If those promises fall through, remember that you could be held liable.

The key point here is that you can be held *personally* liable—the rats that got you into this whole mess in the first place can leave you holding the bag!

One Last Line of Defense

Perhaps you're still thinking of getting into one of these plans, or some other shady business opportunity. Then despite all you've learned here, at least take advantage of the business opportunity laws your home state may have in place. As of 2004, 23 states have business opportunity laws. Most of these laws prohibit sales of business opportunities unless the seller gives potential purchasers a presale disclosure document that has first been filed with a designated state agency. Since they have to file with the state, it's harder for scam artists to fold their tents in the middle of the night and skedaddle with your money.

If you are considering purchasing a work-at-home or other business opportunity, or buying into a multilevel marketing plan, and you live in a state with a business opportunity law, you really should find out more about the protection provided by your state statute before you invest. And if the state you live in doesn't provide this protection, just call the closest state on the list and see what information they may have about the opportunity you're looking into. Spending just a few minutes on the phone could save you some money and heartache down the road.

Marching Orders for Bad Business "Opportunities" to Avoid

✔ If you're considering a business opportunity, match it up against the Action Items and see if it can hold up to scrutiny.

✔ Be very, very skeptical about multilevel marketing plan claims. In fact, ignore them!

✔ Use government resources and Better Business Bureau available to you to make sure your business opportunity is legitimate.

22

Cashing In on Cash Flow

> *Opportunity is missed by most people because it is dressed in overalls and looks like work.*
>
> —Thomas A. Edison, inventor

Now we come to something close to home for me and one of my favorite parts of this book, where I get to discuss the business that I engage in everyday—the cash flow industry. Although this business has been the strategy that enabled me to win my personal Cash Flow War, for the purposes of this book I'd just like to offer some information on the industry as an alternative to the franchise route we spoke about in Chapter 20. If, after reading about this industry, you'd like to learn more about it, you will find information at *www.winningthecashwar.com*; there I provide some suggested reading and Web links.

What Is the "Cash Flow Industry?"

Simply put, the cash flow industry is the buying and brokering of privately held income streams in a secondary market. An income stream exists whenever somebody receives payments from somebody else; when the person who receives the payment is a person or a business, it's called a privately held income stream.

Let me simplify a bit. On one end of the financial spectrum there are banks. Banks are in business to lend people and businesses money. Banks don't buy privately held income streams. I, as a Cash Flow Specialist, on the other end of the financial spectrum, don't lend money. I buy and broker privately held income streams. And as a result of that, banks often refer business to me because I'm able to help their customers in ways they can't.

The cash flow industry has its roots in two seemingly unrelated methods of finance—owner financing and factoring. In an owner-financed sale, the seller accepts a promissory note as a portion of the purchase price for real estate or a business. The note is then secured by placing a lien on the property or business being sold. So the seller of the property now has a privately held income stream. Today's Cash Flow Specialist buys that income stream from the property estate seller at a discounted price, and then collects the money owed at full value from the purchaser of the property.

The second method of finance that impacted the development of the cash flow industry is factoring. Factoring has actually been around for hundreds of years but it's only recently that average folks have access to this market. It's fairly simple. When a business sells something to another business it sends the second business an invoice in order to collect the money due. The first business can either wait for the invoice to be paid (eventually), or it can sell the invoice to a *third party* (the factor, or Cash Flow Specialist) for a reduced amount. This is called factoring.

By the Numbers

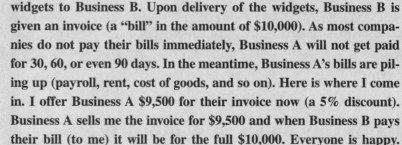

Here is an example of factoring: Business A sells $10,000 worth of widgets to Business B. Upon delivery of the widgets, Business B is given an invoice (a "bill" in the amount of $10,000). As most companies do not pay their bills immediately, Business A will not get paid for 30, 60, or even 90 days. In the meantime, Business A's bills are piling up (payroll, rent, cost of goods, and so on). Here is where I come in. I offer Business A $9,500 for their invoice now (a 5% discount). Business A sells me the invoice for $9,500 and when Business B pays their bill (to me) it will be for the full $10,000. Everyone is happy. Business A received cash today (for a slight discount), Business B received the widgets, and I received $500 for a short-term investment.

Obviously this is a simplified example which doesn't go into how I financed the whole transaction, but it illustrates what the business is about. It's actually fairly simple.

For smaller deals you can fund the whole thing and keep all the profits yourself. For larger deals, you'll need to learn about funding sources. But if we started talking about that, you'd have a whole different book in your hands.

Here is another example of how the cash flow industry works in real life: Let's imagine a guy named Michael owns a house and wants to sell it. His friend Bill says, "Michael, I'd be willing to buy your house, and I'd buy your house for the $120,000 that you're asking for it. However, Michael, I'm not going to write you a $120,000 check this evening. Instead, I'll give you a $20,000 check, and I'll give you my promise to pay you, evidenced by a promissory note, the other $100,000 over the next 30 years. I'll pay you with interest, and I'll pay you $877.57 per month, okay?"

Let's say that Michael accepts that offer, and Bill gives Michael the check and a promissory note for $100,000, and Michael gives Bill the deed to the house. At that point, Bill owns the house. By the same token, Michael no longer owns the house, but he does own something. He owns a $100,000 promissory note backed by a mortgage against the property, which gives him the right to receive payments from Bill of $877.57 per month.

The only thing that Michael cannot do with that note is go to the bank and trade that note for cash. Typically, at some point the Michaels of the world have a cash need and would prefer to have a lump sum of money. I buy cash flows at a discount. So I may pay Michael 90 cents on the dollar, or $90,000 for his $100,000 note. Michael walks away with cash and I get a good return on my investment.

Let me show you a bit of the money behind the scenes. This is the note as it exists in the beginning.

N	I	PV	PMT	FV
360	10	−100,000	887.57	0

Now, let's say I pay $90,000 for Michael's note.

N	I	PV	PMT	FV
360	???	−90,000	877.57	0

I am going to collect the same 360 payments of $877.57 but, since I purchased it at a slight discount ($10,000 in this case), I will effectively get a slightly better yield.

N	I	PV	PMT	FV
360	**11.3**	−100,000	877.57	0

Nothing changes for Bill, the purchaser of the house. He still pays $877.57 per month (only to me instead of Michael). Michael is happy because he gets a lump sum of money; Bill is happy because he gets the house, and I am happy because I get 11.3 percent on my money. If I didn't have the money to buy the note from Michael, than I could "broker" the note to a funder who will pay me a finder's fee for the note (often $1,500 to $4,000).

If it sounds like a good business, that's because it is.

Figuring Out Where You Might Fit into the Cash Flow Industry

To be successful in the cash flow business you need to have a focus. If you market for mortgage notes one week, then retail installment contracts the next, then viatical settlements the next, you will be going in all different directions, and chances are that you will never locate a prospect, let alone close a transaction.

A former student of mine recently created a Web site for his business. That part is good because I really believe you need some sort of Internet presence—whatever your business. But it needs to be targeted. On the site, he lists more than fifty different debt instruments that he transacts—meaning that he's trying to buy income streams in fifty different markets. While his intentions are good, he clearly has not chosen a niche. Until he does, it is doubtful that his marketing efforts will be successful because he doesn't know exactly *who* he's marketing his cash flow service to!

An informal self-assessment can help you decide which cash flow areas you want to pursue as your niche. Take a moment to examine the experience and skills you already have acquired. Then, consider how you could translate that knowledge into a cash flow opportunity.

Suppose, for example, you have worked in the construction industry. Could you use your knowledge of that field to refer construction receivables? Or perhaps your background is in health care. Could you use your understanding of the health care industry to refer medical receivables? Maybe you've worked with life insurance. Could use your experience to refer viatical settlements? Perhaps you have a background in real estate and are interested in private mortgages.

Even if you have no practical job experience that seems to lend itself to the cash flow industry, you still can choose a successful marketing niche. The fact is, many people who get into the industry had no prior experience in it. If your past experience seems irrelevant, simply evaluate your personal interests. Are you interested in helping individuals or businesses? Do you want to work with real estate? Or boats? Or judgements? Your interest level can effectively drive your decision about which debt instruments to focus on.

If you are still unsure which area of cash flow is best for you, ask yourself the following questions:

- Am I more comfortable in a casual or professional environment?

- Would I prefer having several repeat clients or many one-time clients?

- What contacts do I already have? Do I know a lot of real estate professionals, doctors, or attorneys?

- Do I communicate better with business people or consumers?

- Would I prefer to meet with clients in an office or at their kitchen table?

- What needs do I see in the local marketplace that are not being met by anyone else?

The way you answer these questions will guide you to an area that's right for you. For instance, if you like to work with people in need, viatical settlements may be your niche. If you prefer to work with business owners, business notes or business factoring may be better for you.

Action Items

Defining Your Marketing Niche

When you have a general idea which area will be your cash flow niche, you can hone in on your *marketing niche*. You can define your niche one of two ways—horizontally or vertically.

Horizontally

Defining your niche horizontally means choosing one cash flow service and providing it to as many prospects as possible. For example, you may choose to transact delinquent debt portfolios. You will seek clients in all types of businesses, as long as they are holding delinquent debt.

Vertically

Defining your niche vertically means choosing a specific type of prospect or referral source and offering many services. You may choose to market to attorneys, for example, and refer every type of income stream attorneys would encounter.

This "vertical marketing" strategy is becoming increasingly popular, especially among brokers who market for business-based income streams. Rather than finding many clients and offering one service, these brokers find very specific clients, and then provide a full range of business funding services. They may offer factoring, asset-based lending, and equipment leasing, and also refer their clients' delinquent debt accounts and retail installment agreements.

Narrowing Your Scope

After you define your marketing niche in broad terms, you need to *narrow your scope*, or refine your marketing niche, to make it more specific. To narrow your scope, you might consider such factors as:

- Geography (prospects or income streams in a particular city, county, or state).
- Industry or field (medical, international, legal, manufacturing).
- Size of transaction (transactions above or below a certain dollar amount).
- Annual sales revenue or number of employees (if marketing to businesses).
- Payors (only business payors, only consumer payors, or only government payors).

If possible, consider *more than one* of these factors and narrow your scope even further.

The concept of narrowing your niche can be illustrated by an inverted triangle. At the base (top) of the triangle is the broad overview of your prospects. At the point (bottom) of the triangle is a very detailed description of your prospects.

- Top: Businesses that generate more than $500,000 in annual sales.
- Middle: Businesses that generate more than $500,000 in annual sales and provide products or services under a government contract.
- Bottom: Businesses that generate more than $500,000 in annual sales, provide products and services under a government contract in the four surrounding counties.

At the bottom of the pyramid, your marketing niche should be so specific that with very little research you can compile names, addresses, and phone numbers for your potential prospects.

Identifying Prospects

Once you have defined your cash flow niche—and more specifically, your marketing niche—you are ready to identify qualified prospects. Who are qualified prospects?

In general terms, they are:

1. Individuals and businesses that currently hold the types of income streams you transact.

2. Individuals and businesses that are likely to hold those types of income streams in the future.

Identifying qualified prospects means pinpointing by name these individuals and businesses uniquely suited for your services. Why is it important to identify your prospects by name? Because you want your marketing efforts to be efficient and effective.

Suppose, for example, you decide to make lottery payments your cash flow niche. Very few people have use for your service. (Very few of us win the lottery.)

If you communicate to the general public through newspaper ads and mass mailers your marketing efforts would produce minimal results (if any). If, however, you identified exactly who had won the lottery in the past five years, and focused on communicating with those individuals, your marketing would prove much more effective.

Identifying prospects means more than simply having a general idea of the types of prospects you are seeking. It means having a list of the prospects you want to reach with their names, addresses, and phone numbers.

This Is Not for Everyone

Obviously, not every industry is suited to everyone, and this is certainly not a get-rich-quick industry. It requires work, but I have found most people are not afraid of work. I happen to like the cash flow industry—I like structuring deals, I like the rush I get when I close a transaction. I like helping people and I even like the negotiations that I engage in to finance my cash flow deals.

Allies

> If you would like to learn more about the cash flow industry, check out *cashflowwar.com* for ideas and links to other great Cash Flow Industry sites.

Marching Orders

Marching Orders for Cashing In on Cash Flow

✔ **Consider the cash flow industry as a business opportunity.**

✔ **Think about how your former experience may help you get started.**

✔ **Visit *www.winningthecashflowwar.com* for more info on the cash flow industry.**

23

The Real Estate Industry

> *Buy land. They've stopped making it.*
>
> —Mark Twain, author

I have always loved this quote. A large percentage of millionaires in this nation have made their fortune in real estate, so why can't you?

If you're thinking about going into the real estate industry, you're thinking about an area that holds a lot of promise for a Cash Flow Warrior. You're also thinking about an industry that really needs another whole Cash Flow book written about it! With that said, what I'll do in this chapter is to give you an idea of the different types of real estate investing that you can do, and then if you're still interested you should do some extra reading.

Picking your first investment property can be intimidating. It's hard to keep your emotions out of the equation. If you recognize that your emotions have taken over, don't get too freaked out. It's easy to figure out why emotions come into play when you're scared of losing your money.

Many veteran real estate investors can develop tunnel vision while they're making money in real estate. If someone is doing well buying small apartment buildings, the odds are good that they won't even consider investing in larger apartment buildings, condominiums, single-family homes, commercial strip malls, or industrial properties. But there are opportunities to make money by investing in all kinds of property. In this chapter, I will give you a guided tour of the entire market so you can choose the venue that is best for you.

The Demand for Land

Mark Twain was right—land is almost always a good investment. When you own real estate, it's really the land that holds value of your property. A house in a key downtown area that goes up in value every year isn't appreciating because the wood that went into building is worth more annually. It is appreciating because the demand for the location is increasing the demand for the land.

The great American dream has always been to own vacant land, and you can make some money investing in vacant land if you know what you are doing. For example, you could buy a vacant tract of land and subdivide it into lots, and sell the lots at a profit. Or you could buy vacant land and develop it—in other words, build on the land. This is also a good strategy, but unfortunately it's not what most investors do. Typically, an individual will invest in vacant land, do nothing with it for eight or ten years, sell it for twice the purchase price, and think that a lot of money has been made. They are mistaken—they've left money on the table!

> **With vacant land, there is no income to offset any of your expenses. That means potential interest is lost on the cash you invested. For instance, you pay interest on the money you borrowed to buy the land. In addition, you must pay real estate taxes, selling expenses, maintenance costs, liability insurance, special assessment costs, and sometimes even perform maintenance according to city and county codes. On top of all those direct expenses is the indirect "cost" of inflation. Money that you receive when you sell the property is going to be worth less than what it's worth today.**

In addition, investing in raw, vacant land has problems associated with it. First, it is a capital-intensive investment. You have to start with a lot of money and be willing to wait a long time for any financial return. Many investors buy property in areas that are predicted to have long- or short-term growth. Sometimes money is made, but more often than not, investing in vacant land is not a good investment strategy unless you have a plan to increase its worth within five years.

Profits with In-Fills

An "in-fill" project is a type of investment that involves buying a vacant lot surrounded by existing buildings of one type or another. The idea is to buy the lot, build something useful on it, and then sell it off for a profit. Compared to a raw land investment, these projects have less risk for the investor because these opportunities are found in areas that are already developed.

Allies

In many cases, a home or business owner has held a vacant lot next to his home or business either for privacy or for possible expansion. If it's a residential property, the homeowner may be moving and would part with the lot separate from the house. If it's a commercial lot, the owner may be retiring, or may have just decided he didn't want to expand his business. In either case, he decides to sell. This is where you come in.

Even though this type of investment is safer than the purchase of vacant land, you need to do the same kind of research you would do if you were buying raw land. Check to make sure that the property is zoned for what you want to do with it.

One important issue that comes up when doing an in-fill deal in a commercial area is determining whether there are any pollutants in the soil. Most cities require developers to do extensive environmental testing. These tests are expensive, and if any problems are found, the cost of removal could be huge.

Enemies

Opportunities to Redevelop Property

A redevelopment opportunity is when a piece of property is worth more for the value of the land itself than it is with the structure that sits on it. In this situation, you are not looking for vacant land to build on as you did with the in-fill project. Instead, you are looking for a bargain property that could be torn down eventually. Like an in-fill, however, once you have an empty dirt lot, the goal is to build on it and then sell it off for a profit.

If the structure sitting on the lot is already producing income when you purchase it, great! You can buy the property and continue renting out the structure until the time is right to hire a builder and begin the development process.

Mail Call

A friend of mine who is successful in real estate simply looks for property to "bring to the next level." If it is raw land, he subdivides it into lots and sells them individually. He may look for an old residential house that is now in a commercial area and convert that. He may look for an apartment complex and turn the units into condos (and sell them individually—oftentimes to the people who are already renting them). Do you see something in your area that can be brought to a "higher level"?

Income Property

Whether you are a beginning investor or have some experience, there is no question that you are better off buying properties that generate rental income.

Here's a list of several types of properties, all of which could help you accomplish your goals:

- Office buildings
- Shopping centers/strip malls
- Stand-alone stores
- Warehouses
- Hotels and motels
- Apartments
- Nursing homes
- Mobile home parks
- Restaurants
- Single-family homes and small residential properties

While most people are aware that apartments and office buildings are owned by investors, they are generally not aware that many restaurants, stores, and even post office buildings are investor-owned. Some congregations will even lease their church from an investor. Many hotels and restaurants are operated out of buildings that are owned by investors. The range of choices is obviously very big.

As an investor, you should buy within your comfort level. This applies not only to the type of property, but to the size as well.

Mail Call

> **For the new investor, single-family homes generally represent the best investment opportunities. Not only are single-family homes lower in cost, they are also plentiful in the marketplace (which also makes them easy to sell if you need to). And you will find that flexible sellers own many single-family homes.**

Information is easy to acquire about the single-family home market for making a good investment. Your information will tell you that they are increasing in value faster than most any other single segment of the marketplace. In addition, these homes are easily rented and stay rented.

What about Condominiums?

Warning — Land Mines

> **I don't recommend adding condominium investing to your arsenal of real estate strategies except perhaps beachfront or lakefront condos. The main reason is that as an owner, you are limited in what you can do to the property to increase its value. When buying real estate, the idea is to buy a property, find ways to add value to it, and then eventually sell it for a profit. With condominium ownership, however, most associations will not allow you to make any improvements at all to the outside of your unit.**

Most condominiums are not bought to turn a profit; they are bought as a first home or vacation home. If you want to buy a condo as a home, that's not a bad idea, but if you are looking for a home *and* an investment, a single-family home is the best way to go.

The Single-Family Home Is King

If you really want to create extra profit for your efforts, the single-family home is probably the way to go. The principle reason for this is the common desire many people have to own their own plot of land. In addition, the diversity of most single-family properties offers many chances for you to add value. With the exception of wealthy communities and historic districts, there is rarely a requirement for a single-family home to look just like the neighbor's. Check the local zoning regulations to see whether there are any building restrictions.

Getting Started

- Research your market. Identify areas that have some diversity in the homes and that sell well. You don't want to go with a restrictive area with strict homeowners' association rules and no variation. Good bargains are usually found in neighborhoods with lots of variety—different interiors, exteriors, floor plans, and so on.

- Take a trip to City Hall. Find out how difficult the permit requirements are. Obtaining permits can be easy and inexpensive or costly and time-consuming. Answers to these questions will tell you if it's worth the trouble.

- Talk to your real estate agent and get his opinion about what underpriced houses are out there in the single-family residence market.

Finding the Right Property

One of the keys to finding the right property is to survey the market and get a feeling for the kind of style and amenities that seem to command the highest rent per square foot. Your goal then will be to acquire that type of property or one that can be converted at a minimum cost.

In finding the right property, it is important to pay particular attention to your potential expenses. Look for properties that:

- Have all the utilities metered separately. This way, tenants will pay the utility bills instead of you.

- Have individual laundry hookups versus common laundry rooms. If your tenants purchase and maintain their own appliances, it will save you a lot of money over the years. And frankly, the bigger the items your tenants move in, the less likely they are to move out.

- Will generate the greatest profit within the two years following your purchase. Consider a house in a new growth location, property with an extra lot that you can sell off separately, or even the traditional fixer-upper.

- Have not been renovated. Jon Richards once told me, "If you would personally live in it, you probably want another investment property." In other words, you are looking for the properties that have *not* been fixed up yet. That is where you can make even more money. This is where you have to keep emotion out of the picture.

Many, many investors choose a property for investment purposes but choose to live in it first. Their strategy may be to fix it up while they live there, or just live there temporarily doing minor exterior enhancements until they find their next investment property. If this appeals to you, it's often a good way to start out, especially if you can avoid the exemption provided on profits from the sale of property that served as your primary residence for two years.

If you are not able to find single-family–style properties (which probably means you are not looking hard enough or need to lower your standards), you may want to look for standard apartment-style buildings. These usually are two-story buildings with a couple of units downstairs and a couple more upstairs. A parking area usually is either attached or separated, depending on the size of the lot. You also often find former single-family residences split into two to four units. Because of the great financing available, two- to four-unit buildings can be huge money-makers.

Pros and Cons to Renting Out Single-Family Homes

There are both advantages and disadvantages to owning single-family homes as investments.

Pros

- Easier in that you only have one primary tenant to deal with.

- Tenant can be responsible for all utilities, general maintenance, and minor expenses. Of course, you have to pay for major items such as new roofs and broken water heaters, but the tenant should basically live in the house as though he or she owned it.

- Tenants feel a sense of privacy. If given a choice, most people would like to live in a house if they can afford it.

- You can use fences to create privacy between properties that have separate units on the same lot. Even if fences do not separate the units, these kinds of apartments give tenants more privacy than a three- or four-unit building.

- As a general rule, the more private you can make the rentals, the more tenants will look at the unit as their home rather than a temporary residence, and the less the tenants will call and ask for things to get done.

Cons

- The return on a single-family residence is usually less than that from an apartment investment.

- When a tenant vacates a single-family home, your vacancy rate is 100 percent. If you own multiple units and a tenant vacates, the cash flow from the other units can help sustain you as an investor.

Five Units and Up

As an investor, there are inherent advantages when you graduate to a property that has five or more units.

Pros

- Economies of scale; it does not cost twice as much to run 20 units as it does 10, and so on.

- By turning a five-unit building into a four-unit building, you can turn a property that required a commercial loan into one that only requires a residential loan.

- Vacancies are of less impact to you as an investor because the remaining tenants provide you with multiple streams of income.

Cons

- Limited availability of financing (requires commercial loan).
- Diligent research to know in advance what kind of permits are required and what costs are involved.
- May need the professional expertise of a builder and architect to help you determine whether the project is worth the expense.

Big Apartment Buildings

Plenty of loans are usually available for big apartment buildings. But when it comes to commercial loans like these, investors usually have to come up with a significant chunk of change for a down payment.

Tenants who rent in larger properties are usually looking for similar types of living arrangements as those who live in large condo developments. They want nice amenities and benefits without having to maintain them. Items that attract tenants to larger apartment complexes include:

- Recreational amenities (pool/jacuzzi, racquetball/tennis courts, clubhouse, car wash, and so on)
- Laundry room
- Appliances provided
- Tenant camaraderie/social functions
- Walk-in closets
- Private balcony or porch
- Air-conditioning
- Fresh paint, clean carpet, well-maintained and functional fixtures
- Upscale amenities (wet bar, fireplace, and so on)
- Cable or satellite TV
- Attractive exterior and well-maintained grounds
- Secure parking and grounds

Renters will pay top dollar in apartment complexes that provide amenities like these and maintain them well. But as you move into larger properties, you will be leaving the "mom-and-pop" phase of real estate investing and entering the "business" phase. The properties produce good and consistent income but must also be aggressively managed just as any large apartment complex is. In short, there is a lot of money to be made but big apartment buildings require huge down payments and intensive management.

Commercial and Industrial Properties

Investing in commercial and industrial properties is a great real estate strategy. Businesses need a roof over their heads, just like home renters. In fact, many experts maintain that these properties are simply a "home for a business." Here are some examples:

- Parking lots
- Garages
- Warehouses
- Stand-alone stores
- Shopping centers/strip malls
- Office buildings
- Mobile home parks
- Specialty commercial (restaurants, gas stations, and so on)
- Small factories
- Larger industrial buildings

Going Head to Head: Commercial versus Residential

Commercial and industrial properties have some distinct advantages and disadvantages when compared to residential purchases.

Pros
- Long-term tenants
- Limited management

- Consistent return on investment
- Consistent appreciation in value

Cons

- Limited availability of tenants
- Limited availability of financing

Now that you've got an idea of the sort of real estate you might want to invest in, I'll talk a tiny bit about financing. Remember, this is just Real Estate 101—you need to look into this in a more in-depth fashion before you proceed. With that said, you would be surprised how many people believe that you have to pay 20 percent of the price of the house as a cash down payment. In an area where the average home price is $100,000, that means you would have to accumulate $20,000 in your savings account before even thinking of buying a house. The good news for you when you want to sell a starter home is that there are many first-time homebuyer and down payment assistance plans that make the down payment a non-issue for many buyers.

First-time buyer plans don't work for an investor, however, so we need to consider other strategies. Fortunately, as an investor you have a variety of options. Certain lenders provide a percentage of what the property is worth rather than the purchase price so if you can negotiate a price below that percentage the lender provides everything you need. Sometimes the seller is so motivated that you can get seller financing for at least enough to cover the down payment.

A Word about "No Money Down" Deals

I have many colleagues who talk about "no money down" deals. These are properties that you purchase with—surprise—none of your own money. These are often a numbers game (in that you are going to make a lot of offers before one is accepted). There is certainly a time and a place to do No Money Down deals. But make sure you follow two rules.

1. It *must* be Cash Flow. Don't buy spec (speculative properties) in a negative cash flow situation unless you have an immediate out. I have seen time and time again where a property sells for an inflated value because

someone "believes" there is a new race track, mall, or amusement park going in across the street (but of course there has been no formal announcement or proof). Make sure you are getting a good deal out of the gate—not based on some other factor having to happen for you to be successful.

2. Use the positive cash flow to pay down the debt. I get a kick out of watching a popular infomercial that shows a guy owning almost all the properties on his street (that he purchased for no money down). He has all the properties rented, a couple thousand dollars in positive cash flow burning a hole in his pocket, and still owes 100 percent of the value (as in no equity). No worries, right? Well, what happens when one of them is vacant for a couple months and you still need to make that mortage payment? What happens if two of them need new roofs for about $15,000? There goes your positive cash flow. Sometimes it can fall like a house of cards. Make sure that you have other means to pay bills and let the "cash flow" pay down the debt. Once paid off, you are in a great situation!

With that said, if your cash flow is limited, certainly pursue No Money Down deals, but make sure you have access to funds for repairs, and then you can reasonably expect the property to appreciate based on prior track history.

Allies

> **Most likely, in your town, there is a local real estate investor group. They are a great source for contacts, networking, and learning what works in your area!**

Bottom Line

Although I've told you twice now that you need to know a little more before you invest in real estate, don't suffer from paralysis due to analysis. You will never know everything there is to know about real estate, nor should you. To succeed in real estate, you have to go out and make deals. If all you do is keep learning and preparing, nothing will ever happen. To begin with, the best thing to do to get started is to start small. You can then build upon what you already know and continue to progress beyond that. Now don't go out and acquire a 100-unit apartment complex or an eight-story commercial building right away. Simply do what you can do, keep learning, keep your eyes open, and take small steps.

With all that said, this is why, for the most part, I like to invest in real estate notes. I own the debt. The owners have to pay me, and I don't get any calls about leaky sinks, have to deal with vacancies, or any other problems. You don't get to call the bank when something is wrong with your house!

Marching Orders for Real Estate

✔ Investigate your options and learn all you can about real estate.

✔ Choose your properties with an eye towards income streams.

✔ Find a local real estate investor group.

✔ Start small.

Taxes and Your Business

On April 15th you count your blessings and then send them to Washington.

—Milton Berle, comedian

If you are like me, you probably looked at the title of this chapter and were about as enthused to read this as a chapter titled "Spiders, Bugs, and other Fun Pets" or "Things Your Teenager Won't Tell You." Amazing as it may seem, if you decide to take an entrepreneurial approach to your Cash Flow War battles, the IRS can actually be your friend. Okay, that may be a little bit much, but let's just say the IRS doesn't exactly have to be your enemy. And they go out of their way to prove that they're not your enemy by posting a great number of informational tax publications on their Web site.

Keep in mind that any IRS booklet or publication that I refer to in this chapter can be found simply by going to www.irs.gov and typing the name of the publication into the search engine on the home page. If you don't have a printer attached to your computer, you can call 1-800-TAX-FORM (1-800-829-3676) and they'll mail hard copies of whatever you want.

Before we really get going, here is my *big* disclaimer: Taxes and their preparation are different for everyone. Each person has a unique situation. I wrote this chapter to give you an idea of the wonderful benefits associated with owning your own business and the tax implications with them. However, I am not offering tax advice. You must contact your tax professional to see how your individual circumstances apply.

Whew! Now that we have gotten that out of the way...

Mail Call

> **Most financially independent people own their own business—even if it is part-time and out of the house. These are people just like you, who probably live on your street, who are able to take advantage of tax benefits specially geared towards business owners.**

Tax Advantages of Owning a Home Business

Once you have a company set up, most likely out of your home, you can begin to realize the benefits of additional tax deductions. For example, if you have a 2,000-square-foot home and a 200-square-foot office, you could deduct 10 percent of many expenses. Of course you need to consult with a tax expert, but it is likely you may realize some of these deductions:

- A percentage of your rent if you rent or lease.
- A percentage of your mortgage interest if you own your home.
- A percentage of real estate taxes and homeowners' association fees.
- Household supplies and cleaning services for the business portion of your home.
- Repair and maintenance of your home office.
- Utilities (electricity, gas, water) attributable to the business use of your home.
- Trash collection.
- Furniture in your household that you convert for use in the home office.

- Phone services, minus the base local service for the first line into your home. (Lines devoted to the Internet and faxing may be entirely deductible.)
- Business use of your automobile.

The list goes on and on. Anything that can be *legitimately* used in the context of your new company may be considered for deduction. Each of these items will also potentially lower your taxable income. Taking all the deductions you're eligible for can offset the higher cost of health insurance you have to pay as a self-employed person. For more information, see IRS Publication 587, Business Use of Your Home.

Just imagine if you earned $10,000 in your first year of your own business, but you can also prove that you purchased $10,000 worth of computers, phones, etc. In the end, you most likely will not have to pay tax on the $10,000 you earned because you also spent $10,000 on equipment. In other words: You broke even. This advantage of owning your own business is often overlooked. One quick example: You may be able to deduct a significant portion of your cable bill if you have a high-speed Internet connection and a TV in your home office. (You may be able to justify deducting a portion of the bill if you use the Internet predominantly for your home business.)

Recent Legislation Changes That Can Really Help You Out

There have been some new tax laws enacted in the past few years. Cash Flow Warrior Entrepreneurs can really get some big business tax savings as a result of the recently enacted Jobs and Growth Tax Relief Reconciliation Act of 2003. This law allows for a huge increase in the first-year depreciation allowance for qualifying property. Under this law, entrepreneurs can immediately deduct 100 percent of the cost of most new and used business equipment instead of depreciating it over several years. What this means is that you can upgrade your home (business equipment computers, fax, and so on) and deduct almost the entire cost.

Under prior law, the allowance was limited to $25,000. Now, under the new law, the annual allowance for taxable years beginning in 2003, 2004, and 2005 quadruples to $100,000.

Don't neglect to look into the tax breaks available for buying certain new or used "heavy" SUVs, pickups, and vans used more than 50 percent for business. They qualify under the $100,000 Section 179 allowance. If you can prove you need a Hummer to run your small business (good luck), you can buy one and deduct it on your taxes. Not so bad! Another big plus for business owners who operate as sole proprietors, partnerships, or S-corporations is the fact that they will directly benefit from the new law's reduction in marginal tax rates.

Putting Your Family to Work

For Cash Flow Warriors with lots of mouths to feed, or with an older parent they are financially responsible for, you can (in some cases) put them on the payroll of your small business. If you *pay* your family what you would normally give them for general expenses you can use the payroll expense as a deduction against your business earnings.

Allies

> **A word of advice: Don't get too crazy here! You can't put a six-year-old kid on your payroll to any great degree, however if you have a 16-year-old you may be in luck.**

As a small-business owner, you have an opportunity to hire your spouse, your children, and even your parents as a way of minimizing your family's tax burden. By shifting taxable business income to a family member, you can move money from your higher tax rates to their lower tax rate and thereby create some real tax savings for you and your business.

Under age 18 (and at least seven, the age the IRS has approved for employing your children), your children are exempt from Social Security and unemployment taxes through an unincorporated business.

The catch is that you can only pay your children when they perform legitimate work in your business. But legitimate work can be stuffing envelopes or sweeping up! You can pay minors wages that are tax-deductible to your business, and tax-free to them (up to the $4,750 standard deduction), and you still get to claim your children as dependents on your personal income tax return. If you decide to shift more than $4,750 to them, their beginning tax rate is only 10 percent.

> **Pay your children and parents weekly and in the same manner as any other employee—on a regular basis by check.**

Allies

You can pay your parents' wages (for legitimate work) with tax-deductible dollars from your business. These tax-deductible (before-tax) dollars can replace the after-tax dollars that you otherwise might have given them for expenses. Because you are paying them with your business's pretax dollars, there are definitely more of these dollars to give them than you otherwise would have had available for them.

Hiring a Tax Accountant

Despite all of the free help the IRS will give you, once you have a small business that is really cranking along, it's in your best interest to hire someone to do your taxes. Just remember that you need to keep good records to hand over to your accountant or they won't be able to use the full extent of their knowledge when seeking deductions for you. They can only work with what you give them!

A good accountant is worth his or her weight in gold. Just to give you an example, my wife and I had the same accountant for years. He was inexpensive and seemed to do a good job. Each year we paid whatever he said and moved on. One year, on April 4, we received a large envelope with all of our tax information and a letter from the accountant saying that "our taxes were too difficult

Allies

Mail Call

to do" at this point (we had property investments, notes, and so on). April 4th! Not even a phone call! Oh, and by the way, "I think you owe around $20,000 this year."

Needless to say, at this point we had to scramble to find an accountant who could file an extension and do our taxes in the summer. In the end, we found a great accountant. Dan (the new accountant) has a fee that is about ten times the old one but he knows what he is doing. Dan even found items that our original accountant had overlooked and in the first year saved us from overpaying taxes in the amount of around $15,000! I guess I owe my first accountant a "thank-you-for-being-an-idiot-and-quitting-on-April-4th" card.

A good accountant will always be worth the money. To this day, despite moving all over the country, the same person does our taxes. Just like most of the licensed professionals you'll run across as an entrepreneur, most tax return preparers are honest and provide excellent service to their clients. But since you're the person who will ultimately be responsible for whatever your accountant files for you, you'll need to check this person out thoroughly. Here are some suggestions to consider when hiring a tax professional:

- Avoid preparers who claim they can obtain much larger refunds than other preparers. There's only so much these guys can do legally, and if they do it illegally, you're responsible!

- Avoid preparers who base their fee on a percentage of the amount of the refund. It seems like that may be too much of a temptation for some of the shadier characters out there.

- Get references, and ask questions from clients who have used the tax professional before. Were they satisfied with the service received?

- Make sure you use a reputable tax professional who will sign the tax return and provide you with a copy for your records. If the professional won't sign the return, you know he or she is a little shaky at best.

- How long has this person been doing this? You need to consider whether the individual or firm will be around to answer questions about the return months, even years, after the return is filed. The IRS has up to five years to review your taxes.

- You must be able to view the person's credentials. It makes a difference if a person represents him- or herself as an accredited tax preparer, enrolled agent, certified public accountant (CPA), licensed public accountant (LPA), or tax attorney. The attorneys, CPAs, and enrolled agents can represent you before the IRS in all matters including audits, collection, and appeals. LPAs and accredited return preparers may only represent taxpayers for audits.

> **Never, ever sign a blank tax form or sign a completed form without reviewing it and making sure you understand all the entries.**

Unfortunately, sprinkled in amongst the vast majority of good folks, there are some pretty shady tax return preparers out there and they can cause considerable financial and legal problems for their clients. When somebody gets a little cute with your taxes, like claiming inflated personal or business expenses, false deductions, unallowable credits or excessive exemptions, it can have serious repercussions for you. Some preparers even manipulate income figures to obtain fraudulent tax credits, such as the Earned Income Tax Credit.

> **Tax evasion is a felony crime punishable by up to 5 years imprisonment and a $250,000 fine. Remember—no matter who prepares a tax return, the taxpayer is legally responsible for all of the information on that tax return. Even if you don't do any jail time, having a felony conviction on your record can severely damage your credit and your credibility for the rest of your life.**

> **Tax laws are very involved and it is worth your while to hire someone trained in this area to do your taxes. My accountant has covered his fee to me ten times over in finding benefits.**

If you run into a tax accountant who doesn't quite meet the criteria I have laid out, check the professional out more thoroughly or move on to a different one.

The government even provides free tax help in certain situations. It's worth your time to check out IRS Publication 910, the Guide to Free Tax Services. This booklet identifies the many IRS tax materials and services available to you, and how, when, and where you can get them. It's pretty surprising how many programs are free and available year-round through the IRS. Tax education and assistance programs, which are fairly in-depth and valuable to small business owners, and tax tips are covered in this guide. The guide also lists telephone numbers for recorded tax information, automated refund information, and IRS mailing addresses.

Another important resource for you to investigate when you're trying to figure out the tax implications is *www.sbaonline.sba.gov/sbdc/*. This is the home page for the Small Business Resources section, and it contains many additional links to federal government agencies and programs. All in all, Uncle Sam has laid out some pretty big bucks to put together some programs that can really help a budding Cash Flow War entrepreneur figure out his or her taxes. Additionally, this section offers a list of specific resources for minority- and women-owned businesses.

Marching Orders for Taxes and Your Business

✔ **Check out *www.irs.gov*. Uncle Sam has put up loads of good tax information on this Web site.**

✔ **Keep abreast of changing laws that can help you out.**

✔ **Hire a reputable tax accountant. They're always worth the money!**

Declaring Victory in the Cash Flow War

> *Our business in life is not to get ahead of others, but to get ahead of ourselves...*
>
> —Stewart B. Johnson, from *Cole's Quotables*

I want to congratulate you again. No matter how many people eventually read this book, you will still be part of a small, elite group when compared to all the people who go through life not realizing that they can have something better.

I want to leave you with three things: A short story, the six key mindsets for Cash Flow War success, and, lastly, your "medals of honor."

The Wedding, the Ring, and Life's Lessons

It is funny how you learn life's lessons in some of the most unexpected circumstances—if you are just paying attention. Have you ever had a position of importance in a wedding? By position of importance, I mean best man, maid of honor, required attendee, and so on. Let me tell you about being a best man in a wedding. As a best man in a wedding I had three responsibilities:

1. Throw a good "bachelor" party

2. Make sure the groom shows up at the church

3. Hold on to the ring until it's time to give it back to him (during the ceremony)

Let me tell you, the first two went off without a hitch. We had a great party and it was no problem making sure that he was at the church on time for the wedding. I did have a little problem with the ring, however.

When I was given the ring, I had 43 minutes until I had to hand it back. It was in my hand; I was ready to go.

They say you get 15 minutes of fame, right? I can personally tell you that it takes only 13 minutes to lose a ring. Now, you may also think, hey, how much could you have done in 13 minutes that you can't retrace your steps? And the big deal is how can you go retrace your steps so that nobody knows what you're doing?

30 minutes remaining...

I had 30 minutes to find the ring. The search began. What did I do during those 13 minutes? I ate half of a cucumber sandwich, we had a celebratory toast of champagne, and I needed my bow tie tied. (Apparently, only women know how to tie bow ties, which makes no sense to me whatsoever, because they don't wear them, but okay...)

I realized, with only 30 minutes remaining until the ceremony, that I was in a bit of a time crunch. I needed a couple of assistants to help me find this ring.

23 minutes remaining...

We found nothing by the cucumber sandwiches and nothing by the champagne...

19 minutes remaining...

I now needed to look where someone tied my bow tie (which was in the "bride's area," where all of the women were working away getting ready). So I go there to look for the ring.

11 minutes remaining...

I was down to 11 minutes. I heard warm-up music, I didn't have the ring, and just about everybody was looking at this point. And no one was happy with me.

Surprisingly, at that moment, no one seemed to care that I pulled off two of my three responsibilities. The bride did not seem thrilled that we had a great party and that I got him to the church—go figure.

Then they started talking about pretending to put on a ring. That is when I knew I was in big trouble.

Time is up!

At that point, just about everybody was involved in the search. The flower girl came up to me. She wasn't more than four years old. I believe at that point she was the only one not involved in the search.

She said, while tugging on my jacket, "Can I help?" Well, what do you say to someone looking up at you and carrying flowers for an hour and a half because she knows that this is her job? What are you going to say? "Sure you can help," I said.

And then she immediately said, "Well, I know where it is." And I asked, "Where is the ring?" "It's in your hand," she answered.

It took a minute to register in my brain, but I opened my hand, and there it was. Apparently I had it the whole time.

It was at that very moment that I realized, in the end, most of our day-to-day issues are in our hands. Whatever the problem, whatever the solution, it is in your hands. You can control the final outcome.

Your success and financial freedom are not dictated by your friends, coworkers, me, or anyone else. It's all in your hands. You have the power and you now have the knowledge to change your path. You can choose not to accept what life throws at you but to make your life what you want it to be.

It is in your hands, and as I learned, it always had been—don't let *anyone* tell you differently.

The Mindset for Cash Flow War Success

In the final analysis, it all boils down to one thing: a commitment. In order to be successful, you need a commitment to have the right attitudes in your life—in everything you do. Whether you're trying to create wealth in your life, get ahead in your job, or strengthen your relationship with your family, the right attitude is everything.

I learned long ago that there were six attitudes I needed to have in order to reach my goals. These go beyond strategies, because these attitudes affect how I handle the application of every strategy. I truly believe that without these attitudes I would not have achieved the level of success I now enjoy.

I strongly urge you to adapt the following six attitudes in everything you do:

1. **Professional Competency.** Know your speciality inside and out—it's one thing to pursue knowledge, but it's another thing to strive to be the best available in what you choose to do.

    You don't have to be the very best at everything. But whatever you do, you should do it well. Take this attitude to heart in everything you do and you will find yourself ahead of your competition.

2. **Single-Mindedness of Purpose.** Flowing out of the first attitude, there also comes a single-mindedness of purpose—a focus. You should narrow down the scope of what you want to do.

    If you're constantly trying to do multiple projects, you will rarely finish any of them. The old saying about having "too many irons in the fire" is true. Without a focus, you'll only succeed in burning yourself or burning out.

3. **Personal Responsibility.** Personal responsibility is something that is a touchy subject for many people. In a nutshell, we must all realize that we are the cause of most everything in our lives. I am the product of everything I have done in my life, and so are you.

    If we make a mistake, so be it. Learn from it, accept it, own up to it, and move on. You could spend a lifetime playing the "blame game" and get absolutely nowhere. If you truly want to get ahead, the sole resource of accountability must rest on your shoulders.

4. **Effective Conduct.** You simply need to have an objective, realistic understanding of where you *are* at the present moment. Once you have that, you need to understand with precise clarity where you *want* to be.

    Set your goals exactly, and then provide for a specific plan for implementation. By doing this you will achieve what you've set out to do effectively.

5. **Perseverance.** Rome wasn't built in a day. Achieving your goals takes time, and you need to understand that. Every single success happens after

countless individual failures. Unless you give yourself the chance to be successful by sticking to what you're doing, it will never happen.

If you continue doing what you need to, however, you will succeed. Just remember, it only takes one success to overshadow every past failure. Every "yes" is built on a solid foundation of "no's."

6. **Integrity.** Abide by the highest truth, because just about everyone can spot a fake. And while you can fool people some of the time, eventually the truth will come out. That is why I urge people to *always* be truthful and practice whatever they do with integrity.

Your word and integrity are some of the few things that no one can ever take away from you; use them wisely.

If you stick to these six mindsets, I truly believe you cannot fail in anything you attempt. Just about anything can be achieved if you keep the proper attitude and perspective on the objective. These six mindsets will help you do just that.

Congratulations—You're a Medal of Honor Winner

I can't tell you when it will be time for you to declare victory in the Cash Flow War. Different people have different ways of defining their goals. But what I can tell you is now you have everything you need in your Cash Flow War arsenal to get started to achieve your goals—now keep learning! I've given you the weapons you need, and the basic training you need to bring those weapons into play. The rest is up to you.

I am excited for you. With *Winning the Cash Flow War* in hand, you have a golden opportunity to go from a casualty of war to a master of it. Once you have done that, your financial goals and dreams can become a reality. If you implement just half of what you have learned in this book, you will truly be able to declare your financial independence.

We have started a Web site where you can go to share your experiences with other Cash Flow Warriors—people just like you who are dedicated to Winning the Cash Flow War, people just like you who have won their Medals of Honor.

Log on to *www.cashflowwar.com* and sign up for my free e-letter, share your stories of victory, add your name to the list of "Generals," and find resources designed to help you continue your battle and win once and for all. The Web site is a community of like-minded Cash Flow Warriors sharing their experiences and offering each other hints, tips, and opportunities. It's a great resource, it's free, and it's one you should take advantage of.

Once again, congratulations. I look forward to the day when you and I can meet and share stories. Your training is complete, the battle has begun; now go win the war for yourself and your family!

All the best,

Frederic M. Lewey

Suggested Resources

Print

Allen, Robert. *Creating Wealth,* New York, Simon and Schuster, 1986.

Allen, Robert G. *Multiple Streams of Income: How to Generate a Lifetime of Unlimited Wealth,* 2nd ed. New York, Simon and Schuster, 2004.

Goodman, Jordan E. *Everyone's Money Book,* 3rd ed. Chicago, Dearborn Trade, 2001.

Hagstrom, Robert G. *The Warren Buffett Way: Investment Strategies of the World's Greatest Investor,* New York, John Wiley & Sons, Inc., 1997.

Morris, Kenneth M. *The Wall Street Journal Guide to Understanding Personal Finance,* New York, Lightbulb Press, 1999.

Morris, Kenneth M. and Virginia B. Morris. *The Wall Street Journal Guide to Understanding Money & Investing,* New York, Lightbulb Press, 1999.

Pino, Laurence J. *Cash In On Cash Flow*, New York, Simon and Schuster, 1998.

Tyson, Eric. *Personal Finance for Dummies,* 4th ed. New York, John Wiley & Sons, Inc., 2003.

Online

American Capital Exchange
http://www.americancapitalexchange.com/

American Cash Flow Association
http://www.americancashflow.com

Bison
http://www.bison1.com/

Car Buying Tips
http://www.carbuyingtips.com/

CNN Money
http://money.cnn.com/

Consumer Action
http://www.consumer-action.org/

Consumer Guide to Debt Consolidation and Debt Management
http://www.edebthelp.org/

Credit Champion
http://www.creditchampion.com/

Diversified Investment Services
http://www.diversifiedinvestment.com

Entrepreneurial Resource Board
http://www.wtamu.edu/academic/bus/mmgb/ern.html

Federal Citizen Information Center
http://consumeraction.gov/caw_money_general_tips.shtml

Federal Trade Commision
http://www.ftc.gov

Franchisor Organization
http://www.franchising.org/

How Stuff Works
http://home.howstuffworks.com

International Franchise Association
http://www.franchise.org/default-flash.asp

IRS
http://www.irs.gov

Kiplinger
http://www.kiplinger.com

Loansaver Finance
http://www.loansaver.org/

Office of Consumer and Business Affairs (Australia)
http://www.ocba.sa.gov.au/scams/01_scams.html

Pyramid Scheme Alert
http://www.pyramidschemealert.org

Small Business Advisor
http://www.isquare.com/

Smart Biz
http://www.smartbiz.com/link/category/1/

Smart Money
http://netscape.smartmoney.com/

Solutions for Growing a business
http://www.entrepreneur.com/

Tax Advice
http://www.isquare.com/fhome10.cfm

The Riley Guide
http://www.rileyguide.com/steps.html

Uncle Fed's Tax Board
http://www.unclefed.com

University of Missouri
http://muextension.missouri.edu/explore/miscpubs/mp0630.htm

What's Wrong With Multi-Level Marketing?
http://www.vandruff.com/mlm.html

Winning the Cash Flow War
http://www.winningthecashflowwar.com

Glossary

3/1, 5/1, 7/1 and 10/1 ARMs: Adjustable-rate mortgages in which rate is fixed for 3-, 5-, 7-, and 10-year periods, respectively, but may adjust annually after that.

401(k) plan: A cash or deferred arrangement (CODA) that lets an employee contribute pretax dollars to a company investment vehicle until the employee retires or leaves the company.

403(b) plan: Similar to a 401(k), a cash or deferred arrangement (CODA) that lets an employee of a tax-exempt education or research organization or public school contribute pretax dollars to an investment pool until the employee retires or terminates employment.

7/23 and 5/25 mortgages: Mortgages with a one-time rate adjustment after seven years and five years, respectively.

A

Acceleration: The right of the lender to demand the immediate repayment of the mortgage loan balance upon the default of the borrower, or by using the right vested in the Due-on-Sale Clause. Also a term in which the payer makes increased payments to reduce the debt.

Accrued interest: The amount added to a bond or other fixed-income security between the last payment and when the security is sold, or any intermediate date. The buyer usually pays the seller the security's price plus the accrued interest.

Adjustable-rate mortgage (ARM): A mortgage in which the interest rate is adjusted periodically based on a preselected index.

Adjustment interval: On an ARM, the time between changes in the interest rate and/or monthly payment, typically one, three, or five years, depending on the index.

Amortization: Means loan payment by equal periodic payment calculated to pay off the debt at the end of a fixed period, including accrued interest on the outstanding balance.

Annual percentage rate (APR): Measurement of the full cost of a loan including interest and loan fees expressed as a yearly percentage rate.

Annuity: A series of fixed-amount payments paid at regular intervals over the period of the annuity; or a contract by which an insurance company agrees to make regular payments to someone.

Appraisal: An estimate of the value of property, made by a professional appraiser.

Ask price: The price a seller is willing to accept for the security; also called the offer price.

Assessment: Local taxes for a specific purpose, such as a sewer or street lights.

Asset allocation: Dividing your investment portfolio among the major asset categories. The most important decision you will make.

Asset: A resource that has economic value to its owner. Examples of an asset are cash, accounts receivable, inventory, real estate, and securities.

Assumption: The agreement between buyer and seller where the buyer takes over the payments on an existing mortgage from the seller.

B

Balance sheet: The firm's financial statement that provides a picture of its assets, debts, and net worth at a specific point in time.

Balloon mortgage: A loan that is amortized for a longer period than the term of the loan. Usually this refers to a 30-year amortization and a five-year term. At the end of the term of the loan, the remaining outstanding principal on the loan is due. This final payment is known as a balloon payment.

Beta: A measure of a stock's risk relative to the market, usually the Standard & Poor's 500 index. The market's beta is always 1.0; a beta higher than 1.0 indicates that, on average, when the market rises, the stock will rise to a greater extent and when the market falls, the stock will fall to a greater extent. The higher the beta, the greater the risk.

Bid price: The price a buyer is willing to pay for a security.

Blanket mortgage: A mortgage covering at least two pieces of real estate as security for the same mortgage.

Blue chip stock: Stock of large, well-known companies.

Bond fund: A fund that holds mainly municipal, corporate, and/or government bonds.

Bond: A certificate of debt, usually issued by corporations or governments; or a security that obligates the issuer to repay the principal amount upon maturity and to make specified interest payments over specified time intervals to the bond holder. The issuer can be a corporation or a governmental entity.

Borrower (mortgagor): One who applies for and receives a loan in the form of a mortgage with the intention of repaying the loan in full.

Broker: One who assists in arranging funding or negotiating contracts for a client but who does not loan the money. Brokers usually charge a fee or receive a commission for their services.

Buy-and-hold: A strategy in which the stock portion of your portfolio is fully invested in the stock market at all times.

Buy-down: When the lender and/or the home builder subsidize the mortgage by lowering the interest rate during the first few years of the loan.

C

Capital gain: An increase in the value of a capital asset such as common stock. If the asset is sold, the profit is a capital gain. A capital gain may be short-term (one year or less) or long-term (more than one year.)

Caps (interest): Consumer safeguards that limit the amount the interest rate on an ARM may change per year and/or the life of the loan.

Caps (payment): Consumer safeguards that limit the amount monthly payments on an ARM may change.

Cash balance plan: A defined-benefit plan in which each participant has an account that is credited with a dollar amount, generally a percentage of pay. Each participant's account is credited with earned interest. The plan provides the benefits in the form of a lump-sum distribution or annuity.

Cash investment: Very short-term (usually 90 days' maturity or less) obligation, such as a money market fund or very short-term CD, that provides a return in the form of interest payments.

Cash or deferred arrangement (CODA): A CODA is a defined contribution plan that allows participants to have a portion of their paycheck contributed pretax to a retirement account, such as a 401(k), 403(b), or 457.

Certificate of deposit (CD): A short-term security with a maturity from a few weeks to several years; interest rates are established by market demand and competition.

Closing: The meeting between the buyer, seller, and lender (or their respective agents) where the property and funds legally change hands; also called settlement. Closing costs usually include an origination fee, diccount points, appraisal fee, title search and insurance, survey, taxes, deed recording fee, credit report charge, and other costs assessed at settlement. Closing costs are usually about three to six percent of the mortgage amount.

COFI: ARM with rate that adjusts based on a cost-of-funds index.

Commission: Broker's fee for buying or selling securities, or a realtor's fee for selling property.

Common stock: A security issued by a corporation that represents ownership.

Compound interest: Interest credited on both principal and previously credited interest.

Compound sum of an annuity: Constant payments are made at equally spaced time periods and grow to a future value.

Compounding: The ability of an asset to generate earnings that are then reinvested and generate their own earnings (earnings on earnings).

Construction loan: A short-term interim loan to pay for the construction of buildings or homes. These are usually designed to provide periodic disbursements to the builder.

Contract sale or deed: A contract between purchaser and a seller of real estate to convey title after certain conditions have been met. It is a form of installment sale.

Conventional loan: A mortgage not insured by FHA or guaranteed by the VA.

Current yield: Annual income (interest or dividends) divided by the current price of the security. For stocks, this is the same as the dividend yield.

D

Debt-to-income ratio: The ratio, expressed as a percentage, which results when a borrower's monthly payment on long-term debts is divided by gross monthly income.

Deed of trust: In many states, this document is used in place of a mortgage to secure the payment of a note.

Default risk: The risk that a company will be unable to pay the contractual interest or principal on its debt obligations.

Default: Failure to meet legal obligations in a contract, specifically, failure to make the monthly payments on a mortgage.

Deferred annuity: An annuity not yet paying income because money is still accumulating on a tax-deferred basis.

Deferred interest: When a mortgage is written with a monthly payment that is less than required to satisfy the note rate, the unpaid interest is deferred by adding it to the loan balance.

Defined benefit plan: Each employee's future benefit is determined by a specific formula, and the plan provides a guaranteed level of benefits on retirement. The employer makes regular contributions to the entire plan to fund the future benefits of the participants. Usually, the promised benefit is tied to the employee's earnings, length of service, or both.

Defined contribution plan: Employers generally promise to make annual or periodic contributions to accounts that are set up for each employee. Sometimes there are only employer contributions, sometimes only employee contributions, and sometimes both. The benefit payable at retirement is based on money accumulated in each employee's account. The final retirement amount reflects the total of employer contributions, any employee contributions, and investment gains or losses.

Delinquency: Failure to make payments on time. This can lead to foreclosure.

Discount bond: A bond that is valued at less than its face amount.

Discount broker: A stockbroker who charges a reduced commission and provides no investment advice.

Discount rate: The interest rate used in discounting future cash flows; also called the capitalization rate.

Diversification: The process of accumulating securities in different investments, types of industries, risk categories, and companies in order to reduce the potential harm of loss from any one investment.

Dividend: A cash payment financed by profits that is designated by a company's board of directors to be distributed among stockholders.

Dollar cost averaging: A system of putting equal amounts of money in an investment at regular time intervals to lessen the risk of investing a large amount of money at a particularly inopportune time.

Dow Jones Industrial Average (DJIA): Price-weighted average of 30 actively traded blue-chip stocks, traditionally of industrial companies.

Down payment: Money paid to make up the difference between the purchase price and the mortgage amount.

Due-on-sale-clause: A provision in a mortgage or deed of trust that allows the lender to demand immediate payment of the balance of the mortgage if the mortgage holder sells the home.

E

Earnest money: Money given by a buyer to a seller as part of the purchase price to bind a transaction or assure payment.

Employee Retirement Income Security Act of 1974 (ERISA): Designed to secure the benefits of participants in private pension plans through participation, vesting, funding, reporting, and disclosure rules, and the creation of the Pension Benefit Guaranty Corporation. ERISA provided added pension incentives for the self-employed through changes in Keoghs and for persons not covered by pensions through individual retirement accounts (IRAs).

Employee Stock Ownership Plan (ESOP): ESOPs are defined contribution plans, that provide shares of stock in the sponsoring company to participating employees' retirement plans.

Entitlement: The VA home loan benefit is called an entitlement (that is, entitlement for a VA guaranteed home loan). This is also known as eligibility.

Equal Credit Opportunity Act (ECOA): Federal law that requires lenders and other creditors to make credit equally available without discrimination.

Equity: Another word for stock (or similar securities representing an ownership interest). *or*

The difference between fair market value and current indebtedness.

Escrow: Account held by the lender into which the home buyer pays money for tax or insurance payments. Also earnest deposits held pending loan closing.

F

Face value: The stated principal of a bond or other debt instrument.

Family of funds: A group of mutual funds under the same management company.

Fannie Mae: Federal National Mortgage Association (FNMA): A tax-paying corporation that buys and sells conventional residential mortgages as well as those insured by FHA or guaranteed by VA. This institution, which provides funds for one in seven mortgages, makes mortgage money more available and more affordable.

Farmers Home Administration (FmHA): Provides financing to farmers and other qualified borrowers who are unable to obtain loans elsewhere.

Federal Housing Administration (FHA): Division of the Department of Housing and Urban Development that insures residential mortgage loans made by private lenders. FHA also sets standards for underwriting mortgages.

FHA loan: A loan insured by the Federal Housing Administration open to all qualified home purchasers.

FHA mortgage insurance: Requires a fee (up to 2.25 percent of the loan amount) paid at closing to insure the loan with FHA. In addition, FHA mortgage insurance requires an annual fee of up to 0.5 percent of the current loan amount, paid in monthly installments.

Financial planner: An investment professional generalist who helps individuals delineate financial plans with specific objectives and helps coordinate various financial concerns.

Firm commitment: Promise by FHA to insure a mortgage loan for a specified property and borrower. A promise from a lender to make a mortgage loan.

Fixed annuity: A traditional insurance investment vehicle, often used for retirement accounts, that guarantees principal, a specified interest rate, and may also offer dividends.

Fixed-rate mortgage: The mortgage interest rate will remain the same on these mortgages throughout the term of the mortgage for the original borrower.

Fixed-income security: An investment vehicle that provides a return in the form of fixed periodic payments and return of principal; examples are bonds and certificates of deposit.

Foreclosure: A legal process by which the lender or the seller forces a sale of a mortgaged property because the borrower has not met the terms of the mortgage.

Freddie Mac (Federal Home Loan Mortgage Corporation) (FHLMC): Agency that purchases conventional mortgage from insured depository institutions and HUD-approved mortgage bankers.

Fundamental analysis: Valuing stocks based on fundamental factors, such as company earnings, growth prospects, and so forth, to determine a company's underlying worth and potential for growth.

G

General obligation bond (GO): A municipal bond backed by the full faith, credit, and taxing power of the issuing municipality rather than the revenue from a given project.

Ginnie Mae (Government National Mortgage Association) (GNMA): Provides sources of funds for residential mortgages, insured or guaranteed by FHA or VA.

GNMA (Ginnie Mae) pass-through certificate: Fixed-income securities that represent an undivided interest in a pool of federally insured mortgages put together by GNMA.

Going public: Selling privately held shares to new investors on the over-the-counter market for the first time.

Government bond: A debt obligation issued by the U.S. government.

Government paper: Any debt security, such as a Treasury bill or a Ginnie Mae, either guaranteed or backed by the U.S. government.

Graduated payment mortgage (GPM): Flexible-payment mortgage where the payments increase for a specified period of time and then level off. This type of mortgage has negative amortization built into it.

Growth stock: The shares of a company whose earnings are expected to grow at an above-average rate.

Guaranteed investment (interest) contract (GIC): Debt instrument sold in large denominations often bought for retirement plans. The word guaranteed refers to the interest rate paid on the GIC; the principal is at risk.

Guaranty: A promise by one party to pay a debt or perform an obligation contracted by another if the original party fails to pay or perform according to a contract.

H

Hazard insurance: Fire insurance and similar coverage.

Housing expenses-to-income ratio: The ratio, expressed as a percentage, that results when a borrower's housing expenses are divided by his/her gross monthly income.

I

Impound: That portion of a borrower's monthly payments held by the lender or servicer to pay for taxes, hazard insurance, mortgage insurance, lease payments, and other items as they become due; also known as reserves or escrow.

Income replacement ratio: The percentage of income that an individual needs to maintain the same standard of living during each year of retirement.

Income statement: The financial statement of a firm that summarizes revenues and expenses over a specified time period; a statement of profit and loss.

Income stock: Those stocks having a history of regular dividend payments that contribute the largest proportion of the stock's overall return.

Index: A published interest rate against which lenders measure the difference between the current interest rate on an ARM and that earned by other investments which is then used to adjust the interest rate on an adjustable mortgage.   *or*

A statistical measure of the changes in a portfolio representing a market. The Standard & Poor's 500 is the most well-known index, which measures the overall change in the value of the 500 stocks of the largest firms in the United States.

Indexed rate: The sum of the published index plus the margin. For example, if the index were 9 percent and the margin 2.75 percent, the indexed rate would be 11.75 percent.

Individual Retirement Account (IRA): An IRA provides individuals an opportunity to save for retirement on a tax-deferred basis. The amount that is tax-deductible varies according to an individual's pension coverage, income tax filing status, and adjusted gross income. Account balances distributed from one IRA or from a qualified retirement plan may be rolled over to another IRA.

Insider trading: Trading by management or others who have special access to unpublished information. If the information is used to illegally make a profit, there may be large fines and possible jail sentences.

Interim financing: A construction loan made during completion of a building or a project. A permanent loan usually replaces this loan after completion.

Investment adviser: A person who manages assets, making portfolio composition and individual security selection decisions, for a fee, usually a percentage of assets invested.

Investor: A money source for a lender.

J

Joint-and-survivor annuity: This type of benefit payment provides the spouse with monthly income equal to at least one-half the amount of the participant's benefit. To reflect the cost of the survivor protection, the participant's benefit is usually reduced.

Jumbo loan: A loan that is larger than the limits set by Fannie Mae and Freddie Mac. Jumbo loans usually carry a higher interest rate.

Junk bond: Bond purchased for speculative purposes. They are usually rated BB and lower, and they have a higher default risk.

K

Keogh plan: A Keogh plan is a retirement plan for self-employed individuals and their employees to which tax-deductible contributions up to a specified yearly limit can be made if the plan meets certain requirements of the Internal Revenue Code. Keogh plans, also called H.R.10 plans, may be defined benefit or defined contribution plans.

L

Lien: A claim upon a piece of property for the payment of a debt or obligation.

Liquidity: The degree of ease and certainty of value with which a security can be converted into cash.

Loan-to-value ratio: The relationship between the amount of the mortgage loan and the appraised value of the property expressed as a percentage.

Lock: Lender's guarantee that the mortgage rate quoted will be good for a specific number of days from day of application.

Lump-sum distribution: The distribution of a participant's entire account balance or of the entire value of a participant's accrued benefit (under a defined benefit plan) as a single cash payment to the participant (or beneficiary).

M

Margin: The amount a lender adds to the index on an adjustable rate mortgage to establish the adjusted interest rate; or the use of borrowed money to purchase securities (buying on margin).

Market capitalization: Number of common stock shares outstanding times share price.

Market risk: The volatility of a stock price relative to the overall market as indicated by beta.

Market timing: Attempting to leave the market entirely during downturns and reinvesting when it heads back up. Requires a crystal ball to be effective.

Market value: Highest price that a buyer would pay and the lowest price a seller would accept on a property.

Maturity: The length of time until the principal on a bond must be repaid.

MIP (mortgage insurance premium): Insurance from FHA to the lender against incurring a loss due to borrower's default.

Money market mutual fund: A mutual fund that invests in very short-term financial securities, usually of less than 30 days' maturity.

Money purchase pension plan: A defined contribution plan in which employer contributions are usually determined as a percentage of pay.

Mortgage insurance: Money paid to insure the mortgage when the down payment is less than 20 percent.

Mortgagee: The lender.

Mortgagor: The borrower or homeowner.

Municipal bond: Tax-free debt instrument issued by a state or local government.

Mutual fund: A pool of investors' money invested and managed by an investment adviser. Money can be invested in the fund or withdrawn at any time, with few restrictions, at net asset value (the per share market value of all securities held) minus any loads and/or fees.

N

National Association of Securities Dealers Automated Quotations System (Nasdaq): A computerized system that provides up-to-the-minute price quotations on about 5,000 of the more actively traded over-the-counter stocks.

Negative amortization: Occurs when your monthly payments are not large enough to pay all the interest due on the loan. This unpaid interest is added to the unpaid balance of the loan.

Net asset value: The market value of a mutual fund's total assets, after deduction of liabilities, divided by the number of outstanding shares; the per share price of no-load mutual funds.

Net effective income: The borrower's gross income minus federal income tax.

New York Stock Exchange index: A market value–weighted measure of stock market changes for all stocks listed on the NYSE.

Nonassumption clause: A statement in a mortgage contract forbidding the assumption of the mortgage without the prior approval of the lender.

Nonqualified plan: A pension plan that does not meet the requirements for preferential tax treatment. This type of plan allows an employer more flexibility and freedom with coverage requirements, benefit structures, and financing methods.

O

Office of Thrift Supervision (OTS): The regulatory agency for federally chartered savings institutions; formerly known as the Federal Home Loan Bank Board.

One-year adjustable mortgage: Mortgage whose annual rate changes yearly. The rate is usually based on movements of a published index plus a specified margin, chosen by the lender.

Open-end fund: A mutual fund that continuously sells shares to investors and redeems shares when investors wish to sell. Open-end funds have no limit to the number of shares they can issue.

Origination fee: The fee charged by a lender to prepare loan documents, make credit checks, inspect, and sometimes appraise a property; usually computed as a percentage of the face value of the loan.

Over-the-counter market: A communications network through which trades of bonds, non-listed stocks, and other securities take place. Trading activity is overseen by the National Association of Securities Dealers (NASD).

P

Par value (bond): The face value of a bond, generally $1,000 for corporate issues, with higher denominations for many government issues.

Pension Benefit Guaranty Corporation (PBGC): PBGC was created by ERISA to insure payment of certain pension plan benefits in the event a covered plan fails to pay the benefits. Covered plans or their sponsors must pay annual premiums to PBGC to provide funds from which guaranteed benefits can be paid.

Permanent loan: A long-term mortgage, usually ten years or more.

PITI: Principal, Interest, Taxes, and Insurance. Also called monthly housing expense.

Pledged account mortgage (PAM): Money is placed in a pledged savings account and this fund plus earned interest is gradually used to reduce mortgage payments.

Points: Prepaid interest assessed at closing by the lender. Each point is equal to one percent of the loan amount (e.g., two points on a $100,000 mortgage would cost $2,000).

Power of attorney: A legal document authorizing one person to act on behalf of another.

Preferred stock: A security representing prior claim to common stock on the firm's earnings and assets. Preferred stockholders normally forgo voting rights and receive a fixed dividend that takes precedence over payment of dividends to common stockholders.

Prepaid expenses: Necessary to create an escrow account or to adjust the seller's existing escrow account. Can include taxes, hazard insurance, private mortgage insurance, and special assessments.

Prepayment penalty: Money charged for an early repayment of debt. Prepayment penalties are allowed in many states.

Prepayment: A clause in a mortgage permitting the borrower to make payments in advance of his or her due date.

Present value: The value today of a future payment, or stream of payments, discounted at some appropriate interest rate.

Primary mortgage market: Lenders, such as savings and loan associations, commercial banks, and mortgage companies, who make mortgage loans directly to borrowers. These lenders sometimes sell their mortgages to the secondary mortgage markets such as to FNMA, GNMA, and so on.

Principal: The amount of debt, not counting interest, left on a loan.

Private mortgage insurance (PMI): In the event that you do not have a 20 percent down payment, lenders will allow a smaller down payment. With the smaller down payment loans, however, borrowers are usually required to carry private mortgage insurance.

Profit-sharing plan: A defined contribution plan where contributions are determined at the employer's discretion; these plans are also called deferred profit-sharing plans.

Prospectus: The written statement that discloses the terms of a securities offering or a mutual fund. Strict rules govern the information that must be disclosed to investors in the prospectus.

Q

Qualified plan: Any retirement plan that meets IRS criteria that allow employers to deduct pension costs as a business expense and defer current income tax on its earnings and allow employees to defer income tax on the employer's contributions and earnings.

R

Realtor: A real estate broker or an associate holding active membership in a local real estate board affiliated with the National Association of Realtors.

Recording fees: Money paid to the lender for recording a home sale with the local authorities, thereby making it part of the public records.

Refinance: Obtaining a new mortgage loan on a property already owned; often to replace existing loans on the property.

Renegotiable rate mortgage: A loan in which the interest rate is adjusted periodically. See ARM.

Rescission: The cancellation of a contract. With respect to mortgage refinancing, the law that gives the homeowner three days to cancel a contract (in some cases) once it is signed if the transaction uses equity in the home as security.

Real Estate Settlement Procedures Act (RESPA): A federal law that allows consumers to review information on settlement cost once after application and once prior to or at a settlement. The law requires lenders to furnish the information after application only.

Return: This is the value of income plus capital gains relative to investment. This is another way of defining yield.

Revenue bond: A municipal bond supported by the revenue from a specific project, such as a toll road, bridge, or municipal coliseum.

Reverse annuity mortgage (RAM): A form of mortgage in which the lender makes periodic payments to the borrower using the borrower's equity in the home as collateral for and repayment of the loan.

Risk/return trade-off: The balance an investor must decide on between the desire for low risk and high returns, since low levels of uncertainty (low risk) are associated with low potential returns and high levels of uncertainty (high risk) are associated with high potential returns.

Risk: Possibility that an investment's actual return will be different than expected; includes the possibility of losing some or all of the original investment. Measured by variability of historical returns or dispersion of historical returns around their average return.

Rollover: An employee's transfer of retirement funds from one retirement plan to another plan of the same type or to an IRA without incurring a tax liability. The transfer must be made within 60 days of receiving a cash distribution.

S

Salary reduction plan: See CODA.

Satisfaction of mortgage: Document issued by the mortgagee when the mortgage loan is paid in full; also called a release of mortgage.

Savings or thrift plan: A defined contribution plan in which participants make contributions and to which employers may also contribute, usually fully or partially matching participants' contributions. Contributions are commonly made with after-tax earnings.

Second mortgage: A mortgage made subsequent to (and subordinate) to the first one.

Secondary market: A market in which an investor purchases an asset from another investor rather than the issuing corporation. An example is the New York Stock Exchange.

Secondary mortgage market: The place where primary mortgage lenders sell the mortgages they make to obtain more funds to originate more new loans.

Security analyst: One who studies various industries and companies and provides research reports and valuation reports.

Servicing: All operations a lender performs to keep a loan in good standing, such as collection of payments, payment of taxes, insurance, and property inspections.

Settlement/settlement costs: See closing/closing costs.

Shared appreciation mortgage (SAM): Mortgage in which a borrower receives a below-market interest rate in return for which the lender receives a portion of the future appreciation in the value of the property. May also apply to mortgage where the borrowers share the monthly principal and interest payments with another party in exchange for part of the appreciation.

Simple Interest: Interest which is computed only on the principle balance.

Simplified Employee Pension (SEP/SARSEP): A defined contribution plan created under the Revenue Act of 1978 to help small employers establish a pension plan. SEPs are arrangements under which an IRA is established for each eligible employee. The employee is immediately vested in employer contributions and generally directs the investment of the money. These arrangements are sometimes called SEP-IRAs.

Social Security: The comprehensive federal program of benefits providing workers and their dependents with retirement, disability income, etc. Don't count on it!

Standard & Poor's 500 index: An index of 500 major U.S. corporations. There are 400 industrial firms, 20 transportation firms, 40 utilities, and 40 financial firms. This index is value-weighted.

Stock dividend: A dividend paid in additional shares of stock rather than in cash.

Stock split: The division of a company's existing stock into more shares. In a two-for-one split, each stockholder would receive an additional share for each share formerly held.

Stockbroker: An agent who, for a commission, handles the public's orders to buy and sell securities.

Straight-life annuity: Benefits from a qualified plan that are paid to the participant in monthly installments for the duration of the participant's life.

Survey: A measurement of land, prepared by a registered land surveyor, showing the location of the land with reference to known points, its dimensions, and the location and dimensions of any buildings.

Sweat equity: Equity created by a purchaser working on a property being purchased.

T

Time horizon: The length of time an investment is held.

Title Insurance: Policy which insures a home buyer against errors in the title search.

Title search: An examination of municipal records to determine the legal ownership of property. Usually is performed by a title company.

Title: Document that gives evidence of an individual's ownership of property.

Treasury bill: Short-term debt security issued by the federal government for periods of one year or less.

Treasury bond: Longer-term debt security issued by the federal government for a period of seven years or longer.

Treasury note: Longer-term debt security issued by the federal government for a period of one to seven years.

Truth-in-lending: Federal law requiring disclosure of the annual percentage rate to home buyers shortly after they apply for the loan. Also known as Regulation Z.

Two-step mortgage: A mortgage in which the borrower receives a below-market interest rate for a specified number of years (most often seven or 10), and then receives a new interest rate adjusted (within certain limits) to market conditions at that time. The lender sometimes has the option to call the loan due with 30 days notice at the end of seven or 10 years; also called Super Seven or Premier mortgage.

U

U.S. savings bonds: Backed by the full faith and credit of the U.S. government, savings bonds are registered and nontransferable securities.

Underwriting: The decision whether to make a loan to a potential home buyer and the matching of this risk to an appropriate rate and term or loan amount.

Usury: Interest charged in excess of the legal rate established by law.

V

VA loan: Long-term, low- or no-down payment loan guaranteed by the Department of Veterans Affairs. Restricted to individuals qualified by military service or other entitlements.

VA mortgage funding fee: Premium of up to 1⅞ percent (depending on the size of the down payment) paid on a VA-backed loan.

Valuation: The process of determining the current worth of an asset.

Value line index: The index represents 1,700 companies from the New York and American Stock Exchanges and the over-the-counter market. It is an equal-weighted index, which means each of the 1,700 stocks, regardless of market price or total market value, are weighted equally.

Variability: The possible different outcomes of an event. As an example, an investment with many different levels of return would have great variability.

Variable annuity: An annuity that fluctuates based on the market performance of an underlying securities portfolio. Unlike fixed annuities, there is no guarantee of principal or rate of return.

Variable-rate mortgage (VRM): See ARM.

Verification of deposit (VOD): A document signed by the borrower's financial institution verifying the status and balance of his/her financial accounts.

Verification of employment (VOE): A document signed by the borrower's employer verifying his/her position and salary.

Vesting: Vesting is a process in a qualified retirement plan where participants earn a right to accrued benefits (under a defined benefit plan) or account balances (under a defined contribution plan) by the completion of specified years of service.

W

Warehouse fee: Many mortgage firms must borrow funds on a short-term basis in order to originate loans that are to be sold later in the secondary mortgage market (or to investors). When the prime rate of interest is higher on short-term loans than on mortgage loans, the mortgage firm has an economic loss that is offset by charging a warehouse fee.

Wilshire 5000 Equity Index: A stock market measure comprising 5,000 equity securities. It includes all New York Stock Exchange and American Stock Exchange issues and the most active over-the-counter issues. The index represents the total dollar value of all 5,000 stocks.

Wraparound mortgage: Results when an existing assumable loan is combined with a new loan, resulting in an interest rate somewhere between the old rate and the current market rate. The payments are made to a second lender or the previous homeowner, who then forwards the payments to the first lender after taking the additional amount off the top.

Z

Zero-coupon bond: A bond that generates no periodic interest payments and is issued at a discount from face value. All return is realized at maturity.

Note: This glossary has been adapted primarily from The American Savings Education Council Web site (*www.asec.org*), Us MortgageShop, Lion Inc.'s *Loansolve.com*, and American Association of Individual Investors (*www.aaii.com*).

Following are two pages of the Calculator Worksheet for your use. Please refer to Chapter 12 for guidance in completing these worksheets.

Calculator Worksheet

N	I	PV	PMT	FV
———	———	———	———	———
———	———	———	———	———
———	———	———	———	———
———	———	———	———	———
———	———	———	———	———
———	———	———	———	———
———	———	———	———	———
———	———	———	———	———
———	———	———	———	———
———	———	———	———	———
———	———	———	———	———
———	———	———	———	———
———	———	———	———	———
———	———	———	———	———
———	———	———	———	———
———	———	———	———	———
———	———	———	———	———
———	———	———	———	———
———	———	———	———	———
———	———	———	———	———

Calculator Worksheet

N	I	PV	PMT	FV
_____	_____	_____	_____	_____
_____	_____	_____	_____	_____
_____	_____	_____	_____	_____
_____	_____	_____	_____	_____
_____	_____	_____	_____	_____
_____	_____	_____	_____	_____
_____	_____	_____	_____	_____
_____	_____	_____	_____	_____
_____	_____	_____	_____	_____
_____	_____	_____	_____	_____
_____	_____	_____	_____	_____
_____	_____	_____	_____	_____
_____	_____	_____	_____	_____
_____	_____	_____	_____	_____
_____	_____	_____	_____	_____
_____	_____	_____	_____	_____
_____	_____	_____	_____	_____
_____	_____	_____	_____	_____
_____	_____	_____	_____	_____
_____	_____	_____	_____	_____

Index

Looking for more information or want to share your victory with others?

Visit *cashflowwar.com* and sign up for your free e-letter.